Information Systems
A Management Perspective

CW00434933

Information Systems

A Management Perspective

Christopher Martin and Philip Powell

McGRAW-HILL BOOK COMPANY

London · New York · St Louis · San Francisco · Auckland · Bogotá · Caracas
Lisbon · Madrid · Mexico · Milan · Montreal · New Delhi · Panama
Paris · San Juan · São Paulo · Singapore · Sydney · Tokyo · Toronto

Published by

McGRAW-HILL Book Company Europe

Shoppenhangers Road, Maidenhead, Berkshire, SL6 2QL, England

Telephone 0628 23432

Fax 0628 770224

British Library Cataloguing in Publication Data
Martin, Christopher
Information systems: a management perspective.
I. Title II. Powell, Philip
658.40380285

ISBN 0-07-707428-9

Library of Congress Cataloging-in-Publication Data
Martin, Christopher
Information systems: a management perspective/
Christopher Martin and Philip Powell.
p. cm.
Includes bibliographical references and index.
ISBN 0-07-707428-9
1. Management information systems.
I. Powell, Philip. II. Title.
T58.6.M3575 1992
658.4'038--dc20   91-28122

34 CUP 943

Typeset by Alden Multimedia Ltd
and printed and bound in Great Britain at the University Press, Cambridge

To Rachel and Nicola

Contents

Preface

Information systems have become a vital part of all aspects of managerial work, and it is hardly possible for the modern manager to do his or her job effectively without a grounding in at least the fundamentals of information systems. This book is designed to provide a comprehensive intermediate guide to the nature of the work which computers perform in organizations, and to introduce the role which information systems can play in the development and management of the enterprise.

The information systems field is a broad one and when writing a text book of this kind a number of different approaches are possible. The materials chosen for inclusion in this text have been carefully selected to provide a broad appreciation of the key aspects of information systems (IS). The book has been written for a wide readership, with students of management, accounting and the management sciences especially in mind. The aim is for the reader to reach an intermediate level in information systems, so the book will be suitable for a wide range of students in higher education as well as to people already working in industry. The text will be applicable to courses run by accounting and professional bodies including CIMA and ACCA.

There is a wide-ranging debate on the nature and syllabus of information systems as a topic of study. For example, the two different requirements for training individuals for their own computer use on the one hand, and appreciation of the information needs of the enterprise as a whole on the other hand, has brought into focus a number of problems associated with the choice of a coherent IS syllabus. What does the IS field consist of exactly, and what should be taught at entry level, intermediate level and beyond? One way to attempt to answer this question is to look at the information system needs and knowledge of business managers.

Managers and information systems: eight requirements

The organizational manager of today needs information systems knowledge to help in the following tasks:

1. Communicating with IS specialists, who are responsible for the organization and management of the information resource.
2. Using a personal computer or terminal, either as a stand-alone device or linked to the organization's mainframe.
3. Making decisions about information received, in terms of its value and reliability. Managers need to understand how the information has been selected, processed and communicated.
4. Making decisions with information; this may involve data manipulation in model-based decision support systems, or scanning different views of data in advanced executive information systems.
5. Discussing the manager's own information requirements, and especially participating in the specification of information flows and processing, in the systems for which he or she is responsible.
6. Understanding the potential of new and upcoming information technology in all its forms; this technology may profoundly affect the organization's efficiency and competitive advantage in the future.
7. Being aware of the importance of information as a strategic resource within the organization.
8. Being aware of the social consequences of information systems, in terms of the principal effects on people's jobs and working lives.

These requirements call for a deeper and, especially, a broader appreciation of information systems than has been necessary in the past; it is this broader perspective which this book aims to cover.

The text is organized into chapters which are grouped in six parts. Part One introduces theoretical foundations and discusses information and decision-making as the context for information systems. Part Two provides a background in the technology of information systems and examines computer technology. Software and its use in creating information system applications is described in Part Three while Part Four focuses on information system development. Part Five introduces management issues which are special to the control of information systems in the organization. Finally, Part Six looks at the leading edge—and beyond—of information system applications, and discusses the impact of information systems on society. Each chapter concludes with a list of key terms and suggestions for further reading. The suggestions include books and journal articles which are seminal, or which provide wider information on the topics covered. The key terms act as a reminder of materials covered, and can be used for revision.

Chris Martin, the prime mover behind this book, tragically died during its production. It is published as a memorial to his enthusiasm for, and knowledge of, information systems.

PART ONE

Information systems foundations

1
The role of information systems

Information systems and management

Most organizations, even down to the very smallest, utilize computers in some way or another. The uses to which the computers are put vary enormously, ranging from word processing and elementary accounting systems through to on-line enquiry, sophisticated decision support systems and mathematical modelling for corporate planning. It is probably true that many of today's businesses simply could not function effectively without automated information processing systems of some form or another. The costs and delays arising from manual processing methods would be truly daunting without automated data processing; consider, for example, the raw data processing involved when next you write a cheque or buy a plane ticket. Increasingly, information systems are seen as a strategic resource within the organization; that is, they have an important impact on key operations which determine the livelihood of the organization.

But it would be wrong to overemphasize the role of computers alone. In practice, most management information systems are an amalgam of human and computer-based activities, where man and machine have different but complementary roles to play in achieving the successful working of the system. The question as to which aspects are best done by machine and which are best done by people is a fascinating one, and, of course, the answer is changing constantly with rapid advances in technology. Table 1.1 compares some of the different capabilities of human and computer as information processors.

The advantages of computerized information systems

There are several distinct advantages which can accrue from the successful use of computer systems. We use the word *can* carefully here; it is not certain that

3

Table 1.1   Humans and computers compared

	Human	*Computer*
Overhead costs	expensive	cheap
Running costs	expensive	cheap
Performance over time	deteriorates	constant
(stamina)		
Reliability/consistency	poor	excellent
Computation ability	poor	excellent
Handling the unexpected	good	poor
Commonsense abilities	excellent	poor
Language abilities	good	poor

any benefits will accrue just because a computer is installed: far from it. In practice it is necessary to plan computer systems with great care and to implement them skilfully in order to realize the full benefits. This book is intended to provide guidance for realizing those benefits and for avoiding some of the pitfalls which may arise.

There are significant advantages to be achieved from the successful implementation of computer-based systems; but these can take several different forms, and it is worth while being quite clear as to which benefit(s) are being sought. Generally, the concrete advantages fall into four categories:

1. information cost-effectiveness;
2. enhanced business growth potential;
3. the automation of decisions;
4. enhancement of decision quality.

INFORMATION COST-EFFECTIVENESS

Computers have greatly reduced the need for clerical data processing; at the same time new work roles have arisen, and new information workers have appeared to fill them. In general, computers can process raw data very much more cheaply and accurately than human beings, and this has meant a dramatic reduction in the costs of elementary data processing. Many organizations have justified the introduction of computer systems on the basis that specific cost savings will accrue as a result of a direct saving in clerical effort. Most mature organizations will by now have already shed or relocated clerical effort where this can be directly replaced by automated systems and so further cost reductions here are not so easy to achieve. In practice, the direct replacement of human data processing by computers is rarely straightforward and clerical cost reductions must be balanced against a whole host of new costs associated with the new systems.

ENHANCED BUSINESS GROWTH POTENTIAL

Many organizations find that they are hampered in their search for growth by

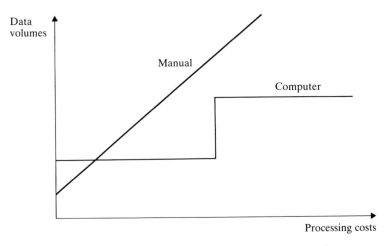

Figure 1.1   The effect of increasing data volumes on processing costs

their administrative paperwork systems, or by the lack of consistent informa-tion. The introduction of computer-based systems can overcome these hurdles and allow growth in sales to occur. The costs of manual data processing tend to rise linearly with the volumes of data; i.e. ignoring any learning effects, it costs twice as much to cope with 200 documents as it does to cope with 100. This is usually because the dominant cost element is people. However, this will not be the case with a computer system; once initial installation costs have been overcome it may cost little to expand the system to cope with extra volumes of data. This effect is sketched in Fig. 1.1.

It can be seen that with small data volumes the computer system initally costs more than an equivalent manual system, because of the capital outlay on equipment and set-up costs. However, as data volumes rise, so the manual system costs rise with them while the computer costs remain roughly constant. This is because more data needs more people, but the computer can take on more work until its capacity is reached. At a certain point, the computer will have reached its limit and will need enhancing or replacing, resulting in a step-change in costs. Thus there is an area of the graph where the computer costs are constant while manual costs are rising. A carefully designed system will exploit the capacity of the computer to soak up increased volumes with little cost increase. (This is of course a simplification of reality, and in reality the people function will be a stepped cost also and there will be a host of other factors to consider.)

THE AUTOMATION OF DECISIONS

The work of an organization can be seen as being made up of countless elementary individual decisions. Most of these decisions are usually quite straightforward, but the decisions must be taken none the less, and good solutions arrived at or the organization cannot function. Examples of these elementary decisions are legion, but include the allocation of sales discounts to customers depending on previous sales records, or the calculation of PAYE income tax depending on earnings and tax code. A computer system can handle such decisions accurately and tirelessly, according to a fixed set of rules called an algorithm. A great advantage of the computer is that it can make decisions no matter how complex the decision factors are, always providing that these factors can be defined. This enables consistency and accuracy to be achieved in the organization's work and enables management and staff to concentrate on aspects requiring human judgement and skills.

ENHANCED DECISION-MAKING

Much of the development work in information systems for management is aimed at improving the quality of human decision. This is a different matter altogether from the automation of decisions discussed in the previous section. The intention now is to provide information to enable the manager to make a decision, which, based on more accurate information or assisted by a computer model of the factors involved, will permit him or her to achieve better outcomes than if the decision was made unaided.

Recent developments in decision support systems (DSS) and executive information systems (EIS) have had far-reaching effects on strategic decision-making by senior managers. Decisions which have crucial long-term effects on the organization can be supported by computer-generated information and decision models so that the long-term effects of different options can be reviewed. Further enhancements to decision quality are possible as a result of developments in the comparatively new field of computer-based artificial intelligence and expert systems.

In addition to these cited advantages, information systems are increasingly being considered as strategic; in overall terms they can crucially affect an organization's survival. This aspect will be considered in more detail in Chapter 17.

Types of information system

Already in our discussion of the role of computers in management, we have seen a broad range of possible applications. Since these different applications often have quite different aims and objectives it is essential to discriminate among the five main groups of information systems: data processing, management information systems, decision support systems, office automation systems, intelligent knowledge-based systems.

DATA PROCESSING (DP)

The aims of data processing are to process large amounts of data quickly, cheaply and accurately. Automated data processing (ADP) was the first major application of computers in management, and, indeed, automated data processing of one kind or another had been carried out long before computers became generally available in the 1950s. The punched card was developed in the late nineteenth century by Herman Hollerith so that the results of the US population census could be processed by machines. The improvements which these punched-card methods produced were adopted by many of the larger business organizations, who sought to reduce the costs of their elementary data processing tasks. Payroll and elementary accounting systems were among the first and most popular systems to be automated. The electronic digital computer greatly improved the scope and cost-effectiveness of ADP, and the new technology became known as electronic data processing (EDP). Now it is taken for granted that the elementary data processing tasks of a business will be performed wherever possible by computer; indeed for many firms it is an essential part of their competitive business strategy.

MANAGEMENT INFORMATION SYSTEMS (MIS)

MIS grew naturally out of the earlier simple data processing systems. While processing data quickly and economically, it was a small extra step to summarize and select information which would help managers make decisions. For example, while processing the payroll, there is little extra computer processing involved in producing totals of overtime payments, or an analysis of days worked by each department.

In time, it came to be seen that information produced by the computer system could be produced to standards of speed and accuracy which were just not possible before, and that this information could act as a platform achieving a far more efficient business organization. There came to be a special emphasis on the value of management information and this resulted in systems being designed specifically for their information outputs, rather than purely for the data processing benefits. These systems were planned so as to create all (or almost all) the information needed for the monitoring and controlling of an organization's affairs.

Although there is some dispute over the definition of these terms, MIS usually means a system which contains large amounts of information which has been structured to assist management in decision-making. (The relationship between data and information will be defined more precisely in Chapter 2.) Typically, the information is held on some form of database, consisting mainly of financial data from internal company systems, and is used mainly by middle management in monitoring and controlling the organization's business. Management information systems are essentially historic, being concerned with past actions and outcomes.

In recent years there has been a swing away from large-scale MIS systems. It was found that these large, integrated systems were very expensive to build, cumbersome in operation and did not always achieve all the benefits that were expected. Today, it is probably fair to say that there is still an important role for the MIS, but it is no longer seen as the ultimate and final expression of the organization's information needs. Rather, the MIS takes its place among the other types of computer-based information systems which an organization may utilize.

DECISION SUPPORT SYSTEMS (DSS)

These systems were created, at least in part, as a response to some of the perceived failings of MIS. The MIS, because it was based mainly on internal financial data, did not directly address the needs of top management, or of strategic decision-making. A DSS usually contains specially designed models which provide the user with the means of assessing the consequences of decision. An example of this is known as a 'what if?' facility: given the task of deciding between various forms of investment, for instance, the system user can see the consequences of each option when the system evaluates the effect on profitability using a financial model of the organization's finances.

OFFICE AUTOMATION SYSTEMS

Information technology (IT) is a broad term which has been coined to refer to the range of electronic facilities used in modern management. These facilities include personal computers, word processing and desk-top publishing (DTP), electronic mail, electronic point of sale (EPOS) and electronic funds transfer (EFT). Many of these techniques remove the need for paper-based filing systems of communications, and have given rise to the expression 'the paperless office'. However, most offices are still anything but paperless and the strength of the technology lies primarily in the utilization of computer and communications technology together in information processing and transmission.

INTELLIGENT KNOWLEDGE-BASED SYSTEMS (IKBS)

The search for a means of creating human-like computer systems has been carried out in research departments of universities since the very earliest days of computers. In recent years this has been supplemented by substantial commercial development, particularly in expert systems. The capacity of computers to reproduce human skills and abilities is known as artificial intelligence (AI). A number of special techniques have been developed over the years which enable computers to go some way towards emulating these skills. IKBS utilize AI techniques in order to provide specialist expert systems. It is now possible to store the knowledge of human experts in a computer and to enable the knowledge to be tapped by an enquirer who consults the computer. The system reviews the problem, asks questions if necessary and provides a diagnosis and suggestions for a solution (see Chapter 21).

Summary

Computer-based information systems are now used by virtually all organizations. Information systems can be used for a number of different purposes. The advantages of automated systems include information cost-effectiveness and efficiency, improved business growth potential and improved decision-making; information systems are increasingly considered to be strategic. A broad grouping of information systems includes: data processing, management information, decision support, office automation and intelligent knowledge-based systems.

KEY TERMS   Artificial intelligence (AI)   Data processing (DP)   Decision automation   Decision quality   Decisions support systems (DSS)   Electronic office   Expert systems (ES)   Information cost-effectiveness   Information technology (IT)   Intelligent knowledge-based systems (IKBS)   Management information systems (MIS).

Further reading

Boddy D., McCalman J. and Buchanan D.A. (Eds), *The New Management Challenge: IS for Improved Performance*, Croom Helm, London, 1988.
Davis G.B. and Olsen M.H., *Management Information Systems*, McGraw-Hill, New York, 1984.

2
Information and management

Any discussion about information systems inevitably involves using the words data and information. But what exactly are these? In normal speech the words are often used interchangeably, but in talking about computer-based information systems it is necessary to make a careful distinction between the two.

Data and information

Data is the raw material of organizational life; it consists of disconnected numbers, words, symbols and syllables relating to the events and processes of the business. Data on its own can serve little useful purpose; in fact, a serious problem for the manager is the need to make sense of the deluge of data that threatens to overwhelm him or her in the normal course of the job. The ability to select those items of information which are truly necessary from the flood of irrelevance is a key management skill. The extent of the information explosion can be seen from the fact that 75 per cent of all information available on the earth today has been created in the last 20 years! And it has been estimated that the total amount doubles every 10 years or less!

THE NATURE OF DATA PROCESSING

Information comes from data that has been processed to make it useful in management decision-making.

$$\text{data} \rightarrow \text{PROCESS} \rightarrow \text{information}$$

The task of data processing is one which has been performed by people since the earliest days, whether we consider the stone tablets of prehistoric man or the quill pens of Dickensian England. Now, increasingly, this task is being undertaken by computers, but the steps are essentially the same whether the process is undertaken manually or electronically.

STAGES IN DATA PROCESSING

Origination

At some point, new data comes into existence. This could be when a customer rings in to a sales department and places an order for a product; at this time new data relating to the customer and his or her needs is identified, where none existed before. From this point on, these data items are processed, partly electronically by formal computer and communication systems and partly by other less formal means such as word of mouth and manipulation in manual records.

Input

If data exists only in somebody's head, then the input will have been via one or more of the body's five senses. Computer systems require an extra step whereby data is converted into a machine-sensible form before being input. Computer systems have a number of different input methods available which are discussed in more detail in Part 2.

Processing

Data can be manipulated in an infinite number of ways, but, in practice, most data processing tasks can be described in surprisingly simple terms. Data items can be sorted into appropriate sequences; one item can be compared with another and decisions made on the basis of the comparison; numerical data can be maintained by calculation; and, finally, data can be summarized, i.e. condensed into a form showing less detail.

Storage and retrieval

A prime need of any business is the storage and retrieval of data. Large organizations can require the filing of staggering amounts of data: think of the accounting records of a national utility such as British Gas plc, or the personnel records of the Civil Service. We now take for granted that such a mass of records will be stored and retrieved using automatic systems. A major contribution of electronic computer systems in management has been the cost-effective storage and efficient retrieval of data which electronic storage systems provide.

Output

When data has been processed, or retrieved from a storage system, then it will be communicated to a data user in some way. This could be achieved by word of mouth, or in the form of a written report or diagram. Computer systems employ a number of methods for outputting data, including display on a VDU screen and printing reports and documents.

INFORMATION AND UNCERTAINTY

The main (but by no means the only) criterion for deciding about information is its usefulness in decision. This point has a number of considerations: firstly, if information is to be useful, then clearly its value depends to a large extent on the recipient and how it is to be used. Information is only useful to *somebody* and a prime criterion of its value relates to decision. Of course, the decision in question may not be immediate; information can be useful when it informs decisions to be made at some time in the future. In fact, learning is about storing information which may be useful at some time in the future.

All this implies that information which is useful to one person may be quite useless to somebody else, thus we may say that one manager's information may be another manager's data. Consider the staff in a sales office checking sales orders to allocate trade discounts: in this situation, details such as the customer's name and type of business may be items of information used to make a decision about the discount allowable. Now consider the sales manager in the same office as he or she decides whether to allocate more salespeople for the amount of business to be achieved that month: in this instance, the total order value achieved so far may be the key piece of information and the details of individual customer names are irrelevant to the decision.

If we were to tell you that, today being Monday, tomorrow is Tuesday, then this piece of information will not be very valuable to you! The information has no surprise value, it tells you nothing you do not already know. Information is of more or less value to the extent to which it reduces our uncertainty about our world. If you were considering placing a bet on the favourite in the 3.30, then there would be uncertainty as to the outcome. If there were not, then you would find it hard to place a bet, because everybody would have knowledge of the result. But there is always uncertainty about the outcome of future events (in management as well as in horse racing). The information you receive about the race and about the horses may act to reduce this uncertainty, and is more or less valuable accordingly. For example, knowing that a horse is favourite tells you something about the possible outcome. Of course, just because the horse is favourite does not mean that it will win; but to a certain degree, your uncertainty about the outcome has been reduced. Knowing the odds, then, on the horses in a race reduces to some extent our uncertainty about the outcome (even if not very much) and hence this information has a certain value.

Desirable characteristics of information

In order that it should be valuable to the recipient, information must be of sufficient quality to make it useful in decision. But what is information quality? In practice, there are several rule-of-thumb criteria which help to create better information:

1. *Relevant information*. The need for information to be relevant to the purposes

of the recipient in decision-making cannot be overstressed. Irrelevant information constitutes a substantial problem, because it distracts attention from important issues and wastes managers' time. It should be remembered that information which is relevant to one person may well be quite irrelevant to another who has different responsibilities. A further point is that information which is relevant now may become less so over time.

2. *Accurate information.* Information should be accurate enough for the purposes in mind. Clearly, wrong and misleading information can only have harmful consequences, and perhaps is worse than no information at all. However, at the same time, unnecessary numbers of decimal positions which add spurious accuracy will serve no purpose. The level of accuracy, therefore, should be chosen to suit the circumstances: sterling values to the nearest penny are necessary for personal payslip details; values to the nearest pound may be suitable for supervisors' reports; values accurate to the nearest thousand are usually chosen for the company's published accounts. This point is reinforced in the next paragraph.

3. *Concise information.* The problem of an 'information explosion' for management has already been mentioned. An essential quality of useful information is that it should represent the minimum necessary to convey what is required for the decision in hand. Anything extra beyond what is essential serves only to add to the manager's information overload, and also acts to increase processing costs unnecessarily.

4. *Timely information.* Information which arrives after a decision has been made is clearly of little use, however accurate and relevant it may have been. Hence the value of most information reduces sharply over time. Computers have often been introduced to lend their very fast processing speed specifically in order to improve the timeliness of information flows.

5. *Well-presented information.* The manner in which information is presented to the recipient has a dramatic effect on its usefulness in decision-making. If key information is hidden in huge volumes of printouts, or if tables of numerical statistics are issued to show trends which might have been better displayed on a graph, then the decision-maker will not have been given the necessary assistance in his or her understanding of the information. Apart from these general points, there is some evidence to show that individuals have certain preferences for information types; for example, some people respond better to information presented visually in the form of pictures or graphs while others are happier if the same information is supplied in a verbal or textual form.

6. *Complete information.* In order to make a decision, the manager needs all the information relevant to that task; if key parts of the information set are missing then this will obviously detract from its value.

7. *Up-to-date information.* Information must reflect the current known facts relating to a decision; if it shows details relating to the past when more recent information would be of greater use, then, in a sense, it is no longer accurate.

8. *Cost-effective information.* Providing information always costs money (although often the true costs of creating it may be hidden); any decision, however important, can only have a certain value. Information which costs more to provide than the value that can result from a better decision, is not cost-effective. Often it is just as difficult to ascertain the true benefits from use of information as it is to evaluate the cost of producing it (this point will be taken up in the next chapter.) Nevertheless, the creation and processing of information is a large item of expense for most organizations, and it is necessary to be careful that the benefits derived are not outweighed by the costs of production.

The computer, when employed with care, can assist in the achievement of these desirable characteristics. The successful design and implementation of information systems is rooted in an understanding of how these characteristics can be achieved.

Clearly, the creation and provision of information which has one or more of the above qualities may result in conflict with the other characteristics. For example, to produce information which is complete in all respects may well take too long, so that the information is no longer timely; or to take the extra care required to make sure it is well presented may result in the information no longer being cost-effective. In practice, producing information requires us to select a suitable compromise between the desirable characteristics, which represents the best we can do in a given situation.

Information value and costs

Assessing the value of information is not always easy, and there are different views as to how this should be done. Nevertheless, an attempt must be made to consider this point because providing information certainly entails outlay. If you consider the cost of a large computer system and the specialist staff required to run it, then the costs may be very high indeed. How are we to judge whether the cost is worth while without knowing the value of the information provided?

Returning to our racing example, if we could entirely reduce your uncertainty about the outcome of the horse race, then the information would surely have a specific (and possibly very high!) value. The point is that you could calculate quite specifically how much it would be worth paying to have that information. In general, we try to apply the same principles to estimating the value of information in management, i.e. by attempting to assess the value arising from decisions which could be taken more accurately on the basis of the information provided.

In a management setting, information can clearly be seen to have value if it results in somebody taking action which increases profitability. If that extra profit can be measured, then we have a direct assessment of the value of the information which achieved it. For example, if we provide information about optimum stockholding levels and the information can be acted upon so that a direct reduction in stockholding costs of £10 000 per year ensues, then we can claim that the information is worth that much, i.e. it would pay us to spend up to that value to obtain the information.

Unfortunately, the issues are rarely so clear-cut in the management world. The value of information is usually dependent on the recipient's needs and abilities to act in a given situation, and so there is usually no absolute or constant value of any piece of information. This is particularly true for management information systems where information may relate to decisions which in themselves are hard to quantify, or to situations which might arise in the distant future.

In practice, then, the costs of information systems are usually justified using qualitative as well as quantitative arguments about the benefits which are to accrue.

Managerial use of information

Of course, individuals differ in the ways in which they respond to information and this inevitably affects the way in which decisions are taken. It has been shown, for example, that people have different cognitive styles, i.e. some people prefer information which is structured and follows a clear path from beginning to end (analytic or systematic style) while others prefer a more intuitive approach and like to see where the information as a whole is going (intuitive or heuristic style).

An oft-quoted example of this style difference is shown in the case of two people who are planning for a car journey. One prefers to drive to the approximate location to see if he can find it—the intuitive/heuristic approach —while the other person prefers to trace a map route from beginning to end —the systematic/analytic approach. Either approach may be more or less effective and successful depending on the circumstances; but the individual's response to information will, of course, be different. Differences such as this call for information systems which are tailored to the cognitive styles of the people who are to use them. However, this degree of sophistication in business systems design is rather rare.

FORMAL AND INFORMAL INFORMATION SYSTEMS

Because we concentrate a great deal on formal information systems: accounting reports, computer printouts and so on, we tend to forget that, in fact, managers pay a lot of attention to other, less formal, sources of information. These include managers' own observations of events, and especially the face-to-face and telephone contacts they have with the people around them. In fact, the typical manager spends most of the time gathering information in this way (or being exposed to it) and hence the informal information sources make up a significant part of the manager's world (Table 2.1).

Of course, the informal information is completely different from the sort of

Table 2.1   Formal and informal information systems compared

Formal	Informal
How communicated	
printed reports	word of mouth, gossip,
computer terminals	hearsay
How created	
MIS, computer-based systems	personal contacts, 'grapevine'
By whom created	
staff specialists	managers' interpersonal
IS department	networks, including
corporate planning	colleagues, subordinates,
department	superiors, friends and allies
Information types	
quantitative	qualitative
financial	personal
economic	non-economic
Information characteristics	
regular, scheduled	unscheduled, chance contacts
summarized	disaggregated
aggregated, selected	fragments of detail processed

thing which we usually think of as 'management information'. It consists of word-of-mouth reports about events and people in the organization, usually reported verbally and with little quantitative content. Often the information is inaccurate, it comes from 'the grapevine' and tends to be newsy with snippets of detail about people and events which are of general personal interest.

The informal information system has obvious drawbacks as regards accuracy, validity and reliability. Nevertheless, managers seem to prefer their informal systems to the formal systems for some aspects of their information needs. The reasons for this are not hard to find: the informal information usually has a more immediate character to it, i.e. it relates to the here and now; also, it may be easier to digest and to act upon than a complex report or financial summary. In extreme circumstances informal information may be more trusted than the formal information passed down by senior management.

In fact there are circumstances where informal information is of the utmost importance to managers. Consider the sales director who visits his office in the morning and reads the monthly sales analysis for his division; this report—from the formal information system—tells him which customers have placed orders, and for how much. In the evening he plays a round of golf with a friend from one of his most important client companies; his friend tells him of a rumour —the informal information system—that the client company may be about to place its business elsewhere. This is serious and worrying news (if true) which the sales director acts on the next day by contacting the client directly.

Clearly, the informal information system has a tremendous importance in this instance because it advised the sales director of possible future events. The formal information system would have told him of the problem only after the client company had withdrawn its custom. The issue here is that informal information systems serve a key purpose for most managers, and that formal, computer-based systems have a complementary role. They do not necessarily replace all previous information systems.

Summary

A primary purpose of information systems is to process data into information. Information is used in order to reduce uncertainties about events. This information should be, *inter alia*, relevant, accurate, concise and timely and managers will receive it both from formal and informal sources.

KEY TERMS   Cognitive style   Formal and informal information   Information characteristics and value   Interpersonal network   Uncertainty reduction   Value of information.

Further reading

Ackoff R.L., Management MIS information systems, *Management Science*, **4**, pp. 147–156, 1967.
Benbasat I.B. and Taylor R.N., The impact of cognitive styles on information system design, *MIS Quarterly*, **2**, 2 June, 1978.
Cherry C., *On Human Communication*, MIT Press, Cambridge, Massachusetts, 1957.
Feltham G.A., The value of information, *The Accounting Review*, Oct, pp. 684–696, 1968.
McKenny J.L. and Keen P.G.W., How managers' minds work, *Harvard Business Review*, May/June, pp. 79–90, 1974.
Mintzberg H., *Impediments to the Use of Management Information*, Society of Management Accountants of Canada and NAA, Canada, 1975.

3
Managers, decisions and organizations

In order to understand the development of computer-based information systems in management, it is essential that we understand how these systems are to be used. Most developments in information systems are intended to assist management decision-making in one form or another. But what exactly is decision-making? How do managers make decisions, and how can the information system help them in this task? We have already seen the link between computers and information in the last chapter, where we examined the desirable attributes of information for management use. Now we must take this a stage further and look more directly at management's task and the decision-making process.

Characteristics of management

What do managers do? This question has been addressed many times by management theorists, often with widely differing conclusions about what management behaviour really is. In the context of information systems it is useful to consider two distinct views of management behaviour: firstly, a normative view of what management should be about and, secondly, a research-based, empirical view which indicates the roles that managers actually play. Fayol gives us an example of the first approach and Mintzberg provides an example of the second.

MANAGEMENT FUNCTIONS

Henri Fayol, writing in the 1920s, was one of the first to discuss management in systematic terms and his simple schema of management functions has been popular ever since (for further discussion on Fayol, see Brech 1970). According to Fayol the function of management should be seen as a number of distinct tasks; in a modernized form these tasks are as follows.

1. *Planning*   Management considers the objectives of the organization and decides how these are to be achieved. Planning is undertaken at all levels of management, but usually with a different time span in mind. Low level management deals primarily with immediate problems, higher management with long-term plans.
2. *Organizing*   Having arrived at a plan of the organization's activities, management can consider the ways in which the necessary tasks to be undertaken can be separated or combined so that they can be assigned appropriately to individuals or groups.
3. *Directing*   This involves motivating the workforce, communicating effectively so that the necessary tasks are properly understood, and coordinating efforts to achieve the planned objectives.
4. *Controlling*   Inevitably, if the operations of the organization are left to themselves, there will be a drift from the desired outcomes. Management must monitor the activities of the organization and identify any discrepancy between outcomes and planned objectives in order to take corrective action.

Clearly, all these activities require information for their successful fulfilment. Often, it is the last mentioned management activity, that of controlling, which receives the lion's share of information system development; but it can be seen that the other management functions merit close attention too, and, in fact, information systems have a crucial role to play in all of them.

MANAGEMENT LEVELS

The functions of management described above are important at all levels of management. But the emphasis of these functions in a manager's job differs according to his or her level in the organization. Management level is partly a function of seniority, partly a function of position in the hierarchy; clearly it depends crucially on the type of management structure pertaining in the organization. Nevertheless, it is useful to distinguish three distinct levels, depending on the general character of the management decisions undertaken (Fig. 3.1).

Top management is involved in strategic decision-making; essentially these decisions have far-reaching consequences which involve substantial amounts of money or are very significant to the organization in other ways. Examples are the decision as to whether to merge with another organization or whether to address some crucial overseas market. These decisions often relate to events or outcomes on a time-scale of years or even decades into the future. Middle management is more concerned with tactical decisions; these involve implementing the strategy conceived by top management. For example, where top management has decided to move into an overseas market, middle management would implement the strategy and decide on manning levels and annual targets. A major concern of middle management is the monitoring and control of organizational outcomes. Typically, tactical decisions involve smaller financial

Figure 3.1   Management levels and decision

considerations than strategic ones, and will have effect weeks or months into the future. Supervisory management makes operational decisions about day-to-day activities in the organization. Continuing the example from above, supervisory management would effect the daily disposition of the sales force in the new marketing effort. The financial effects will be smaller than in the other decision types, and the time-scale correspondingly shorter, perhaps measured in hours or days.

Clearly, it would be wrong to imagine that decisions can be placed too rigidly into watertight compartments; there will be many instances of overlapping responsibilities and decision activities in the hurly-burly of organizational life. Nevertheless, it is useful to remember that there are substantial differences in management approach and function and these emerge in different information needs. It would be quite wrong, for instance, to provide a top manager with the kind of detailed, daily operational information required by supervisory management.

MANAGEMENT ROLES

A very useful insight into management comes from considering managerial behaviour in terms of roles and role requirements. A role can be considered simply as a set of requirements on the individual, together with the perceptions of role occupant, and others, as to the part the individual has to play. Most people have very many different roles which they occupy at work and at home. For example, a University student may play all of these roles: daughter, sister, friend, student, learner, teacher, listener, presenter and so on.

Managers also play many different roles. Mintzberg (1973) outlined a set of ten managerial roles, based on empirical research into the behaviour of working managers. Mintzberg identified six characteristics of managerial work which gave rise to the roles identified. Managerial work is typified by high-speed, high-volume tasks: up to 600 different tasks in one day. These activities are brief, fragmented and of considerable variety; attention must be rapidly switched from one activity to another as priorities change due to *ad hoc* problems that arise. The manager is the linchpin between his organization and a diverse network of contacts. Managers show a strong preference for verbal media, that is, meetings and phone calls, not mail and memos. Despite the above calls on their time, managers appear to have a reasonable amount of control over their daily agenda. From these characteristics of the work that they perform, Mintzberg derived the following managerial roles.

Interpersonal roles

- Figurehead: linked to the manager's status; the manager acts as a symbol, saying when signing certain documents or presiding over formal meetings.
- Leader: the manager exercises power; he or she influences the organization by giving commands and by expressing norms and values and encouraging desired behaviour.
- Liaison: a role characterized by the network of relationships which the manager creates and maintains.

Informational roles

- Monitor: the manger continually seeks relevant information about the organization so that he or she can detect opportunities and threats.
- Disseminator: information is transmitted within the organization; the manager often has special access to information from a wide variety of sources, and acts so as to filter and transmit this information.
- Spokesperson: this role involves transmitting information outside the organization or local department; because of his or her position the manager is expected to act as spokesperson to various external groups, e.g. customers, suppliers or shareholders.

Decisional roles

- Entrepreneur: the manager initiates decision activity at his or her own discretion; he or she is engaged in planned and systematic changes.
- Disturbance handler: the manager reacts to events and takes the necessary decisions; he or she is engaged in a reactive or involuntary action.
- Resource allocator: perhaps the most prominent managerial role; the manager is deciding how to utilize organizational resources, including money, materials and, especially, people.
- Negotiator: the manager is making arrangements with others, e.g. union representatives, customers, external consultants.

Clearly, all these roles require the role incumbent to use information of various kinds. Which of these roles is most usually supported by information systems? Monitoring and resource allocation are activities which are most often addressed by classical MIS. But as the other managerial roles are also important, should not information systems be devised to support these roles too? Another important consideration arising from these 10 roles is that only four of them are explicitly about decision-making. Clearly, a manager does many important things which are not formally concerned with decision-making in its narrow sense. It would be wrong, therefore, to consider information systems as being only concerned with decisional behaviour. Managerial activity is about many other things apart from decision-making, and information systems should therefore be expected to play a broader part in the manager's working life. Nevertheless, decision-making is a key managerial activity which is directly addressed by information systems and it is necessary to examine this aspect of managerial behaviour in more detail.

It should also be appreciated that managers can be classified by their function (for example, finance, production, marketing) as well as by their roles or place in the hierarchy. Such a financial classification is very restrictive as it explains little of what managers do or need by way of information; the foregoing analysis is of more relevance to our study of information systems.

Models of the decision process

PROGRAMMABLE AND NON-PROGRAMMABLE DECISIONS

A very useful categorization of decisions was first described by Simon (1960). Simon's idea was that all decisions made by managers can be regarded as falling along a continuum ranging from programmable at one end through to non-programmable at the other (Table 3.1). Programmable decisions are routine decisions which have been clearly defined. For example, when creating a sales invoice the decision as to how much VAT to charge is defined by law; the decision mechanism, together with the necessary data about VAT rates, is easy to program into a computer (hence the term programmable).

Non-programmable decisions, on the other hand, are more messy and harder to define completely. For example, the decision on whether to marry your girl/boy friend will involve criteria which are very hard to define (and have certainly not been so defined in law, at least in the West), together with

Table 3.1 The programmable decision spectrum

Programmable	*Non-programmable*
Routine	Novel
Repetitive	Once-off
Clearly structured	Not structured
Procedures defined	Procedures unknown
Complete information	Uncertainty
Reliance upon rules and regulations	Reliance upon judgement and creativity

information which could be very hard to come by! Another important consideration is that the method of making the decision may not be at all clear; you may not have made this decision very often in the past and so have little experience to guide you!

In fact, in a management context it often appears that the more interesting, important and difficult decisions are of the non-programmable type.

DECISION CHARACTERISTICS

In management, examples of decisions which clearly fall into the two categories are not hard to come by. Programmable decisions include those undertaken in the work of invoicing and elementary accounting, in factory machine-scheduling and stock control. Non-programmable decisions depend to some extent on the particular organization involved, but for many businesses these difficult decisions occur in take-overs or mergers, in the creation of long-term marketing strategy and, particularly, in the decisions involving people and social and ethical issues.

Of course, many decisions will not fall neatly into one category or the other; there will be occasions where the information required is only partly complete, or where the decision procedures have been gone through once before so that the situation is not entirely new.

An important part of the work of people involved in management information systems is the moving of decisions from the non-programmable end of the continuum to the programmable end; when that has been achieved in a certain circumstance, then the decision may be readily undertaken by computer. But in general terms this work is by no means complete; there are very many decisions in management which are not programmable, and plenty which may never be programmed. Looking on the bright side: there will always be plenty of challenging situations for people engaged in developing management information systems. Also, the likelihood is that there will always be the need for creative managers, at all levels.

But what exactly is a decision? Although there are very many different definitions, we can identify certain elements which will be present in all decisions:

ELEMENTS OF DECISION

1. Problem space: a certain situation in which the decision problem is embedded.
2. Decision-maker: an individual, or group of people, who 'owns' the decision problem.
3. Goals or objectives: desirable outcomes which the decision-maker wishes to obtain.
4. Alternatives: a set of choices from which a decision will be made.
5. Choice: the selection of an alternative.

Table 3.2 The decision-making process

Phase	Function
1 Intelligence	Scanning the environment
2 Design	Generating solutions
3 Choice	Selecting an alternative
4 Implementation	Putting the choice into effect
5 Review	Monitoring outcomes

There have been many attempts to define the organizational decision-making process. A simple model which recognizes five distinct phases (Table 3.2) is useful for considering the impact of information systems. The first three phases are based on the famous model due to Simon (1960); this has been extended to show the two extra steps usually found in normative decision models.

Phase 1: intelligence

This phase relates to the manager scanning his or her environment, looking for opportunities and problems about which he or she needs to make a decision. Inevitably, the process involves processing information; essentially it is a problem-finding process.

Phase 2: design

Here the decision-maker needs to create or design possible solutions to the problems or opportunities that he or she has identified. It is also necessary to design methods for developing criteria, decision methods and the means of testing the solution. Part of the process is the very important step of defining clearly what the problem is, so that subsequent phases do not operate on the wrong problem.

Phase 3: choice

This is the part of the decision-making process which has received the most attention from management scientists and business theorists. The emphasis is on evaluating and selecting among known alternatives or solutions, and there are a number of methods available for doing this so as to achieve optimum outcomes. These methods include: mathematical equations, linear programming, dynamic programming, queuing theory, inventory control equations, decision tables, break-even analysis, minimax rule, decision analysis (decision networking), game theory, and there are many others. A detailed discussion of these methods is beyond the scope of this book, but interested readers are referred to suggested texts in the Further reading at the end of the chapter. Because of the emphasis on the mathematical derivation of economically optimum solutions, the computer has traditionally been routinely involved in this phase of the decision process.

Phase 4: implementation

Having identified a problem and selected a solution, the next (and vital) step is to ensure that the solution is implemented. In a management setting this may well involve the introduction of a number of new issues to do with organizational and social problems which are themselves difficult to incorporate into economically optimum decision processes. Essentially, the process is one of planning and organizing the events required of the decision solution, taking into account the individuals and groups who will be involved and the special needs of the specific situation.

In fact, the implementation of computer systems themselves (say, as part of the solution to an information overload problem) is an important special case of the implementation problem, and one which is dealt with in greater depth in a later chapter.

Phase 5: review

When the decision solution has been successfully implemented, there is the ongoing need to check that the solution is working (and continues to work) in the way that was expected. This involves carefully assessing the present situation and comparing this with the anticipated outcomes which were to be achieved from the decision solution chosen. This is effectively a monitoring process, and this idea ties in well with the earlier description of middle-management functions. The computer has traditionally been employed in the detailed task of comparing and contrasting information arising from the present situation against information about objectives expressed in the form of targets or budgets.

COMPUTER SUPPORT FOR DECISION

Clearly, computer-based information systems have a crucial role to play in the managerial decision process. With the five-phase decision model in mind, we can see more clearly how this can be achieved.

The intelligence phase requires scanning of key environmental information; the computer can help here by storing and presenting information for scan, and perhaps by performing routine scanning tasks in order to report by exception when situations arise which require management action. The use of advanced data filing systems, such as database, are important here.

The design phase involves creating potential solutions; this has not traditionally been an area where computers have been helpful, but, for example, recent developments in decision conferencing have resulted in systems which aid the' process of creatively addressing solutions. Decision support systems are an important growth area, and this topic is given special attention in a later chapter. There is little doubt that this is an area of tremendous potential for the development of new computer systems.

The choice phase is one where computers have traditionally been very effectively employed, using a whole range of different techniques. The important issue here for the information system user is to select the appropriate mathematical or management science technique for the decision situation; in practice this is often quite difficult to do, and it may be advisable to seek the advice of a management science specialist. The operation of the technique usually involves the use of a software package (e.g. for linear programming), and once the appropriate data has been gathered the evaluation of different options may be quite straightforward.

The implementation phase of the decision process is very much a management operation, involving the balancing of economic- and people-issues and other intangibles. Computer-based systems can help here by storing and displaying data on past decisions and their consequences, and by keeping management up to date on the progress of the implementation. A well-tried and popular technique for controlling the implementation of large projects is the critical path method (CPM), also known as project evaluation and review technique (PERT).

Reviewing the results of decision implementation is a task particularly suited to computer-based information systems. Data from the organization which relates to the solution implemented can automatically be compared against data relating to the organization's objectives, and discrepancies highlighted for management action. Many accounting and budgetary systems are designed with this principle in mind.

NORMATIVE VERSUS DESCRIPTIVE DECISION MODELS

Thus far we have considered the management decision process in terms of three simple decision models (the word 'model' is used here to mean a simplification of reality, and elementary 'theory'). Of these, the five-phase decision process model is perhaps the most significant; but all of these models represent important (and above all useful) tools for understanding management's information requirements.

However, this is not the whole story. The human decision process is a subtle and complex one, and psychologists and scientists from several disciplines are still grappling with the task of attempting to understand the intricacies of human behaviour in organizations. The five-phase decision model is a normative one, in the sense that it represents the way in which managers are supposed to act in a decision situation (Fig. 3.2). In practice, things may be very different because managers respond as individuals to personal and political issues. In other words they are human beings, and who among us can claim that they behave in a completely rational way all the time?

It is important, therefore, to look at the work of researchers who have examined the way real managers behave in real organizations, in order that we are not misled about the nature of the situation in which information systems are to operate. Theories of management decision which have been arrived at in this way are known as descriptive theories, because they represent what actually

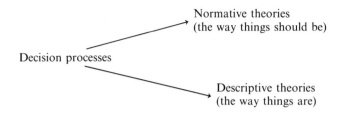

Figure 3.2 Normative and descriptive theories

happens rather than what ought to happen. This descriptive work will be described in the next chapters.

Human decision-making

One of the most useful features of computer systems is that they can provide facilities and capabilities which humans do not have, for example, the ability to accurately store and retrieve thousands of items of information very rapidly, and to perform complex calculations in a fraction of a second. By the same token, humans have distinct abilities which are very hard to reproduce in computer systems, for example, the ability to work with incomplete data, and the use of heuristics. This last point will be discussed in more detail later.

A human being processes information by means of three cognitive mechanisms: the perceptual subsystems, short-term memory and long-term memory (Fig. 3.3). There is evidence that information is processed serially (i.e. one item at a time), and that the short-term memory holds only seven items at any one time (note Miller's magical number 7). The human long-term memory is an amazing device which has an extraordinary capacity with a subtle and

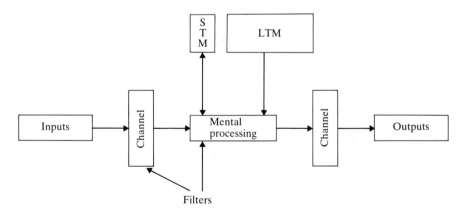

Figure 3.3 The human information processing system

complex mechanism for linking items stored; once information has entered long-term memory it appears to be stored for ever (although the linking mechanisms can change so that we can seem to forget things if the items are not frequently accessed).

Although the human brain is a phenomenally sophisticated and powerful device, it has a number of limitations with respect to information processing, and it is possible to augment these by providing computer-based support.

The limitations of short-term memory mean that a human's ability to process symbols and digits without error is extremely limited. For example, the six- or seven-digit postcode is just within the capacity of short-term memory. LE11 3TU is a postcode, a sequence which can be remembered, but only after some rehearsal (i.e. it has been stored in long-term memory); certainly most people cannot mentally manipulate or memorize several postcodes at the same time at all easily.

The same phenomenon is illustrated by telephone numbers and local dialling codes. If somebody gives you their six-digit phone number, you may be able to use this without difficulty; if the number is preceded by a new four-digit local code then the internal processing task is much more difficult. In fact humans process data in 'chunks' rather than in digits and symbols, and the exact details of the cognitive limitations are not at all clear.

Computers, in contrast to humans, have a tremendous capacity for manipulating symbols and digits with great speed and accuracy, and many management applications involving these manipulations are performed by computer.

Another well-researched human limitation is the inability of most people to make good decisions with information involving probabilities rather than absolutes. This leads to significant errors of judgement in important decision tasks. For example, most gamblers will study the past run of results on a roulette wheel before placing a bet, even though they probably know that past results cannot possibly affect future outcomes.

Most people unconsciously bias their judgements in various ways, for example, by using information which is readily available rather than seeking out new relevant facts. Some of the limitations of human information processing for decision are shown below.

- Processing limitations:
  - processing capacity easily overloaded,
  - inability to make use of probabilistic information,
  - poor discrimination between causality and correlation,
  - lack of ability to integrate information from multiple sources.
- Biased filtering of information:
  - preference given to available data (availability bias),
  - preference given to explicit concrete, factual data over intangibles (factual bias),

- preference given to most recent data (recency bias),
- past preferences affect judgement (hindsight bias),
- preference given to data which has familiar units (units bias).

There are certain other characteristics of the decision-maker which are worth noting. The theory of cognitive dissonance (Festinger, 1957) explains why people will revise their views in order to conform with an action which they have already taken. For example, people who have recently bought a new car will pay most attention to adverts for the same make, because this acts as a means of reinforcement of their choice. This was shown in a famous experiment in which students were offered various amounts of money to write an essay encapsulating rather unpopular views; the students who had been offered the least money (and therefore suffered the most cognitive dissonance in having to express distasteful opinions) changed their views in line with the essay more than the ones who had been offered most money. In other words the students who had least monetary inducement needed to justify their actions in another way, and the only way to do this was to change their views.

DECISIONS IN ORGANIZATIONS

Management decisions are rarely made by individuals acting entirely in isolation. Most people are influenced, directly or indirectly, by others in the organization in which they work. This idea leads to considering how organizations as a whole behave when decisions are made. Simon (1960) showed that, in fact, organizations do not behave in a perfectly rational and economic manner; rather, they make decisions which are 'good enough' for the purposes at hand but which are not necessarily optimum. This process of finding a solution which is satisfactory, but not necessarily the best, is known as *satisficing*.

Taking this idea a stage further, Lindblom (1959) described how organizations rarely make decisions which would involve a substantial change of direction; instead, they move forward in small, limited steps towards their goals; in other words, they are 'muddling through'. Lindblom argues that this is an appropriate response for large organizations which need to achieve stability, and effectively he justifies satisficing as an appropriate organizational decision strategy.

A further aspect of decision-making involves the consideration of organizational politics. Inevitably, when considering objectives, it is necessary to ask: whose objectives are these? In any organization there will nearly always be different views about how the organization is to be run, and different interests at stake; inevitably there will be conflict between individuals or groups of individuals who have different ideas about how the organization's resources are to be utilized. These conflicts lead to political behaviour; this behaviour involves the use of power together with political skill to achieve outcomes desirable to the individual or group concerned. Information is used as a means to achieving political ends, as well as being a key resource in its own right.

The information provider needs to be very much aware that information is a double-edged sword, and that it is not always utilized for strictly rational purposes. Indeed, there is an increasing trend (see Robey and Markus, 1984) for management theorists to view decision processes in organizations from a political viewpoint rather than from within traditional economic or rational frameworks.

Summary

Information systems attempt to assist managerial activities. These activities include planning, organizing and controlling, and may take place at different organizational levels. The manager will have a number of roles of an interpersonal, informational and decisional nature. The decisions faced may be programmable or non-programmable; the type of computer support needed being dependent on this. It should further be noted that human decision-takers differ in their abilities and style of information processing and a useful information system should take account of this.

KEY TERMS   Bias   Cognitive dissonance   Cognitive filtering   Discrimination   Five-stage decision model: intelligence, design, choice, human information processing (HIP), long-term memory (LTM)   Management functions: planning, organizing, directing, controlling   Normative and descriptive decision models   Programmable and non-programmable decisions   Role theory   Satisficing   Short-term memory (STM)   Strategic and tactical decisions.

Further reading

Anderson D.R., Sweeney D.J. and Williams T.A., *An Introduction to Management Science*, West, New York, 1985.

Anthony R.N., *Planning and Control Systems: A Framework for Analysis*, Harvard Business School, Boston, Massachusetts, 1965.

Brech E.F. (Ed.), *The Principles and Practice of Management*, Longman, London, 1970.

Cyert R.M. and March J.C., *A Behavioural Theory of the Firm*, Prentice Hall, New Jersey, 1963.

Festinger L., *A Theory of Cognitive Dissonance*, Row and Peterson, Evanston, Illinois, 1957.

Janis I.L. and Mann L., *Decision Making*, The Free Press, New York, 1977.

Lindblom C.E., The science of muddling through, *Public Administration Review*, **19**, 1959.

Lucey T., *Quantitative Techniques*, DP Publications, Eastleigh, Hants, 1985.

Miller G.A., The magical number seven, plus or minus two: some limits on our capability for processing information, *The Psychological Review*, **63** (2), 81–97, 1956.

Mintzberg H., *The Nature of Managerial Work*, Harper and Row, New York, 1973.

Mintzberg H.A., Raisinghani D. and Theoret A., The structure of unstructured decision processes, *Administrative Science Quarterly*, **21**, 246–275, 1976.

Pettigrew A., *The Politics of Organizational Decision Making*, Tavistock Publications, London, 1973.

Robey D. and Markus M.L., Rituals in information systems design, *MIS Quarterly*, March, 1984.

Simon H.A., *The New Science of Management Decision*, Prentice-Hall, New Jersey, 1960.

Stewart R., *Managers And Their Jobs*, Macmillan, London, 1967.

4
The systems approach

The word system is in common use as well as in an information context; we refer to the education system, or the national transport system, for example. In an information context one could refer to a computer system,or perhaps to a wider set of elements – the information system – meaning all aspects of information provision, including human processing. In fact there is a separate field of study, quite apart from computers, which seeks to understand how the world works in terms of the general properties of systems. This field of study examines the world using a set of principles known as general systems theory (GST), or the systems approach. This area provides an important set of insights into the way that systems work generally, and is especially useful when considering how computers and people in organizations work together.

General systems theory

The essence of general systems theory is that it provides a different way of thinking about problems. It originated in thinking from philosophy, engineering and biology and some of its ideas are recognizably rooted in the original disciplines. It is usually couched in rather abstract terms, which makes it somewhat difficult to get hold of: in the following discussion concrete examples will be given wherever possible in order to make the topic more approachable.

What is a system? In order to discuss this question it is useful to consider some examples:

- Solar system: the sun, moon, earth and planets all connected by gravitational forces.
- Traffic system: roads, vehicles, drivers, rules and regulations all forming a complex working pattern.

- Computer system: hardware elements and software working together to produce information.

These are examples of concrete systems; they all have in common the idea of a set of elements (the planets, say, or vehicles and drivers) which are connected in some way. Following this, we can now attempt a definition:

A system is a collection of entities which are related to each other and to their environment so that they form a whole.

In other words, a system has a set of parts that are connected in some way which makes the thing as a whole interesting. This is a very broad definition, and systems concepts can be applied to a great many areas of study. It is important to note that systems under study can be defined in different ways; we define a system in a certain way because it is useful to do so, or because it represents the way most people look at it, rather than because of any inherent structure.

A key concept arising from the discussion so far is that the elements of a system, when considered separately, do not provide the essence of the system. One needs to consider the thing as a whole in order to understand it fully; in other words the whole is greater than the sum of the parts. This effect is known as synergy. This is especially true of organizational systems in general, and information systems in particular. For example, a common error is to think only about the computer aspects of an information system, and to ignore the people who are to make use of the information.

SYSTEM COMPONENTS

It is now time to consider an example of a computer-based information system so that we can examine system components a little more closely. The stock control system chosen is shown as a systems map in Fig. 4.1, i.e. the system elements are indicated together with the interconnections between them. Clearly, there are many more connections than are shown here; as explained earlier, the system is defined so as to show the important elements for a given situation or requirement.

The systems map shows key elements of the stock control system and the ways in which these elements interact. A vital consideration is the way in which the system interacts with other systems; for example, senior management, suppliers and customers are not part of our stock control system (as defined here) yet they interact crucially with it.

Key system components include:

- Boundary: this defines the edge of the system of interest; inside the boundary is the system proper, outside the boundary is the rest of the world (environment) with which the system connects.
- Environment: the outside world in which the system exists; business organizations interact with the economic environment.
- Interface: the area of contact between the system and its environment; often

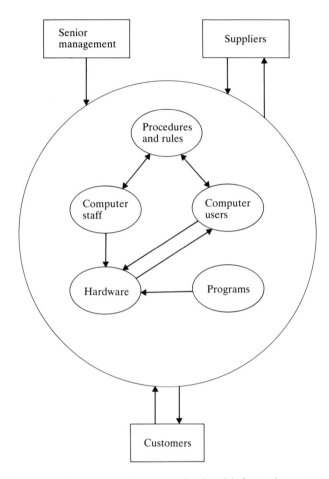

Figure 4.1 Stock control: an organizational information system

this is a key area, e.g. the human/computer interface.
- Inputs: everything taken in by the system from its environment; for an organization this could be raw materials, energy, money, information.
- Outputs: everything discharged from the system into its environment; for a business this could be finished products, money, information, waste energy in the form of heat and so on.

CHARACTERISTICS OF SYSTEMS

A key feature of general systems theory is that it provides useful and important general insights into the way in which systems work. Our discussion on system boundaries and environments leads to the first characteristic, the degree to which a particular system is open or closed.

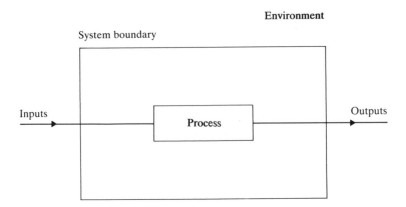

Figure 4.2   Schematic view of the open system

Closed systems

These have no interaction at all with their environment; an example would be a chemical reaction occurring in a specially sealed container. Industrial processing plants attempt to keep their hazardous processes as closed systems. In practice, no system can be completely cut off from its environment (and evidence about pollution from nuclear power stations emphasizes this point). But it is often useful to consider certain systems as being closed, for example, the solar environment, open space, but astronomers can safely ignore these effects when calculating the motions of the planets and can usefully regard the system as being closed.

Open systems

These interchange materials or energy or information with their environments. All forms of life are open systems and interact constantly with their worlds. All organizational systems can be regarded as open, and this is by far the most important category from our point of view. A generalized view of an open system is shown in Fig. 4.2. This figure emphasizes the importance of the interactions between the system and the environment, and introduces the idea of the system transforming inputs by way of some process.

Deterministic systems

These behave in a way such that any state of the system can be predicted if the rules of system behaviour are known. For example, the exact position of the planets in the solar system can be calculated hundreds of years into the future, by the application of Newtonian celestial mechanics. In a business setting, the workings of a computer program are deterministic because the computer follows a set of program instructions in a precisely predictable way (unless it breaks down!).

Probabilistic or stochastic systems

In contrast, these systems do not behave in a precisely predictable way. Here, events occur according to chance and if we are to predict the state of the system we must use the laws of probability and statistics. Many systems of great interest are unpredictable, or at best only partly predictable, for example the weather systems surrounding the British Isles! Another stochastic system is the national economic system, here the fluctuations of economic growth or stagnation are caused by a complex set of factors operating in an uncertain environment and Government can at best exert only a partial influence. All organizational and information systems should be regarded as at least partially probabilistic, if only because they include human elements, these being the least predictable of natural phenomena!

Self-regulatory systems

These react to outside influences in a purposeful manner, in order to achieve some objective. All animals (all living forms, perhaps) act in this way in order to survive, propagate and pass on their genes to the next generation. Organizations, too, can be regarded as self-regulatory, but, of course, when considering the objectives of the organization, one must be careful to ask how these tie in with the goals of the individuals who make up the organization.

Static systems

As the name implies, these are systems which never change their states; a system of laws (such as the biblical ten commandments) might be regarded as static.

Dynamic systems

These are in constant change, and can be viewed as continually moving from one state to another. For example, certain insect populations such as locusts can be considered to be dynamic as they expand or contract according to conditions such as food availability, predator populations and weather.

Dynamic equilibrium

This refers to systems which react to events in their environment by 'attempting' to remain static. To do this they must make continual internal changes, rather like a man balancing on a tightrope who continually shifts his position in order to remain in place. Biological systems which behave in this way are called homeostatic. Many organizations can be regarded as behaving in this way; in order to survive they must adapt and change in order to cope with a turbulent economic environment. This brings in the crucial question of how systems exert control, which will be considered in the next section.

Black-box systems

It is often the case that the detailed workings of a system are just not fully understood (like the cognitive processes of the human brain), or are too complex to be fully described (like the details of weather systems). In these cases it is useful to regard the processing part of the system as a black box, i.e. it has an opaque cover and its internal workings are not open to inspection. Instead, it is useful to discuss the inputs and outputs rather than the precise processing details. For example, in our later discussion on computer hardware we will consider computer components only down to a certain level; we will not examine the details of electronic mechanisms, or the movements of electrons. In this way, we are regarding the computer itself as a black box and we can discuss the characteristics of inputs and outputs without obscuring the business issues with too much technical detail.

Equifinality

This is a feature of systems which organize themselves in different ways to achieve the same result; in other words there may be several different system structures and/or processes which can achieve the same final solution. For example, given the same requirement specification, individual computer programmers may write programs which all achieve exactly the same outputs, but the details of each program may differ substantially. An organization may perceive a number of different ways of achieving its objectives.

Subsystems

We can regard our organizational system in Fig. 4.1 as being made up of five distinct subsystems. For example, we have a hardware subsystem and a subsystem of rules and procedures. If necessary we can regard these separately and examine them in detail as systems in their own right. This look at subsystems is like taking a microscope to our system and examining its components. This concept is much used in information system design where large systems are broken down into manageable subsystems and developed separately.

Coupled subsystems

In separating out subsystems for consideration, we find that they are connected (coupled) to other subsystems in various ways. In breaking down information systems for development, we wish to keep the subsystems separate so that we can work on them independently; in other words we wish to de-couple them. In doing so we are improving overall reliability because the systems are deliberately isolated and affect each other as little as possible; if one subsystem breaks down, others should be able to carry on without being affected.

This need for de-coupling occurs in many business situations; for example,

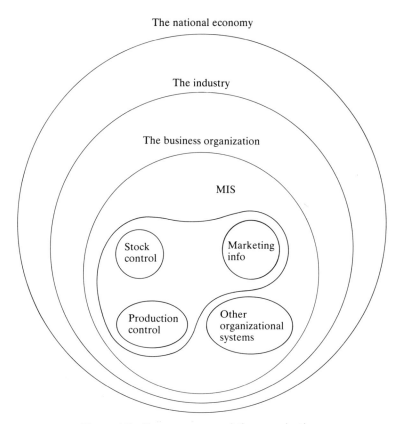

Figure 4.3 Suprasystems and the organization

production and marketing functions are coupled by the requirement to produce goods to satisfy the demands of the market. This may mean that the production system has to work inefficiently to produce short (and hence costly) runs of product to satisfy immediate customer demand; the marketing system may lose sales opportunities by being unable to call for products to meet unexpected sales. The two systems can be de-coupled by providing a stock of goods which acts as a buffer between the requirements of production and marketing; this buffer enables each system to act independently and to achieve optimum working conditions.

Suprasystems

We examine a system under a microscope, as it were, in order to determine its subsystems; by the same token, we can pull back and look at our system through a wide-angle telescope and examine in breadth the hierarchy of systems of which it is itself a part. For example, we can consider the stock control system as being part of the overall business MIS (which might include sales and production information subsystems as well as the stock control system). The overall business MIS is a suprasystem; it is the one above the system we are examining. The MIS in its turn can be considered as part of the business organizational system, which in itself is part of an industry, which is part of a national economy, and so on. Figure 4.3 shows a hierarchy of suprasystems.

Control in organizational systems

The idea of control is fundamental to management, and we have already discussed aspects of control when considering management roles and decision-making. The purpose of this section is to consider control from a systems behaviour viewpoint in order to cast fresh light on the nature of management control in organizations.

We have already seen that systems act so as to achieve their objectives (self-regulatory systems). The question arises as to how this is achieved. Consider again the simplified diagram for an open system; this time a control loop has been added (see Fig. 4.4). The principles behind control loops are very important and are worth careful study.

The purpose of the control loop is as follows: the current state of the system outputs is measured by a sensor (S), and this information is carried back to a control mechamism called a comparator (C); here the state of the outputs is compared to the desired state, or standard; if there is a discrepancy between the outputs and standard, then some change is made to the system inputs by an effector (E).

This mechanism—the control loop—enables the system to control its state. The key issue here is the flow of information from the outputs back round to the inputs via the control mechanism: a closed loop. If the loop is broken at any point then the system can no longer control itself because information about the outputs is not available to control the inputs. Imagine flying a plane with all the cockpit windows and instruments blanked off; you still have a means of changing the system outputs via the usual controls, but with no information on the plane's current state how do you know whether to bank left or right, or whether you should raise or lower the nose? The flow of information about the current system state is crucial in business also, in order that management can see what is happening at any particular time in order to make the necessary changes.

When information about the output state is compared to the desired state, the control mechanism usually acts so as to reverse any discrepancy; if your car wanders too far to the right, then you steer left to correct it. This is known as negative feedback. Most control mechanisms work in this way.

Examples of negative feedback occur throughout the natural and technological world. A commonplace example occurs in the thermostat which controls the boiler in the domestic central heating system. If the room temperature (system output) is too high compared to the thermostat temperature setting (standard), then the thermostat acts so as to shut off the energy supply (input) to the boiler.

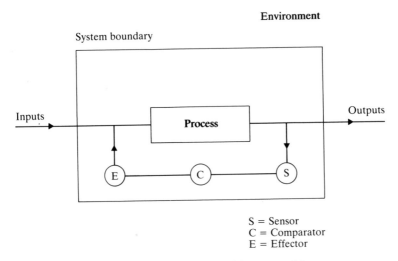

Figure 4.4 The open system with a control loop

If the room becomes too cold, then the thermostat acts so as to increase the energy supply. Successful business operations relay on negative feedback to control their activities; system outputs (in terms of production, or services supplied) are compared to budget or target values and are then adjusted accordingly.

Positive feedback occurs when a system responds to an increase in outputs by increasing the inputs (and vice versa). Usually, this is a recipe for disaster as the system runs wild until halted by some external mechanism. For example, a musician using an amplified public address system may place the microphone too near the loudspeaker; the microphone then picks up the amplified sound and passes it back through the system where it is further amplified, and so on, producing a rapidly increasing noise called howlback (see Fig. 4.5).

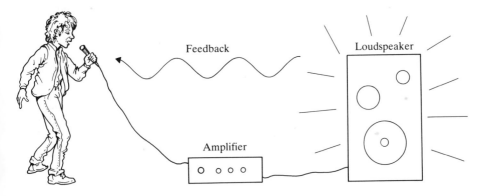

Figure 4.5 Positive feedback

Natural systems may also run wild in this way; a population of insects responds to increased food availability arising from mankind's farming activity by increasing in size. Usually such increases produce an environmental response such as an increase in predator populations, or perhaps man adds negative feedback to the system by spraying pesticides in proportion to the insect population. Of course, no system can respond to positive feedback for very long before some corrective action occurs, arising from within the system itself or from its environment.

It is not unknown for businesses to act as though there were a positive feedback mechanism; increased sales success sometimes results in runaway selling activity (to take advantage of the opportunity) accompanied by attempts to increase production outputs to match. Such an upward spiral is usually halted by cashflow problems, i.e. there is insufficient money in the business to finance the working capital required for the extra sales; firms have gone bankrupt from this cause, which is known as overtrading.

Even negative feedback systems have problems associated with them. Consider first the timing of feedback. As you drive a car, the visual feedback on road and traffic conditions is virtually instantaneous, but suppose there was a 10-second delay between your seeing some obstacle and responding with the footbrake or steering wheel; clearly you would not survive for long in modern traffic conditions. Other feedback systems have to tolerate extended delays; for example, the effect of an advertising campaign may not be known for weeks or months after the campaign has begun, owing to the difficulties of monitoring customer opinion and to delay before customers make purchases. By the time the results have been evaluated and assessed, the current campaigning may have finished and cannot benefit from knowledge of its effectiveness. Most business systems suffer from feedback delays to some extent; customer-based systems can act so as to minimize the delay.

A particular problem arising from feedback delay is the phenomenon of oscillation or hunting. An example of this occurs when we try to control a shower. As the water is turned on it runs cold, so we turn the temperature control up to 'warm'; however, nothing appears to happen immediately (because the hot water takes time to run from the mixer mechanism to the shower head) so we try turning the control to 'hot'. Eventually, hot water comes through, too hot perhaps, so we respond by turning the control back to 'warm'; again nothing happens immediately because of the time for the water to flow through the pipes so we respond by turning the control back to 'cold'. Eventually cold water comes through and we try to compensate by adjusting the control, and the cycle repeats itself. The effects of this over-control are shown in Fig. 4.6.

The cure for the unwanted oscillations is to damp down the exaggerated control responses by undercompensating, or to delay the execution of the effector. The unwanted oscillations due to feedback delay are common in many technological systems, and occur in business systems also. A common example

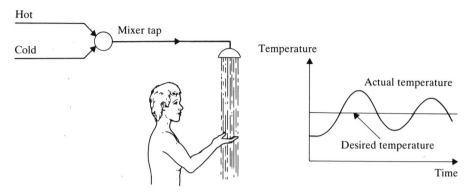

Figure 4.6   The effect of feedback delay

in business occurs in sales performance targeting, where a salesman's annual targets and commission are set according to last year's performance; if he is lucky, the salesman may have an easy year and good commission, only to find that his targets are set much higher next year, when he may have a thin time of it.

FEEDFORWARD

With feedforward, an additional component called a predictor (P) is added to the control loop circuit of Fig. 4.7 (compare this with feedback control in Fig. 4.4). The predictor uses data about the current state of the system together with a predictive model of the process so as to estimate the future state of the system. The prediction about the future (rather than straightforward data about the

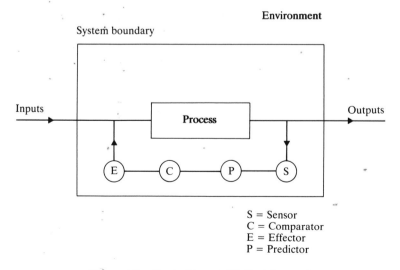

S = Sensor
C = Comparator
E = Effector
P = Predictor

Figure 4.7   Control loop with feed-forward

present state) is then fed to the comparator which compares it to the desired state in the usual way. The comparator and effector will then make adjustments to the system state in the same way as with feedback. Feedforward control mechanisms are not as common as feedback in management situations, although their use is highly desirable.

An example of feedforward is found in stock control using a demand forecasting technique such as exponential smoothing. Exponential smoothing is a simple forecasting technique which bases predictions of the future on past data which is weighted so that the most recent past carries most weight. Data about present stock levels is combined with forecasts about future demand levels to arrive at desirable current stock levels. Thus, action is taken to adjust stock levels using predictions about future states. This is necessary because of the lead times inherent in most stock ordering systems; it would be no good waiting for stocks to run down before adjusting ordering levels if there is a 10-week delay before a supplier can respond.

REQUISITE VARIETY

Ashby's law of requisite variety (Ashby, 1956) states that in order to achieve effective control, a system must be capable of as much variety as the environment in which it exists. Put another way, the control elements in the system must be flexible enough to cope with all the variations with which it must contend. A system which cannot respond with sufficient variability to changes in its environment will respond inappropriately, with the consequence of inefficiency or possible system failure.

An example of system inefficiency due to lack of requisite variety can be seen in the central heating system we considered earlier. Some systems do not have continuously modifiable inputs but simply switch the boiler on or off according to the state of the environment; this leads to fluctuations around the desired mean. This problem is not due to lag but to the lack of sufficient responses available in the system. In this instance, the inefficiency is relatively minor and is acceptable because it enables a simpler (and hence cheaper) system to be used.

Biological systems show an amazingly varied response to their natural environments; indeed, they must do so or they would not survive. However, even these cannot always cope with unexpected circumstances. For example, most living systems cannot cope with ionizing radiation arising from radioactive nuclear sources. In this instance, the ratiation is a new phenomenon on the earth and living systems have not had time to evolve a response to it.

In a business setting there are a number of consequences of the law of requisite variety. If a decision is to be automated and incorporated into a computer-based system, then the system must be supplied with enough control responses to cope with any situations that might arise. A consequence of the failure to do this is that the system acts incorrectly: it has bugs even though it may respond correctly to all the situations for which it has been programmed. The classic example is the billing system which invoices a customer for a zero amount; when the customer sensibly makes no reply to this, the system issues a reminder, followed eventually by a letter threatening legal action if the zero amount is not paid. This situation continues until somebody steps in to supply an alternative response. The problem here is that the computer was not programmed with sufficient variety to cope with the situation.

In practice, it is very difficult to build in sufficient variety into any control system (be it human- or computer-based) and so there must be scope for flexible responses by people to unusual events. A problem with rigidly bureaucratic organizations is that they cannot respond properly to unusual or complicated events. This often seems to happen where difficult individual cases are involved, and from this has arisen the poor reputation of bureaucracies for handling individual problems.

Implications of GST for computer-based systems

General systems theory acts as an important theoretical underpinning for the study of information systems in business. Importantly, it cuts across the boundaries of the many disciplines which are found in business: finance, economics, management science, marketing, organizational behaviour, industrial relations and so on. These subjects all have separate traditions and philosophies, and provide different viewpoints on the management world. GST can provide a global view, not tied to any particular discipline, and offers terms and concepts acceptable to all.

Instances when a systems approach or systems thinking are useful abound, and some examples of these have been highlighted in the text. Some key general points which reflect the importance of the systemic view are given below.

ADVANTAGES OF SYSTEMS THINKING

1. It provides a unified theoretical framework for the study of business and information systems.
2. It emphasizes the importance of regarding information systems as part of an organizational whole.
3. It provides an understanding of control issues in management.
4. It reveals the multiple interactions of a system with its environment, and highlights the importance of subsystems and suprasystems.

Summary

We have seen how general systems theory can be used to provide insights into the nature of systems in general and computer-based systems in particular. The ideas of open and closed systems, sub- and suprasystems were introduced. System behaviour may be altered by feedback and feedforward and by delays in either. Finally, variety is required in a system in order that it may achieve effective control.

KEY TERMS   Black box   Boundary   Closed system   Closed loop   Comparator   Control loop   Coupling and de-coupling   Cybernetics   Deterministic   Dynamic equilibrium   Effector   Entities   Environment   Equifinality   Exponential smoothing   Feedback delay   Feedforward   General systems theory (GST)   Homeostatic   Hunting   Interface   Negative feedback   Open system   Open loop   Oscillation (hunting)   Positive feedback   Predictor   Probabilistic (stochastic)   Requisite variety   Self-regulatory system   Sensor   Subsystem   Suprasystem   Synergy   Systems approach.

Further reading

Ashby H.R., *Introduction to Cybernetics*, Wiley, London, 1956.
Beer S., *The Brain of the Firm*, Allen Lane, London, 1972.
Beishon J. and Peter G. (Eds), *Systems Behaviour*, Open University Press, Milton Keynes, 1976.
Checkland P., *Systems Thinking, Systems Practice*, Wiley, Chichester, 1981.
Cushing B.E. and Romney M.E., *Accounting Business Information Systems and Organizations*, Addison-Wesley, Reading, Mass., 1987.
Simon H.A., *The Science of the Artificial*, MIT Press, Cambridge, Mass., 1981.
von Bertalanffy L., *General Systems Theory: Foundations, Development, Applications*, George Barziller, New York, 1968.

Summary to Part One

Part One has laid the foundations for our study of information systems. This background has involved looking at the information needs of organizations and managers within those organizations. The advantages available from utilizing computer systems were discussed. A central concept is the transformation of data into information: information being data to which meaning has been attached. Different information is needed at different organizational levels, depending on the manager's function. Different processing and delivery systems will be required to provide this information. The manager's function is often related to the type of decision faced. Higher level management often has to address non-programmable problems, while at low levels, tasks can often be delegated to computers.

Managerial problem-solving with computers requires recognition of the complementary nature of their skills. Machines are very good at rapid tedious operations requiring high degrees of accuracy and consistency. Humans, on the other hand, are poor at these tasks, yet adept at inspirational, creative and negotiational activities.

It is important to recognize that the firm is as much a system as any computer. Indeed, the computer, or information system, is a subsystem of the organization. As such both will affect each other. Part Two takes a step into this subsystem, by looking at the components of the technology which underlies information systems.

PART TWO

Information system technology

5
Computer origins

Origins of the computer

Calculating devices of one kind or another have been part of mankind's world since ancient times. The abacus was one of the earliest, dating back to around 1000 BC in ancient China. Table 5.1 shows some of the more important calculators from the last few centuries. The purpose of all these devices was to speed calculation, improve accuracy and take out some of the drudgery of repetitive calculation, although it should be recognized that people were typically very cheap to employ and making life easy for them was not given very high priority.

The modern counterpart of the earlier devices is the simple electronic calculator. The word 'simple' is used in a special sense, not because the calculator itself is simplistic—far from it, in one sense it is an extraordinary artifact of modern technology—but because there is a crucial difference between the calculator, and its antecedents, and a modern digital computer. This difference is reflected in several key features of the modern computer which will be discussed in the sections that follow.

The first significant attempt at developing a true computer was undertaken by Charles Babbage (1792–1871), the English inventor and professor of mathematics at Cambridge. Many of the features of the modern computer were first developed by Babbage and, not surprisingly, modern terminology owes much to him also.

Babbage's first machine was the difference engine. This was designed in response to the requirement for the extensive and complex calculations needed in astronomy, army ballistics tables and certain manufacturing applications of the time. The method of differences is a straightforward mathematical procedure for reducing the calculation of any polynomial to simple additions,

Table 5.1   Early calculating and data processing devices

Inventor	Device	Date
Blaise Pascale	Pascaline adding machine	1642
John Napier	Napier's bones logarithm calculator	1650
Robert Bisaker	slide rule	1650
von Leibnitz	mechanical calculator	1670
Herman Hollerith	punched-card machines for data processing	1880

which can, of course, then be tackled by anybody (or anything) that can add up, even a machine. Hitherto these calculations were performed manually by semi-skilled mathematicians, and the results were slow and error prone. The new machine was not successful in practice (although later versions developed and extended by others were). Babbage himself lost interest after some years of grappling with awkward assistants and limited funding, and turned to the development of a far more ambitious and advanced machine, the 'analytic engine'.

The social and technological background to these developments is important. At the turn of the nineteenth century the English industrial revolution was in full flood; the development of the steam engine resulted in sheer muscle power being replaced by machine. Further, the development of engineering techniques resulted in a number of skilled and semi-skilled manual processes being automated. This was true especially in the cotton spinning and weaving industries in the English Midlands, where the spinning Jenny and steam-powered weaving loom revolutionized the production of cloth. The displacement of labour by machines resulted in riots and the formation of the Luddite movement: a group of people who sought to protect workers' livelihoods by smashing the modern machinery which threatened their jobs.

The automation of skilled manual work in the textile industry required the development of certain engineering techniques. The essential feature of automation is that a process becomes self-regulating, i.e. it does not require continual human intervention. This involves control as well as the replacement of muscle power. The elements of control were discussed in Chapter 4: a direct nineteenth-century application of these principles was the steam governor, a simple device which controlled the speed of steam engines acting under various loads.

But there was something else, too: another engineering idea which has had a far-reaching impact on computer development. In 1804, Joseph-Marie Jacquard (1752–1834) developed a weaving loom which had a new, and subtle, control device. The idea was that the pattern to be woven into the cloth was determined by the pattern of holes punched into a set of cards. These cards were mounted in a reading device where rods passed through the holes (or did not if there was no hole), and thus dictated the pattern of the cloth. When a new pattern was required, a new set of cards was inserted, and the old set was kept until needed. Effectively, these cards represented a stored program which could be used over and over again, or changed or replaced at will. The flexibility offered by this control device gave a tremendous advantage to any machine using it. Similar punched-card control devices were developed for steam organs and player-pianos which could play complex tunes fully automatically.

The crucial point here is that the new control device gave the machine (be it weaving loom or steam organ) much greater scope. Effectively the machine became capable of an infinity of behaviours while working automatically under the control of its stored program. A musical box with a fixed pin-wheel can play but one tune, or perhaps a limited fixed repertoire; but a steam organ with the punched-card control device was capable of as many different tunes as human wit could devise. Using the systems terminology of Chapter 4, we have a control device which is capable of infinite variety. An intriguing feature of these devices is that the tunes to be played, or the pattern of the cloth to be weaved, could be invented long after the machine itself was designed and built. In a very important sense, part of the machine's 'design' had been deferred until later.

A secondary point is that the punched holes in the cards represent a simple binary, yes–no data storage device, and one which has been used extensively during its long history in data processing and in computing. The first data processing application of punched cards came later, in 1890, when they were used to record data from the US census of that year. The cards were processed semi-automatically by tabulating machines designed by Herman Hollerith.

Babbage sought to include the Jacquard control device into his next and most ambitious machine, the analytic engine, started in the 1820s. The idea was that the machine would have a calculating unit which could also make logical comparisons, the mill, and a store which would hold data and intermediate results until needed. The sequence of mathematical processes would be determined by a program held in punched cards. Numbers would be represented by positions on 10-digit wheels and cogs and the machine would be powered by a steam engine. The ideas developed by Babbage for this machine are the direct forerunners of the principles we see in computers today; effectively, Babbage had invented the digital computer.

The principles of programming for the new machine were developed by Babbage together with one of his students, Lord Byron's daughter Lady Ada Augusta, Countess of Lovelace (1816–1852). Lady Augusta became Babbage's collaborator and was the world's first programmer; she developed the programmed loop and other programming techniques which are used extensively today. More than this, she explored the possibility that the machine could handle symbols and logical relations in a way that went beyond mathematics; she envisaged a logical language which could express any relations of objects, so that the machine could, for example, compose music. To honour her contribution to computer science, a programming language—ADA—has been named after her.

The analytic engine was not a practical success. Although conceived with the ideas of the future, it was constructed using the technology of the early nineteenth century, which involved the use of mechanical devices—cogs, wheels, levers and springs—massed together to achieve the design functions. Unfortunately, it was simply not possible then to manufacture components accurately enough to produce a working model, and Babbage's ideas had to wait for a new technology, that of electronics, before finding a practical expression.

The electronic revolution

The development and application of electronics flourished in the 1930s, and found popular expression in the radio receiver. It was during World War II that progress reached a peak with the competitive development of radar and other military devices. At this time a number of electronic and electro-mechanical computing machines were built, primarily in the UK and USA. Some of the most extensive machines built at this time were developed in order to break secret codes, for example a machine called Colossus in the cryptographic unit of the Department of Communications, Bletchley Park, England. This machine was built by a team headed by Alan Turing to crack the secret codes produced by the German Enigma coding device. Colossus was so successful that many secret messages were intercepted and instantly decoded, and this is believed to have had a major impact on the war.

The first true general-purpose, stored-program computer to be built and successfully operated was completed in 1949 at Cambridge University in England. The EDSAC (electronic delay storage automatic computer) was built with about 3000 electronic valves. It had 1024 words of random access electronic memory which held the program and working data and the machine was capable of multiplying in about 6 microseconds.

Similar machines were being developed at about the same time in the USA. For example, the ENIAC (electronic numerical integrator and computer) was built at the University of Pennsylvania, under a contract for the US Army to calculate ballistic tables (there are indeed echoes of Babbage's difference engines here). ENIAC was notable for its sheer physical size: it contained 18 000 valves and used 150 kW of power (equivalent to 150 electric fires). The machine was built in a U-shape, but overall it was 30 metres long and 2.5 metres high. Compare this with a modern desk-top micro which may have many thousands of times the processing capability of ENIAC.

One of the collaborators on the ENIAC project was the American John von Neumann, who did important theoretical work on computer design and whose name is used to describe the architecture of the computer which has been in use up to the present day. He invented (or perhaps re-invented) the stored-program, serial processor concept, which is so important in modern computers. Thus a von Neumann machine means a computer with a serial processing structure that is essentially the same as the one proposed in the late 1940s.

Table 5.2 Key events in the development of computing

Inventor	Key event	Date
von Leibnitz	binary arithmetic	1660
Joseph Jacquard	card-controlled loom	1804
Charles Babbage	difference engine	1823
	analytic engine	1832
Ada Augusta	programming techniques	1836
George Boole	symbolic logic	1854
Herman Hollerith	data processing devices	1880
Thomas Watson	IBM founded	1911
UK team	Colossus code-breaking machine	1942
Alan Turing	principles of universal computing and artificial intelligence	1945
USA team	ENIAC first electronic calculator	1946
John von Neumann	principles of stored-program computer	1947
UK team	EDSAC first stored-program computer	1949
UK team	LEO (Lyons electronic office) first commercial computer used in data processing	1953
John Backus	FORTRAN developed	1956
Intel corp	first microprocessor: the Intel 4004	1971
Micropro	Visicalc and Wordstar, micro-based software packages	1979
IBM	IBM PC	1981
ICOT	Japan announces the Fifth Generation	1982

Another noteworthy pioneer was the English mathematician Alan M. Turing, who first showed theoretically that a machine capable of certain elementary operations could emulate any data processing mechanism; in other words it could be universal in its application. Apart from his contribution to computer design, Turing also discussed the first principles of artificial intelligence at this time (see Part 6).

Computer generations

The development of electronic computers from the late 1940s to the present day has shown an astonishing progression. The principal improvements are characterized by step-changes due to breakthroughs in the design and manufacture of electronic components. Each major change has given rise to a new generation of computers, each generation more powerful, more compact and reliable and, above all, cheaper than its predecessor.

Table 5.3   Step-changes in technology

Generation	Electronic technology	Era	Example machines	Typical memory size	Typical speed (mips)
first	valves	1950s	EDSAC Univac IBM 650	0.4 K	0.01
second	transistors	1960s	NCR 501 CDC-6600 IBM 1410	10 K	0.2
third	integrated circuits (ICs)	1965	IBM 360/30 ICL 1900	64 K	1
	large scale integration (LSI)	1970s	IBM 370/155 Cray-1	512 K	5
fourth	very large scale integration (VLSI)	1980s	IBM 43613 Amdahl 580 IBM pc XT	5 Mbyte	30
fifth	ultra-large scale integration (ULSI) and parallelism	1990s	experimental		

mips: millions of instructions per second.

Each step-change has ushered in a whole new range of computer users, as the reduced cost of machines in the new generation has encouraged fresh entrants to the benefits of automation. Similarly, each generation has resulted in a new range of applications as different uses have become economic, or as improved computing power has made new applications feasible.

THE FIRST GENERATION (1946–1956)

The first generation was based on thermionic valve technology. This involved the linking together of tens of thousands of electronic valves to create the internal logic of the computer. Each evacuated glass valve was several inches high and had an internal heater; the cost of each valve was high, and the reliability was low. Machines were incredibly expensive by today's standards, and were very unreliable; on average, an early machine might work for a few seconds or minutes before a component failure. Thus the mean time between failures (MTBF) might be measured in minutes, or even seconds. Add to this the physical problems of removing large amounts of excess heat, and the intellectual difficulties of programming in machine language and it is easy to see why an early market estimate by IBM showed total world demand for computers at only 20 units!

Nevertheless, these early machines were capable of performing calculations at hitherto unheard of speeds and did useful scientific work. The first commercial data processing application of computing was undertaken in 1953 by the British firm of Lyons, who owned a chain of tea shops and used a first-generation machine christened LEO (Lyons electronic office) to run a payroll application.

THE SECOND GENERATION (1957–1963)

This generation utilized transistors, invented by scientists at Bell Laboratories in the USA as early as 1947. Transistors were far smaller and much more reliable than valves, used less electrical power and cost considerably less to manufacture. Individual transistors were wired to printed circuit boards (PCBs) for ease of assembly.

As well as the significant cost and reliability improvements, the electronic characteristics of the new components enabled substantial computing speed enhancements as well. Main store was built using matrices of ferrite cores; each core retained a magnetic charge to represent binary 0–1 positions. This improvement in store technology provided bigger, faster memories and enabled larger and more sophisticated programs to be run.

A typical commercial machine of the period was the IBM 1401; this machine sold in large numbers alongside its competitors and for many larger businesses represented their first experience of business computing.

THE THIRD GENERATION (1964–1979)

The third generation represented a major step forward which outdistanced previous advances. The technological innovation which supported this breakthrough was the development of the integrated circuit (IC). Hitherto, individual electronic components (valves or transistors) were wired together in large numbers to create the electronic logic of the computer.

Then scientists found a way of simulating the effects of transistors by etching patterns onto a silicon wafer (semiconductor) called the silicon chip (Fig. 5.1). Using advanced photographic techniques, many components could be combined on one single chip. Effectively the computer's logic circuits were combined together: IBM called this solid logic technology (SLT). This technological advance meant that the computer electronics were inherently more reliable and offered substantial improvements in processing speed. When mass produced in large numbers, the chips were much cheaper to manufacture than the equivalent transistors and circuit boards.

Many manufacturers developed new machines at this time, but by far the most famous was the IBM System/360 series. This was a family of compatible mainframe computers ranging from the 360/20, a small-scale entry-level machine suitable for medium businesses, through to the 360/65, a large powerful mainframe for organizations with extensive computing requirements. The machines were the first to incorporate the new technology and became the most commercially successful range of computers seen so far.

The reduced prices and increased performance of third-generation computers led to frantic growth of the computer industry as many companies installed computers to process business data. This in turn led to entirely new industries,

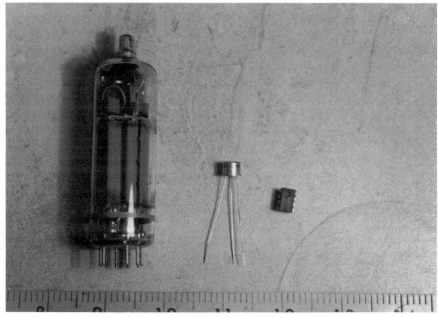

Figure 5.1 Valve, transistor and chip

as entrepreneurs moved in to fill the explosive demand for computer hardware of all kinds, and for computer application software. The result was a plethora of new machines and software, and a substantial shortfall of people with the necessary training to design, program, implement and run the new systems in user organizations.

As the demand for computers, and for computer power, increased, so technological development provided faster and more cost-effective electronics. Integrated circuit (IC) designers incorporated more and more components on each chip in order to gain the improved performance and reduced manufacturing costs which the logic integration represented, until thousands of logic components were incorporated on a single chip (large-scale integration, LSI; Table 5.4). At the same time, developments in main memory technology saw the

Table 5.4 The development of circuit integration

Level of integration		Logic components on each chip
small scale	(SSI)	2–64
medium scale	(MSI)	64–2000
large scale	(LSI)	2000–64 000
very large scale	(VLSI)	64 000–2 000 000
ultra-large scale	(ULSI)	2 000 000 upwards

Table 5.5   The fall in computer costs

Year	Cost per 1 000 000 calculations (£)
1950	7.000
1960	1.444
1965	0.667
1970	0.055
1975	0.027
1980	0.014
1990	0.005

replacement of expensive iron core memories with semiconductor memories at much lower prices, with a corresponding jump in memory sizes and reduction in costs.

THE FOURTH GENERATION (1980–1990?)

Fourth-generation computers utilize very large-scale integration (VLSI) which packs hundreds of thousands of logic components on each chip. Memory chips have also increased in capacity and reduced in cost so that sophisticated software involving very large programs has become possible.

Computer costs in general have fallen to the point where the micro is commonplace in the office and workplace and has a multitude of applications in all areas of industry (see Table 5.5). The personal computer is a massive computer growth area and it has become the standard working tool of managers, professionals and knowledge workers across the whole range of organizational life.

THE FIFTH GENERATION (1990–?)

In 1982 the Japanese Ministry ICOT (Institute for New Generation Computers) announced its intention of setting in motion a vast research programme which would lead to the creation of a new era of computing. The programme would involve organizations from government, academia and industry who would collaborate in the development of the new computers. Many strands of development work in hardware, software and applications would be developed simultaneously. By announcing this effort, Japan boldly signalled her national intention of becoming the world leader in computer technology during the 1990s. Following the Japanese announcement, similar projects were set in train in Europe (ESPRIT), the UK (ALVEY), and the USA.

The fifth generation is not just about faster, cheaper computers. The key to the fifth generation is the realization that current computers, still mainly based on von Neumann architecture, are user-unfriendly and restricted in scope. Fifth generation machines will utilize knowledge, will learn from experience, and will accept inputs through voice and vision systems. Some of the specific goals of the fifth generation are speech recognition and language translation, knowledge-based systems and intelligent data retrieval. To pick up a phone in Tokyo, call London and speak in Japanese, and be heard in English is one aim of fifth generation research. See Chapters 20 and 21 for a discussion on the progress of these techniques. The fifth generation of computers is expected to supersede entirely conventional technology; ICOT are expecting major progress to have been achieved by 1992, i.e. 10 years after the start of the project.

In order to achieve these goals, new computer architectures involving extensive parallelism and greatly increased chip densities and speeds are needed; so also are breakthroughs in the understanding of speech, vision and knowledge capture generally. At the time of writing, the extent of realization of the fifth generation goals is not clear; but it is clear that many new computer hardware and software products are appearing, and that Japan is emerging as a major commercial force in the computer industry.

GENERATIONS IN PERSPECTIVE

The cumulative effect of breakthroughs in technology has been that the cost of computing has been reduced by a factor of 10 roughly each decade, while computing power has increased by a hundred-fold over the same period! One oft-quoted way of putting this is to consider the progress of the car industry in the same terms: if cars had developed in the same way, then a Rolls Royce would cost about £10 and travel at 960 000 km per hour! And there seems to be no end to this progression in sight; on the contrary, the rate of change is increasing, and will continue to do so for the foreseeable future.

There are some absolute theoretical limits to hardware development, for example, there is a fundamental limit to the speed of electronic signals because nothing can go faster than the speed of light. There is also a limit to how small switching components can be made because at a near atomic, quantum level there have to be enough particles to provide a consensus on whether a device is in a 'yes' or 'no' state. Research and development projects which are examining very advanced computer architectures may already be coming across these limits. In practice, the architecture of the fastest computers currently requires that components are packed as closely together as possible in order to reduce the distance travelled, and this brings problems of heat generation in the tightly packed structure. the Cray-1 supercomputer consisted of an open cylinder 2 metres high, with very closely packed components and short wire lengths in order to minimize the distances that the electronic signals had to travel. The dense packing caused a lot of heat to be generated and the machine was cooled by a liquid refrigerant.

Summary

Calculating devices are not a recent invention; in non-electronic form they have existed for centuries. Electronic computers are still in their first half-century, yet they are already on their fifth generation, each one a considerable advance on its predecessor.

KEY TERMS   Analytic engine   Colossus   Deferred design   Difference engine
EDSAC   ENIAC   Integrated circuit (IC)   Jacquard loom   LEO   Luddite
Mean time between failures (MBTF)   Mill   Silicon chip   Stored program
Transistors   Ultra-large-scale integration (ULSI)   Very large-scale integration
(VLSI)   von Neumann machine.

Further reading

Daumas M. (Ed.), *A History of Technology and Invention*, John Murray, London, 1980.
Feigenbaum E. and McCorduck P., *The Fifth Generation: Artifical Intelligence and Japan's Computer Challenge to the World*, Addison-Wesley, Reading, Massachusetts, 1983.
Forester T. (Ed.), *The Information Technology Revolution*, Blackwell, Oxford, 1985.
Kline M., *Mathematical Thought from Ancient to Modern Times*, Oxford University Press, London, 1972.
Pratt V., *Thinking Machines*, Blackwell, Oxford, 1987.
Randell B., *The Origins of Digital Computers*, Springer-Verlag, Berlin, 1973.

6
Hardware foundations

Elements of computer structure

So how does an electronic computer work? Although there have been many machines designed and built over the decades since the 1940s, certain principles are common to most of the machines that are now in general use. The intention of this chapter is to identify and describe those common features in sufficient detail so that the management and information implications of computer architecture can be studied. A word of caution is appropriate: modern electronic computers are subtle and complex devices. In extracting and describing the important principles is not possible to convey all the complexities which would be more appropriate on a computer science course. The aim is to provide sufficient detail to enable a manager to discuss information systems with a specialist, and to enable that manager to make his or her own decisions about information.

The first step is to gain a clear understanding of the meaning of certain key terms. The class of machine we are interested in can be defined as the electronic, general-purpose, stored-program, digital, binary computer. There are many devices available which exhibit variations in these characteristics and it is essential that we can distinguish between them.

The electronic nature of the computer seems obvious, but, in fact, computers could readily be built using other technologies, for example, Babbage's machines (entirely mechanical) could probably be built today using modern engineering techniques. So why aren't they? The main point is speed of operation. Electronic devices can change their states millions of times per second and more, and the raw speed which results is a key feature of the power of the electronic computer. Mechanical components, even the fastest, are many orders of magnitude slower. The Cray-2 supercomputer can perform calculations at the rate of 1200 mips (millions of instructions per second).

Other aspects of electronic components are important too. Physical size, reliability, manufacturing and raw material costs, power usage are all aspects of an economic equation which has promoted the development of ever smaller and ever cheaper electronic devices.

The general-purpose computer is one which can be used for any function or problem that can be programmed, i.e. it is flexible. For example, IBM produce many thousands of their personal computers: each machine rolling off the production line may be identical to its neighbour, yet one will be used in computer-aided design, another to do word processing, another to do stock control calculations, and so on. The applications, present and future, are legion. The computer manufacturer may have no idea in detail as to what any one machine will be used for; the customer redesigns each machine for his or her own purposes by changing the internal structure via its stored program.

This is one of the enabling factors in the exponential growth of the computer industry, because manufacturers do not have to investigate specific applications and markets in great depth before designing their products. It is surely an intriguing thought that perhaps the most interesting and important uses for today's computers probably have not been thought of yet!

Having described the advantages of general-purpose machines, it can now be said that there are many situations where computing devices are used where this general flexibility is not required. For example, electronic control devices are used in planes, cars, watches, calculators, cameras, microwave ovens and many other consumer products. In these circumstances, the functions of the systems are fixed and the controlling device does not need to be reprogrammed. Often, the complete final design in these systems has been deferred by the computer manufacturer and completed by a specialist firm which has special knowledge of the final application. In these cases we say that the computer is dedicated to a certain task.

The electronic computer is the general-purpose, deferred-design device without equal. Its universality and diversity of application have encouraged its rapid spread through all aspects of our lives. This capability is achieved by means of the stored program contained in its memory. The program is a complete and unambiguous specification of the task to be performed. It consists of a detailed list of instructions which directs every action of the computer. The program may be changed at will, either to enable the computer to perform some completely different function or to modify the task which it is presently performing.

The computer can do nothing without a program of some kind. Programs may consist of a few hundred instructions, or, in the case of most commercially useful systems, many thousands of instructions, written initially in a special programming language. Computer programs are given the generic name of software in constrast to hardware, the term which refers to all the physical

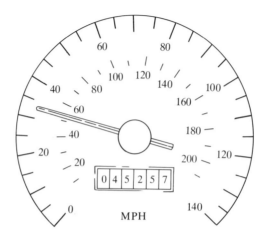

Figure 6.1   A speedometer

components of a computer system. The creation of computer programs is clearly vital to the successful use of computer systems, and a vast new industry has been formed whose business is the manufacturing and marketing of software. This topic is covered in depth in Chapters 10–12.

Most computers in common use in organizations are digital machines, in contrast to analog devices. A digital device represents an item of data by a specific symbol, such as the numeric digits shown on a digital watch, or the numbers shown on a computer screen. In contrast, an analog device represents a quantity by some indirect means, such as an amount of electric current or the physical position of a pointer. A good example of the contrasting types can be found on the dashboard of most cars. The speedometer (Fig. 6.1) is an analog device, representing the car's speed in miles or kilometres per hour by the position of a needle against a scale. The odometer, a digital device, indicates the distance travelled by displaying a group of symbols (digits) which change as the car travels.

There are some crucial differences between analogs and digital modes. Firstly, some items of information, such as temperature, are continuous (i.e. they vary on a continuous numeric scale) and can only be approximated by digital representation. However, in practice we can usually represent such information as accurately as we wish by using as many decimal digits as are necessary. In the odometer mentioned earlier, only one decimal place is shown because that is enough for most purposes; but there is no reason why the device could not be designed to have many more digits if necessary.

The needle on the speedometer in Fig. 6.1 points between two marks on a scale; the driver can judge by eye roughly what the car speed is. This is not completely accurate (though quite good enough for the purpose intended). On most cars, the speedometer needle wobbles between two values. Most analog

Voltage	Numerical value
5.0	| 1
	| 1
4.0	| 1 a device showing a voltage
	| 1 in this band is taken to be
3.0	| 1 showing a 1
	| 1
2.0	| 1
	|
1.0	| 0 a device showing a voltage
	| 0 in this band is taken to be
0.0	| 0 showing a 0

Figure 6.2   Electronic digital representation to binary values

devices are inherently inaccurate, not only because of ambiguity of interpretation, but because even small variations in the state of their components will cause differences in the results shown.

The digital odometer reading, however, cannot be inaccurate, or misinterpreted, in this same way. Digital devices are inherently precise in their operation and in the way that they convey information. (This is not to mean that people might not prefer analog to digital devices. Indeed, there is some evidence that the human brain accepts analog information more readily than digital under certain circumstances; but for machines the inherent accuracy of digital devices is the key issue.)

Thus, we have defined a crucial feature of the digital computer: it handles information internally in a way that is inherently accurate within a range of precision that can be predetermined. The way in which this is done is as follows. The numerical value for 1 is represented by a certain voltage, say $+3.5\,\text{V}$. The value for zero is represented by, say $+0.2\,\text{V}$. Owing to minor inconsistencies in the electronic components, a value of $+3.4\,\text{V}$ might be registered; this will still be treated as 1; in fact anything in the upper band will be treated as the number 1. See Fig. 6.2.

In this way, minor irregularities and discrepancies due to component errors or temperature changes are ignored. Only a gross error will result in the alternative value of zero being incorrectly assumed. For example, the digital signal in Fig. 6.3 may be distorted quite substantially before a wrong value is read. But what about numbers other than zero and 1? In fact, the digital computer does not use them! We will show how this works shortly.

Various analog devices are used in highly specialized scientific and industrial applications to process data. Usually they work by measuring continuous variables and handling data with circuits which perform a fixed transformation before displaying results on dials or other continuous displays. Data

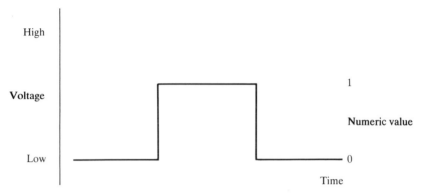

Figure 6.3 A digital pulse signal

is represented internally by the direct measurement of quantities of electric current. Because of this direct representation scheme, minor irregularities in components are reflected directly in the results. (Compare this with the way in which digital computers hold data.)

Analog computers usually do not possess the capability to change functions, i.e. they are dedicated, not general-purpose, devices. Because of their restricted use and limited management application, analog computers will not be discussed further in this book.

Digital computers use binary notation to represent and manipulate data, because the electronic storage components in the machine are capable of only two states, referred to as 0 and 1. This arrangement is chosen because it confers significant engineering advantages in the design and manufacture of computers. There is no theoretical reason why machines cannot be built which represent denary arithmetic directly, but this would add considerably to the complexity, and hence costs, and so binary machines have always occupied the mainstream engineering development path.

Having carefully identified the electronic, general-purpose, stored-program, digital, binary computer from possible rivals, it can be said that this type is by far the most common in a management context. Let us assume from now on that, unless otherwise stated, whenever the word computer is used it is this fully defined device that is being referred to.

Information inside the computer

Information is stored inside the computer in a fashion which has a subtle and crucial effect on information systems. Up to a certain point we can treat the internal workings of a computer as a black-box system, as discussed in Chapter 4. But many aspects of computer display, communications and data storage are characterized as a consequence of this internal representation. In

(a) Binary and denary equivalents

Binary	Denary
0000	0
0001	1
0010	2
0011	3
0100	4
0101	5
0110	6
0111	7
1000	8
1001	9
1010	10
1011	11
1100	12
1101	13
1110	14
1111	15

(b) Binary place values

2^3	2^2	2^1	2^0		Binary place values
8	4	2	1		Denary equivalents

| 1 | 0 | 0 | 1 | | A binary number |
| $8 +$ | $0 +$ | $0 +$ | 1 | $= 9$ | Denary equivalent |

Figure 6.4   Binary number representation

order to appreciate these consequences it is necessary to understand some principles.

The binary place values show a similar logic to denary place values. The rightmost digit is to be multiplied by the denary value of the binary number 1001, i.e. 2 to the power of 0 (which is 1), the next digit by 2 to the power of 1 (which is 2) and so on. Figure 6.4 shows that the denary numbers 1 to 15 can be represented by four binary digits, each of which in turn can be represented by a simple on–off component. Large numbers can be formed by grouping more binary digits, or bits, together and a common arrangement is to have 8 bits, the byte, as the elementary unit of storage.

An alternative term for each unit of storage is the word, and we may speak of a machine which has so many thousands or millions of words of storage. The number of bits in each word is determined by the manufacturer in order to optimize the cost/power characteristics of that machine, and 8, 16 and 32 bit arrangements are common. As a very rough rule of thumb, the larger the word-length the bigger the memory the machine may have and the faster it may process data. However, by the same token, machines with larger word-lengths call for more (and more complex) electronics and so cost more to manufacture.

Having said that numbers can be represented by elementary on–off devices which provide a binary notation, it is worth examining how the computer manipulates those numbers. For example, how is ordinary addition performed? Consider how we add numbers in denary, say 3 + 4 = 7. We know how to do this sum because we remember some elementary rules of arithmetic, in particular we remember all the rules of adding numbers 0 through 10, and probably a great many more besides. If we were to build a computer with denary components, then we would have to 'teach' it all these rules. But in binary, the task is considerably more straightforward because the rules of binary addition are as follows:

Rule 1   0 + 0 = 0

Rule 2   1 + 0 = 1

Rule 3   1 + 1 = 0 and carry 1.

There are no other rules! Rules 1 and 2 are just the first two rules of ordinary denary arithmetic. Rule 3 arises because there are only two digits in binary and so a sum greater than 1 rolls over to the next column. The carry is taken leftwards to the next most significant position in just the same way as in the carry from a sum greater than 9 in denary. Thus adding two numbers in binary is done as follows:

$$
\begin{array}{rl}
0101 & 5 \\
+\ 0100 & 4 \\
\hline
1001 & 9
\end{array}
$$

Taking the rightmost (least significant) column first, 1 + 0 = 1 (rule 2); the second-right column gives 0 + 0 = 0 (rule 1), the third-right column gives 1 + 1 = 0 with a carry (rule 3), which is taken to the leftmost column to give 1 + 0 + 0 = 1 (rules 1 and 2). The sum can be compared with the denary result, as shown. The reader is advised, if this is his or her first experience of binary, to practice several sums in binary and to check the results in denary.

The arithmetic rules are implemented in the computer by the use of elementary electronic components. The electronic devices which perform elementary logical functions are called logic gates. Three of these are shown in Fig. 6.5.

The AND gate is designed so that the output will have a positive value (or 1, or yes) if, and only if, both the inputs a and b have positive values. If only one

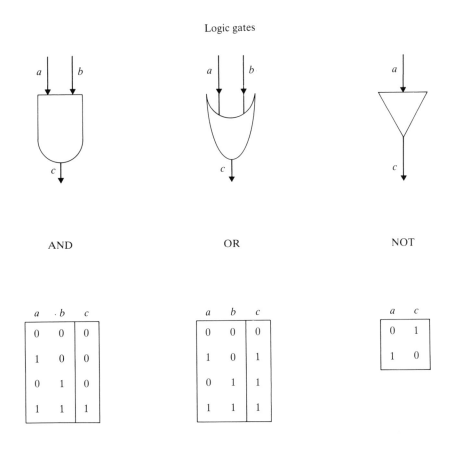

Figure 6.5 Three logic gates: AND, OR and NOT

or the other, or neither, has a 1 value, then c will not have a 1 value. The logical OR gate will show a 1 value at output c if there is a 1 value at either of its inputs. The NOT gate has the effect of showing at its output the opposite of its input: an input of 1 gives output 0 and vice versa.

These components are used in the addition of two binary numbers. The OR gate can be used to implement rules 1 and 2. The AND gate can be used to implement rule 3 (although clearly other components are needed to handle the carry). Figure 6.6 shows a circuit for the addition of bits. The computer is largely made up of a great many of these simple components (and a few others like them) linked together to perform complex logical operations and data transformations. A mass-produced computer will be built using micro-miniaturization

Truth table for the addition of two bits

| Inputs | | Outputs | |
| | | Sum | Carry |
x	y	s	c
0	0	0	0
0	1	1	0
1	0	1	0
1	1	0	1

Implementation in logic gates

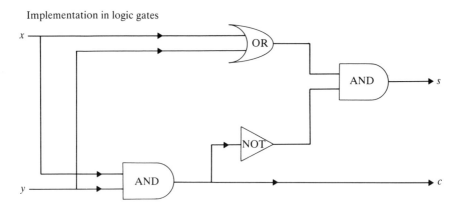

Figure 6.6   The half-adder in elementary logic gates

techniques such that very many elementary components are integrated onto one silicon chip.

   We have seen that computers can use elementary logic components to achieve addition but what about subtraction? In principle we could detail out the rules of subtraction and wire up the necessary components, but in practice what happens is that computer designers use a mathematical trick to simplify the task. It so happens that if you take two binary numbers a and b and you wish to subtract b from a, then this can be done by reversing all the digits in b and then adding 1 to it (this is called complementing). The complement is then added to a to give the desired result.

$$\begin{array}{ll} a\ 0101 - & 5 - \\ b\ 0011 & 3 \\ \quad\ ? & \ ? \end{array}$$

reverse digits in b: 0011 → 1100
increment b: 1100 → 1101

add this result to a:

$$a \quad 0101 \; +$$
$$\text{complement of } b \quad 1101$$
$$\text{result } c \quad 10010$$

(notice that this creates an extra, overflow, digit to the left which is ignored)

$$\text{final result } c \quad 0010$$

These steps in subtraction make use of addition, which we have discussed already, and complementing, the latter being achieved very simply by using the NOT gate to reverse the digits.

So much for addition and subtraction; what about multiplication and division? In fact, many computers cannot do either! That is, they do not have specific instructions for these operations which are directly implemented in hard-wired logic. Rather, they make use of mathematical dodges in order to use circuits and components such as we have already discussed. For example, division may be achieved by the computer obeying a program which involves performing repeated subtractions. The reader may care to write down the rules of binary multiplication (there are not many!) and compare this with the large number of rules of denary multiplication.

Although these arithmetic arrangements simplify design of the hardware it does mean that the computer takes longer to perform calculations than if specialized hardware were used. In most circumstances, the computer is so fast that this simply does not matter, i.e. the computer will spend much of its time waiting for other (mechanical) components, anyway, and there is no time lost. However, some scientific and mathematical applications do require extensive numerical manipulation and in these circumstances special hardware (sometimes called a math co-processor, or floating-point processor) is used to increase calculating speed.

How much simpler life would have been at school if binary had been taught instead of denary! Of course, there is a penalty for using the simplest number system possible, and that is that the number of digits required to represent any given quantity is greater than with a more complex number system. For example, to represent the number 999 takes three denary digits but 10 binary digits (1111100111) in its simplest form. Obviously this adds to the engineering cost of storing numbers. So why not use denary? As a consequence of this logic it would make sense to use an even higher numerical system, such as hexadecimal (to the base 16) or even sexagesimal (to the base 60). However the efficiency of storage possible in these arrangements is more than outweighed by the complexity required elsewhere and, in practice, binary is always the first choice in computer design.

There are several different ways of handling negative numbers in binary. The most usual is to represent a negative number by its complement: we first saw this in the description of binary subtraction. The complement of any binary number is derived by reversing all the bits and then adding 1. Thus the following example shows positive and negative binary numbers and their denary equivalents:

binary	denary
0001	1
1111	− 1
0010	2
1110	− 2
0011	3
1101	− 3
. . . .	

All negative numbers can be recognized as such at once by observing the leftmost bit: if this is 1 then the number is negative. Using this scheme we are using half the numbers available for negative numbers (those starting with 1) leaving the other half for positive numbers (which start with 0). The reader is recommended to complete the above example and verify these statements for himself. What is the complement of 0000, and what does 1000 represent?

The 8-bit byte which is commonly used in computer design can represent numbers from 0 up to 127 positive and − 1 to − 128 negative. What about numbers greater than this? And what about fractions? To represent bigger numbers, 2 or more bytes can be used together to increase the number of bits available. (What is the largest positive number possible with 16 bits, assuming complement representation is used?) Using 2 bytes together in this way is called double-precision representation.

Fractions may be represented in a similar manner to that used in scientific (E-notation) calculations in denary. This representation involves two numbers, a mantissa and exponent to represent very big and very small numbers conveniently; in denary such a number is represented as:

mantissa	exponent
0.8125	9

These two numbers are taken to mean that the mantissa is to be multiplied by 10 to the power of 9, i.e.:

$$0.8125(10^9) \text{ which results in } 812\,500\,000$$

This is usually written as 0.8125 E9 where E9 means 'times 10 to the power of 9'.

This notation can economically show very large numbers, such as 3.6 E99, or very small numbers such as 3.6 E − 99 where the minus sign in the exponent means that the mantissa is to be multiplied by 1/(10 to the power of 99), resulting in a very small number indeed.

The same principle employed in computers is known as floating-point representation and in binary is used thus:

mantissa   exponent

1.000   0111

This means: 'multiply binary 1.000 by 2 to the power of binary 0111'. This gives a result of 256. The fractional point after the first bit in the mantissa is assumed to be present, and always in the same position.

Similarly, we might have the following:

mantissa   exponent

0.100   1110

But what is meant by 0.100 in binary? Following the same logic as for integer representation, the value of the multipliers for fractions is as follows:

$$2^4 \quad 2^3 \quad 2^2 \quad 2^1 \quad 2^0 \qquad 2^{-1} \quad 2^{-2} \quad 2^{-3} \quad 2^{-4}$$

$$1 \quad 0 \quad 1 \quad 0 \quad 1 \quad \cdot \quad 1 \quad 0 \quad 0 \quad 0$$

$$1/2 \quad 1/4 \quad 1/8 \quad 1/16$$

Thus binary 0.1 means 1 times 2^{-1}, which in denary is 1 times $\frac{1}{2}$ or 0.5; binary 0.01 means 1 times 2^{-2}, which gives $\frac{1}{4}$, and so on. Binary 0.11 means $\frac{1}{2} + \frac{1}{4}$, i.e. $\frac{3}{4}$ or 0.75 in denary.

It is possible to increase the accuracy of binary calculations by using 2 bytes for the mantissa (i.e. double precision). Even without this, binary addition becomes much more complicated because of the necessity to manipulate the numbers so that they have the same exponents.

Representing text and pictures

Of course, computers do not just store and manipulate numbers. They also have to handle language, text, special characters and graphics and other information. Most business computers probably handle more text than numbers, so clearly this is an important area. The words in this book were typed onto the keyboard of a computer and were shown immediately on the screen. So how does the computer represent this text internally?

Each character is stored separately in 1 byte, so 'stored' occupies 6 bytes (ignoring the quotes). Each letter is represented by a pattern of the bits in each byte. Every character, number and special character found on a typewriter keyboard has a special pattern associated with it. The byte has 2^8 (256) different possible bit patterns and so there are code patterns available for all the alphabetic characters, upper and lower case, numbers and special characters like ().?⟨⟩* and various other representations.

As long as each part of this computer (keyboard, screen, printer) uses the same codes, it does not really matter what the coding system is, and something completely arbitrary could be thought up. Of course, it makes sense to use a standardized coding system so that computers can communicate with each other, and several codes have evolved. Many computers use either the ASCII code (American Standard Code for Information Interchange), or the EBCDIC (Extended Binary Coded Decimal Interchange Code).

Using an ASCII 8-bit coding system, C.J. Martin is coded in binary bit patterns as follows:

C	11000011
.	10101110
J	11001010
.	10101110
M	11001101
a	11100001
r	11110010
t	11110100
i	11101001
n	11101110

Thus, the keyboard device is designed so that when the letter C is pressed the keyboard device sends the bit pattern 11000011 to the computer.

In order to store and process pictorial data, a picture must be broken down into a matrix of small elements, each of which can be represented by one binary pattern. Each picture element is like a single tile or piece in a mosaic, and is called a pixel (or sometimes pel). An element may be represented by a code which describes its colour and brightness (or its overall brightness, for black and white). See Chapter 20 for more details.

Clearly, the more elements there are, the higher the resolution possible and the better the picture quality. To produce good quality high-resolution images on a computer screen imposes a considerable storage and processing demand on the computer. Machines intended for computer-aided design usually have extensive memory and processing power, far greater than that needed for ordinary business data processing and accounting applications. Examples of such machines include the Sun and Apollo workstations.

The heart of the computer

The internal construction of the computer has changed considerably over the years, and many different arrangements are now current. In particular the size and cost of a computer has a great bearing on the way in which components are designed and arranged. However, as emphasized earlier, certain principles are common to most computers, big and small, and it is to these principles that this section is addressed.

It is useful to consider the computer as having a central element called the central processing unit (CPU), which consists of three key devices (Fig. 6.7):

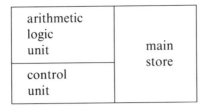

Figure 6.7 The central processing unit

- main store,
- arithmetic/logic unit (ALU),
- control unit (CU).

In the early days of computing the CPU would have been contained in a large metal box which enclosed the three components. Now, miniaturization has reduced the CPU in many computers to a few chips, or even a single chip, the microprocessor.

The CPU is the heart of any computer; its three components act in close harmony together to achieve the rapid and automatic execution of a set of instructions. The instructions are retained in store, along with a small amount of data on which the computer is currently working. The control unit fetches each instruction from store, decodes it and, depending on the detail of the instruction, signals the other components to act. If the instruction is concerned with manipulating numbers, then the control unit signals the arithmetic unit, perhaps to add two items of data. When an instruction has been completed the next instruction is fetched from store. The electronic speed of the CPU enables this cycle of events to be repeated perhaps millions of times per second.

This is the essence of the power of the computer; the engineering concepts have remained unchanged since von Neumann first outlined them in the 1940s, and a direct parallel can be drawn to Babbage's analytic engine of the 1820s with Jacquard control cards acting as the stored program. One major difference is that the electronically stored instructions in the computer can be altered as the program is running which adds a new dimension of subtlety to the variety of which the machine is capable.

The role of the store is to retain instructions and data, and to make these immediately available to the other two components when required. Most of the store is usually engineered in the form of random access memory (RAM); this store is designed so that any part of it can be accessed or read, and any part of it can be overwritten with new information during execution of a program. The quantity of main store available is critically important; it is usually measured in terms of the number of addressable locations, each of which can retain one character. Store sizes are described in terms of kilobytes (Kbytes) where 1 K is 1024 (2^{10}).

As well as RAM memory, it is usual for computers to have a certain amount

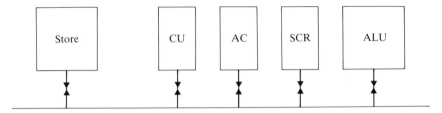

Figure 6.8   CPU showing internal components and connecting bus

of read-only memory (ROM). The purpose of ROM is to retain permanently some commonly used software. This software is installed in the ROM by the manufacturer and typically contains routines which enable the machine to load programs as soon as it is switched on, plus other essential software.

The arithmetic/logic unit (ALU) performs elementary arithmetic operations on data such as adding and subtracting, and forming the complement of negative numbers. It also performs logical operations, i.e. it can compare two pieces of data to see which is larger. This latter class of operation is vital because it gives the computer its decision-making capability. As a result of such a logical operation, the control unit may branch to another part of the program, and thus, for example, one item in a stock inventory list may be signalled as requiring urgent replenishment.

The devices within the CPU are connected by wiring (or its equivalent in integrated circuitry) which carries data in parallel; i.e. all 8 bits from a byte of storage are made available to the control unit at once. This parallel wiring arrangement is called a bus, and buses carrying data, control signals and address information form the vital connections within the CPU. Figure 6.8 shows the components of a CPU with bus interconnections. The components are described in more detail later. This is a simplified diagram of the components and interconnections of a CPU. In practice, there would be several other registers and also a means of handling memory addresses 2 or more bytes long. This latter operation is performed with the help of a device called a multiplexer, which is in effect a switch that acts so as to allow one or the other of 2 byte streams onto the bus, according to the commands of the control unit. In order to handle the addresses of large memories, more powerful machines will have a bus which is able to carry 16 or 32 bits or even more.

We have already seen how data in the form of numbers, text or pictures are represented by patterns of binary digits; what we are interested in now is the format of the instructions which tell the computer what to do. The store is organized as a collection of locations each of which has its own individual address. Thus, we might speak of the location at address 526. As we saw earlier, the contents of one location is a single computer word which may consist of 8, 16, 32 or more bits; to simplify the discussion we will refer only to the 8-bit (byte) arrangement.

Most computers have many thousands of words of storage, and it is usual to refer to the capacity in terms of so many K words or bytes (where K = 1024). Thus we might refer to a computer as having 512 Kbytes of storage meaning 514 048 (512 × 1024). Like the baker's dozen the K has become the computer person's 1000 and is used to describe other quantities. Thus somebody might describe their salary as being £15K, meaning about £15 000. Large computer stores are described in terms of megabytes, where a megabyte (Mbyte) is 1024 Kbytes, i.e. 1024 × 1024 bytes.

As well as the main store itself, the CPU contains several registers; these act like storage locations but have special properties and can be connected to other components in a variety of ways (here a generalized CPU based on a bi-directional bus is shown). The quantity and purpose of the registers differs from one machine to another. We will examine the purpose of only two of them: the accumulator (AC) and the sequence control register (SCR) which both perform roles crucial in the function of the CPU.

The registers are designed so that they can be switched (strobed is the technical term) to accept information present at their input side from the bus, and they can also be separately switched to make information available from their output side. The entire bus will adopt the values of any register whose output lines are switched onto it, so only one register will be switched to show its outputs at any one time.

The instructions that deal with transferring information to and from store work by referring to the accumulator which acts as a staging post for this purpose, and also as the repository for the results of arithmetic operations. The sequence control register contains the address of the next instruction to be executed. It acts as a pointer so that the control unit always 'knows' which instruction comes next.

Although the format of computer instructions varies, certain representative instructions have an operand part and an address part, each held in separate but contiguous bytes of store. An instruction which takes data from the accumulator and writes it to memory is called a store direct instruction, and it may have this binary representation:

1st byte	2nd byte
(operand)	(address)
00111010	00011000
(store)	(24)

The first byte contains the instruction operand (a binary code which the control unit recognizes as the store direct instruction). When fetched from store this operand will cause the control unit to perform several steps including setting the sequence control register (SCR) to point to the next instruction in the program. This sequence of events is called the fetch/execute cycle, and a summary of the steps which are performed is shown below.

Fetch sequence

1. Signal the store to make data available from the location pointed to by the address held in the SCR.
2. Fetch the first half (the operand) of the instruction into the control unit.
3. Increment the SCR to point to the next store location (which contains the second, address part of the instruction).
4. Fetch the second half of the instruction into the control unit.

Execute sequence

5. Signal the store to access the location nominated by the address part of the instruction.
6. Set control lines so that data flows from accumulator to store.
7. Increment the SCR so that it now contains the address of the operand of the next instruction.
8. (This is the end of the cycle, which is now repeated from step 1.)

Some aspects of the fetch/execute cycle will be common to all instructions, but the details of the cycle will depend on the particular instruction involved. This may seem a very complicated sequence of events for the computer to perform in order to achieve the simple objective of moving data from accumulator to store. Nevertheless, the sequence is performed very rapidly indeed.

The store instruction is one of a trio of instructions with similar format which can be compared together and can form a program segment to illustrate how a computer utilizes the components of the CPU.

1st byte	2nd byte	
operand	*address*	*meaning*
load direct	*x*	take the content of memory at location *x* and write it into the accumulator
store direct	*y*	take the content of the accumulator, write this into the memory location *y*
add direct	*z*	take the content of memory at location *z*, add it to the contents of the accumulator and form the new result there

Using these three instructions, a program which adds two numbers together and stores the result would look like Table 6.1 in memory (after the program fragment had been executed).

In this program segment, the control unit will fetch the operand of the first instruction (load) from location 0100: it will then fetch the address part (0106) from location 0101, and execute the instruction by writing the value 23 into the accumulator. Then, the operand of the second instruction (add) is fetched, followed by the second part (0107), and the instruction is executed by adding the

Table 6.1 A program segment in the main store

Store address	Contents	Description
.	.	
.	.	
.	.	
0100	load	Inst.1 operand
0101	0106	Inst.1 address
0102	add	Inst.2 operand
0103	0107	Inst.2 address
0104	store	Inst.3 operand
0105	0108	Inst.3 address
0106	0023	data
0107	0035	data
0108	0058	result
.	.	
.	.	
.	.	

value at 0107 (35) into the accumulator and forming the result there. At this stage the accumulator contains 58. The operand of the last instruction is fetched, followed by the address part (0108) and the accumulator contents are written into location 0108.

Of course, computers have many other instructions apart from these three, and the details of the instruction set will vary from computer to computer. A typical business micro has about 70 different instructions available, each of which performs some elementary function. As well as instructions which refer to memory directly, there are others which refer to indirect addresses, i.e. they refer not to the address shown in the second part of the instruction, but to the address contained in the location at the address shown. Other instructions cause the control unit to jump to different parts of the program, depending on certain conditions.

All the instructions in the instruction set of a particular computer have some part to play in programs which utilize the computer effectively, although the technical details of how this is achieved are beyond the scope of this book. It is a curious feature of the modern computer that it performs very elementary operations, albeit very rapidly indeed, and that in order to perform complex tasks in a business setting it must perform a very large number of very simple operations.

A key objective of this chapter has been to illustrate the relationship between the structure of the computer and the program instructions which it executes. Clearly, the development of computer programs which are to achieve some purpose in the business world requires very careful consideration, and this issue will be taken up in Part Three.

Table 6.2 Classes of computer in order of size

	Approximate price (£1000)	Store size (Mbytes)	CPU speed (mips)	Example machine
micros	1–10	0.1–2	0.01–1	Apple Mac
minis	10–100	0.3–4	0.1–1	DEC
superminis	50–500	1–10	0.5–5	Prime 9955
mainframes	250–5000	2–64	1–30	IBM Sierra
supercomputers	5000–10 000	256–1000	100–500	Cray-3

Computer classes and selection

Although most of the machines which are of interest to us in a business context work along more or less similar lines, there are substantial differences between them in terms of speed and processing power. Clearly, there are different needs for data processing capacity for the manager who uses his PC for spreadsheet work, and the data processing department of a major organization which may need to process millions of records every day.

These different needs are served by a range of different machines supplied by computer manufacturers who tailor their products to suit the requirements of different markets, and at different prices. The current groupings of computer types owes much to the history of computer development, which shows step-changes in technology resulting in the appearance of new types which opened up new markets.

Present-day machines fall into five broad classes according to price: micros, minicomputers, superminis, mainframes and supercomputers (Table 6.2). However, the lines between these classes have become blurred as manufacturers create more advanced products, and as the processing power and memory available relentlessly increase. For example, an ageing 1970s mainframe (many of which are still going strong) might well have a performance inferior to that of a new desk-top micro; considering the different costs involved, this demonstrates the extraordinary developments that have occurred in recent years.

MAINFRAMES

Early computers (1950s–1960s) were designed to be large and powerful; the cost of computers was so high that it made sense to make them as powerful as possible so that one machine could serve the needs of many users. Computer manufacturers tend to specialize in one or more classes, and International Business Machines (IBM), the giant American manufacturer, has traditionally dominated the mainframe market.

Today, mainframes are still designed and built to be very powerful in order to process vast amounts of data, perform extensive scientific calculations and to serve the needs of many users in the same organization. They are usually owned by large commercial organizations, government institutions and universities. They require special housing and siting arrangements with separate power sources, air-conditioning, and false flooring to accommodate a complex net of cables. Mainframes can be upgraded; customers usually buy a minimum configuration and then later add on memory and peripherals as their needs expand. A mainframe is usually supported by a range of peripheral devices; these may include large-capacity disk and tape secondary storage, high-speed printers and several input devices.

A typical mainframe application would be supporting hundreds of terminals, and a communications network to remote processors, while simultaneously processing large amounts of business transactions. In order to run such applications efficiently a sizeable specialist staff is necessary, the members of which require skills in computer operations, programming, software development, systems design and management.

MINICOMPUTERS

Minicomputers emerged in the 1960s. They were designed as scaled-down mainframes in order to capitalize on the latest technology and to open up a new market among business and scientific users for whom the mainframe was too large and expensive. Digital Equipment Corporation (DEC) were among the first to cater for the market and probably are still the major suppliers in the class, although many other manufacturers offer products in this popular range. A typical mini has less power and processing capacity than a large mainframe, fewer peripherals and can support fewer terminals and fewer users, but the machine is available at a substantially lower price.

Many businesses and educational organizations gained their first computing experience on a mini. High-level languages (see later) were also developed around this time in order to make computing available to non-specialist users. The typical mini today will be found in a sizeable department, or as the main computer of a small- to medium-sized company. It will usually have large-capacity disk storage, and one or more high-speed printers and input devices attached. It requires far fewer specialist staff than the mainframe, and probably will not require air-conditioning or special power arrangements.

SUPERMINIS

The supermini was developed in the late 1970s, and like its predecessor, the mini, it emerged as a result of changes in the technology of microelectronics. Essentially, it offers the power of a small mainframe for the price of a large mini, and makes available substantial processing capacity to organizations which hitherto could not justify a mainframe.

Today the supermini offers a price–performance combination which is superior to the small mainframe. However, the ability to upgrade it may be limited and this fact, among others, makes the choice a complex one for the buyer. Many manufacturers compete in this class, among them Prime, Hewlett-

Packard, Wang, and Data General. Conditions vary from machine to machine, but the typical large supermini will have similar peripheral devices and will require similar environmental and staffing arrangements as those of a small mainframe.

MICROCOMPUTERS

More than any other development in computing, the rise of the micro in the 1980s has changed the way in which society in general, and business organizations in particular, work. Its main feature is its very low cost, made possible by developments in high-capacity integrated circuits. Today, the business environment is increasingly dominated by the micro which has become a standard working tool for people in all functions and levels of management. World-wide sales of micros have been predicted to reach 12 million annually from around 1990.

Initially the micro was seen as following the trend of earlier developments in minis, in that the low-cost micro could be brought by even the smallest business. Indeed, costs have become so low that virtually any small business can now afford a micro system, together with its associated software. It requires no special working environment and can be mounted on a desk and plugged into the nearest socket. Backing store was provided by low-capacity floppy disks in early, cheaper versions; current business machines also have fixed Winchester-type hard-disk drives. Input is by keyboard, sometimes augmented by mouse or touch-screen, and output is by low-cost dot-matrix or daisywheel printer. High-level languages and, especially, general-purpose proprietary software packages, removed the need for specialist programming staff and have opened the way to the very wide range of applications for which the machines are now used.

A major shift in emphasis came in the middle 1980s, with the development and marketing of the micro as a tool for the individual: the personal computer (PC). Early developments along these lines were the Apple Macintosh, a machine justly famous for its clever human interface, and the One-Per-Desk (OPD) by International Computers Ltd (ICL) which incorporated advanced telephone-handling features.

IBM then entered the market with the IBM PC and quickly achieved a major slice of the world market. Today, the PC finds its way into the office of many executives and staff workers, and the major buyers of PCs are big businesses and other large organizations which recognize that substantial improvements in productivity can be achieved by making the machines widely available to managers and knowledge workers generally. Today there is little to distinguish the PC (Fig. 6.9) from a micro intended for general business use; and most people simply refer to the micro as the PC in any business context.

Although the IBM PC has become the *de facto* industry standard upon which most proprietary PC software is based, many other manufacturers have sought to compete in this huge and ever-expanding world market by designing machines that work like the IBM PC and, hence, are able to run all the software

Figure 6.9 PC and peripherals

available. Such machines are called IBM compatibles; other manufacturers have sought to duplicate the functions of the IBM PC so exactly that their machines are called IBM clones. A highly successful clone has been the Amstrad PC1512, which overtook IBM in the UK market in 1987. The Apple Macintosh, with its unusual operating system, is about the only business machine to have survived which is not based on the IBM standard.

Competition among manufacturers in this market is so fierce that new products are appearing virtually daily, each offering more power or enhanced features, and/or a lower price. The hardware characteristics of the business micro are therefore constantly changing as new and better products come onto the market. The essential internal features of a busines micro or PC are defined by the following four characteristics.

The type of microprocessor chip which contains the CPU

A small number of specialist chip manufacturers (of whom Intel and Motorola of the USA are major names) supply microprocessors to the computer manufacturers, who then incorporate the devices into their machines. The type of chip used defines the software that can be used on the computer, and also the other CPU characteristics. The more modern chips use advanced techniques which enable faster processing to be achieved (Table 6.3).

It was pointed out in the previous section that arithmetic beyond simple

Table 6.3 CPU chips used in business micros

Microprocessor	Manufacturer	Clock speed (MHz)	Word-length	Computers using this chip
8088	Intel	4–8	8	IBM PC Amstrad pc1512
80286	Intel	8–12	16	IBM PC AT Olivetti M290
68000	Motorola	12–24	32	Apple Macintosh
80386	Intel	16–24	32	IBM PS/2 Compaq Deskpro
80486	Intel	64–96		

addition and subtraction was carried out in the CPU of most computers by indirect methods; usually this is perfectly adequate because most business applications do not involve extensive mathematical calculation. However, in order to increase calculation speed it is possible to have a separate maths co-processor which is connected to the computer's motherboard; this device intercepts maths instructions and performs the calculations directly at electronic speeds. An example is the Intel 80287 co-processor chip which is used in a number of PCs including the various IBM PC models.

Clock speed: the speed at which the chip operates

Computers function by obeying simple instructions very rapidly. As we have seen from the discussion on the fetch/execute cycle, each instruction is itself made up of small steps called micro-instructions. Each tiny step has to be controlled and synchronized so that events follow on at the right time. This synchronization is performed by the control unit which begins each step in time with the signals from an internal clock.

The signals from the internal clock occur at fixed intervals of time, and the speed of the clock, measured in megahertz (MHz, millions of cycles per second), defines the speed of the computer. If the average instruction has about eight steps, then a clock speed of 8 MHz will give about 1 million instructions per second (mips). Clearly, the faster the clock speed the faster the computer will execute instructions. The early Intel 8088 chip operates at 4.4 MHz, and the Intel 80286 can operate at 8, 10 or 12 MHz depending on the application. The 80386 operates at 16, 20 and 25 MHz, making it the fastest chip in general business use at present.

The word-length of the CPU

CPU internal word-lengths may be 8, 16 or 32 bits long, or more. Generally, the greater the word-length the faster the CPU can operate and the larger the main store that can be addressed directly, although at the expense of greater complex-

Figure 6.10   Intel/Motorola chips

ity of the circuitry. Early machines had 8-bit word-lengths, more recent business micros offer 16-bit or 32-bit word-lengths (Fig. 6.10).

The amount of main storage available

The advent of increasingly sophisticated software for PCs has caused the requirement for main storage to increase also. Early business micros had perhaps 128 K or 256 K of main store; more recent business machines offer 640 K minimum, expandable to 2 Mbytes or more. The availability of low-cost RAM has also stimulated the use of main store as a form of high-speed secondary storage; a reversal of the usual roles of storage!

An offshoot development of the PC is the portable or laptop: a battery-powered PC complete with keyboard, screen and disk drives which is designed to be taken and used wherever the manager needs it. Because of their weight and size some early machines were described as 'luggables' rather than portables! However, recent offerings such as the Compaq Portable III are smaller than a document case, and provide keyboard, flat screen and floppy and hard disk drives.

As well as providing computer power to enable the executive to run spreadsheet calculations or word process boardroom minutes while he or she is on the move, in plane or train, the portable may be plugged into a host mainframe by way of a modem which attaches to the public telephone network. For example, a salesman travelling around the country to his customers can use a public telephone to access his host computer at head office and receive data (called downloading) onto his portable about his next customer; he can then calculate quotations and prices while he is with his customer and negotiate more flexibly. The order can then be transmitted directly to the host computer at head office and be processed immediately without waiting for postal services.

SUPERCOMPUTERS

Most recent on the scene are the supercomputers. These machines first appeared in the mid-1980s and offer the ultimate in computer power; indeed so powerful and expensive are they that only a few hundred have been installed world wide. (The latest Cray supercomputer, the Cray model Y-MP, costs around £4M for a single processor.) Table 6.2 shows their principal characteristics in relation to other computers. They are built to perform number-crunching at the highest possible speed and are mainly used for applications involving very extensive and complex scientific or mathematical calculations. In order to maximize the supercomputer's performance, there may be a powerful front-end computer connected to handle all the input–output operations, leaving the supercomputer to concentrate on the calculations. The environmental and staffing arrangements required will be similar to those of the largest mainframe.

An example of supercomputer application is weather forecasting. Meteorologists have developed complex mathematical models which simulate global and local weather systems; these mathematical models represent a picture of the earth's atmosphere in three dimensions, and involve a tremendous amount of calculation. The mathematical simulation of the atmosphere works on a number of regions, each requiring separate calculation in the model. In order to improve the quality of local forecasting it is necessary to perform the calculations over smaller and smaller regions; in other words to use a finer grid in the model. Refining the model in this way results in better forecasts, but creates ever more calculations, and the computing task becomes so immense that only a super-computer can perform the calculations in a reasonable time. These calculation tasks, and others such as the modelling of complex designs in the aircraft and car industries, require truly enormous calculating capability and there is constant pressure for ever-faster machines.

MATCHING COMPUTERS TO ORGANIZATIONAL NEEDS

The broad type of computer which an organization selects is usually roughly in line with the size of its data processing requirements. Big organizations have large processing needs and, therefore, choose mainframes or supercomputers for their main computing resource; small firms have relatively less data to process and may choose a mini or one or more PCs. But the distinction is not at all clear cut. There is considerable overlap in processing capacity between the main computer types, so, for example, a current mini at the top of the range may have as much capacity as a small mainframe, especially if the mainframe is a few years old. There will be organizational considerations which affect policy too. Large organizations may have a decentralized policy so that instead of a central mainframe each division may have its own mini. As its name suggests, the PC is very much the machine for the individual, so managers in a large organization may well have their own individual PCs in addition to the organizational computing resource. Tradition also plays a part. An organization which has been involved in computing for years or decades may have a computing resource based around a central mainframe because it has always done things that way, and because it has developed a fund of skills and experience. Changes in technology that provoke the re-evaluation of IS policy are happening so fast that many organizations lag behind the leading edge.

Towards the future

Research proceeds apace on the development of semiconductor chips, the basic building blocks of computers, which are capable of ever-faster speeds. Super-cooling of components in order to alter their electronic characteristics, and the use of exotic materials such as gallium arsenide, are being explored to produce devices which operate at orders of magnitude faster than conventional components. The Josephson Junction has been researched for many years and offers very fast switching, albeit at temperatures as low as $-269\,°C$.

It was pointed out earlier that the conventional laws of physics might represent an absolute barrier to ever-faster speeds. But recent developments seem to suggest that devices called resonant tunnel resistors can be constructed which utilize the quantum effects found in the vanishing small world of sub-micro-miniaturization. If computers could be built with these devices, called quantum wires, then they would be miniscule with truly phenomenal speeds.

Most of the machines we have looked at so far have in common the computer architecture which was first discussed by von Neumann in 1945. That is, they process instructions one at a time, and thus operate serially. Clearly this acts as a limit on processing speed and computer designers have for many years worked on the development of parallel processors, i.e. machines which process many data items and/or instructions simultaneously. An early commercial machine was the ICL Distributed Array Procesor (DAP) which possessed an array of up to 4096 CPU elements working on different data items simultaneously, in parallel. The Cray supercomputer uses a form of parallelism called pipelining, whereby a set of processors act together to progressively process data items.

There are a number of problems associated with the commercial application of machines of this type, not the least of which is the development of suitable software which can make the most of the computing power available to general problem-solving. However, the ever-increasing demand for more computing power, particularly in scientific and number-crunching applications, will continue to encourage the development of faster and faster computers; it seems certain that to achieve these higher speeds some form of parallelism must be involved.

A recent development in chip technology is the transputer, a VLSI device which comprises 200 000 logic gates on a single chip. The transputer chip is virtually a complete computer; it is different from a microprocessor in that some main memory and communication logic are all incorporated on the same device. Its main use will be as a building block in the development of large transputer networks which can handle extensive parallel processing. These networks may deliver the equivalent power of a supercomputer but at a fraction of the price.

The technology of computing has, thus far, evolved using primarily electronic devices. All the components of modern computers, the logic circuitry, data and control bus, and the memory, rely on electrical signals. Electronic technology replaced the earlier electromechanical devices used in early tabulating machines, and these in turn replaced the mechanical technology of Babbage's clockwork analytic engine. But is the current electronic technology itself about to be replaced by something else?

Present-day telecommunication lines for telephone voice and signal transmission are increasingly being replaced by light-carrying devices, employing fibre-optics. In these systems, information is transmitted in the form of light beams, using lasers. Light-sensitive materials are increasingly being used in secondary storage media, and optical disk technology may eventually replace magnetic disks (see Chapter 8).

Recent developments in optical physics have resulted in the optical equivalents of transistors; these devices, called transphasors, can act as switches in the same way as their electronic equivalents. This creates the possibility of the optical computer, with switching speeds (and hence computing speeds) far in excess of current electronic technology.

Summary

Digital computers are based on binary arithmetic which is used to store and manipulate data in both numeric and textual form. The heart of the computer is the central processing unit which controls processing and interaction with peripherals. There are five types of computers ranging from desk-top microcomputers to massively powerful supercomputers; each has a different role in business information processing.

KEY WORDS Acumulator (AC)   Analog   Arithmetic/logic unit (ALU)
ASCII Binary Bit Boolean algebra Bus Byte Central processing unit
(CPU)   Complement   Control unit (CU)   Dedicated computer   Denary
Digital Double-precision Downloading EBCDIC Fetch/execute cycle
Floating point   General-purpose computer   Generations of computers
Half-adder   Hardware   Instruction operand   Integrated circuit (IC)
Kilobyte (Kbyte) Laptop Logic gates Mainframe Mantissa and exponent

Maths co-processor Megabyte (Mbyte) Megahertz (MHz) Microcomputer Microprocessor Minicomputer Multiplexer Optical computer Overflow Parallel device Parallelism Pipelining Pixel Portable Random access memory (RAM) Read-only memory (ROM) Register Sequence control register (SCR) Serial device Stored program Supercomputers Superminis Transphasors Transputer Word-length.

Further reading

Burger R.M., Cavin R.K., Holton W.C. and Sumney L.W., The impact of ICs on computer technology, *Computer*, October, 88–95, 1984.

French C.S., *Computer Science*, DP Publications, Eastleigh, Hants, 1985.

French C.S., *Computer Studies*, DP Publications, Eastleigh, Hants, 1986.

Grayson A., You thought Laptops were only for loners, *Computerworld*, 23 Feb, 61–62, 1987.

Hayes J.P., *Computer Architecture and Organization*, McGraw-Hill, New York, 1978.

Hockney R.W. and Jessop C.R., *Parallel Computers: Architecture, Programming and Algorithms*, Adam Hilger, Bristol, 1981.

Johnson R., *Microcomputers – Concepts and Applications*, Michell, Santa Cruz, California, 1987.

Makrias S. and Honan P., The complete guide to IBM compatibles, *Personal Computing*, April, 141–143, 1987.

Morris N.M., *Microprocessor and Microcomputer Technology*, Macmillan, London, 1981.

Wilkinson G.G. and Winterflood A.R., *Fundamentals of Information Technology*, Wiley, Chichester, 1987.

7
Input–output devices and applications

The previous chapters have described how computer program instructions act on data in the CPU. The next chapter investigates how large volumes of data are stored externally on secondary storage devices. This chapter looks at how data gets into and out of the computer in the first place. Peripheral devices, linked by electronic interfaces, connect the CPU of the computer to the outside world. Probably the most familiar peripherals are those used on the typical PC: a keyboard connects directly to the CPU for data input, and a visual display unit (VDU) for output from the CPU. Most PCs will also have a low-cost dot matrix or daisywheel printer to give hard copy of results when needed. But there is a wide range of other peripheral devices available, which are necessary under special circumstances.

Input devices and data capture

The computer keyboard is derived directly from the typewriter, and it is an intriguing thought that the usual layout of keys which begins QWERTY . . . was specifically designed by typewriter engineers at the turn of the century because the early machines could not cope with rapid typing; the typewriter arms on which letters were embossed would not fall back quickly enough, so the QWERTY keyboard was designed to slow the typist down! The modern keyboard is still based on the QWERTY layout probably because so many people are familiar with it. Other keyboard layouts and shapes, such as the Dvorak board which is ergonomically designed for keying speed and/or ease of learning, have simply not caught on.

The keyboard remains the main input device for low-volume, on-line data input. Apart from the normal letter keys, there may be a special numeric pad and a number of special function keys; the industry standard PC keyboard has

Figure 7.1 Mouse and Mac with icons

102 keys in all. Applications of keyboard entry range from word processing, PC data input to spreadsheets, programming and program updating, computer operating (all classes), through to on-line data entry and enquiry against computer files on minis and large mainframes. Other devices which supplement the keyboard are the mouse, light-pen and touch-screen (Fig. 7.1).

The mouse is a hand-held device which is dragged across a horizontal surface and causes a cursor to move across the screen. A roller-ball in the mouse sends signals which enable the computer to calculate the coordinates of the mouse as it moves, and one or more buttons on the head of the mouse are used to signal when a selection has been made. The mouse is very useful for drawing shapes in graphic and engineering applications, and for pointing to parts of a document on screen or selecting menu options. It is often supplied as an option for PCs intended for executive use, because it can speed up menu selection in a WIMPS environment (see Chapter 10 on operating systems).

The light-pen is pointed directly at the screen, and a photo-electric cell in the pen provides coordinates to the computer. It is used especially in engineering drawing and computer-aided design (CAD), and similar applications.

The touch-screen is a VDU screen which has infra-red light beams shining across its surface; when the finger points at the screen the beams detect the location selected (Fig. 7.2). It is used where fast and simple selections need to be made. One application is found on the stock exchange where dealers receive

Figure 7.2   Touch-screen application

details of share prices and other information on their screens; the screen offers various selections which the dealers touch in order to access more data and to execute deals. This system is found to be far quicker and more accurate than one where the dealers enter data on a keyboard alone.

The on-line keyboard and its associated manual input devices are usually intended for low-volume human data entry direct to the computer. However, many business data processing applications require high-volume data input and a number of devices have been devised to cater for this requirement.

One of the oldest of the input media is the punch card (see Chapter 5) which was invented long before the computer appeared. Because of the role of the punch card in early data processing machinery, it was adapted as a means of computer input from the very beginning and has been used ever since. It has now largely been superseded by key-to-disk input systems, that is, direct input from the keyboard (although many mainframe installations still have card readers) but it is worth describing now because the principles involved have been reproduced in several more modern input methods.

Data for input to the computer might consist of a number of forms representing stock-take data, for example. This data would be keyed into a card-punch machine which would create patterns in the card for every character keyed; usually one card was punched for each input form. The cards for all the forms would then be fed into a card reader attached to the CPU of the computer; the card reader would then read the cards very rapidly (say 600 cards per minute) and the computer program would process the data and produce a report, or perhaps write data to disk for later processing.

The card punching operation is performed by skilled machine operators who are trained to enter data on the keyboard very rapidly, perhaps 5000 characters per hour, or more, depending on the type of work. Because any manual process is error prone, even when performed by skilled operators, it is usually necessary to verify the data before computer input. Key verification is performed on a special version of the card punch, called a verifier. The verifier operator takes a batch of forms which have already been punched by another operator, and inserts the punched cards for that batch into the verifier. The operator then re-keys the forms exactly as they were keyed originally, while the verifier machine checks that what is being punched this time is exactly the same as the data already in the cards.

Any discrepancy detected by the machine is signalled at once, and usually the keyboard locks to prevent further processing; the operator then checks to see whether the difference is caused by an error in the original key punching. The chances of two different operators making the identical error in the same place are low enough to allow considerable confidence in key-verified data transcription. Of course, the verification operation effectively doubles the cost of the data input task. Key verification is therefore one option to be considered among other types of verification and control (for example hash-totalling and program checking) when designing the complete system. Control is discussed in more detail in Chapters 13–15.

While the key punching and verifying are proceeding off-line, the computer can be employed on other tasks. When the computer becomes available, the cards are read in from the card reader. After the data is computer processed, the cards can be retained as a security measure in the case of loss of the data later on.

Modern versions of this keying and verifying process for bulk data employ the same principles, but the data is keyed to magnetic disk or magnetic tape instead of cards. Key-to-disk and key-to-tape systems usually have several keystations attached to a central disk or tape storage device. The keystations operate independently and usually have a VDU screen so that the operator can see exactly what has been keyed; data is stored on the magnetic medium and can be key-verified as described before. These data-entry systems utilize a microcomputer to handle the data input and comparisons, and are capable of presenting screen record formats to the operator together with programmed duplication and field checking in order to make the keying process more efficient. When a batch of data has been completed, the tape or disk is removed and mounted on a drive connected to the main computer CPU for input.

Off-line manual key punching of data is suitable for large volume data input where other, more cost-effective short-cuts cannot be employed (and some of these will be reviewed shortly). Keyboard entry is a flexible method of data capture in that any data input task, big or small, simple or complex, can be

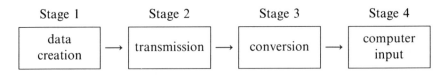

Figure 7.3   Stages of data capture

undertaken without too much pre-planning. Most computers in data processing environments will be serviced by such systems, perhaps in conjunction with other methods for specialist input applications.

What are the key steps of data capture? Figure 7.3 shows the principal stages which normally occur between the origination of a piece of data, and its correct representation inside a computer. Data is created when a customer calls and would like to place an order, or when a examination mark is allocated to a piece of student work, or when an item of stock is moved out of the stores. Perhaps the data is recorded on paper: a source document—for example the customer order may be written to an order form, the student mark noted on a report, the stock item checked against a stock list.

In many circumstances, the data item is then transmitted from the point of capture to where it can be dealt with at the next step. Perhaps the order is sent to the computer department, the student mark given to an examiner over the telephone and the stock list sent to head office through the mail.

The next stage involves the data being converted into a machine-readable form. This can be done by any of the methods described above, all of which require a human being to convert the data manually into a machine-sensible form which can be read directly by the computer. The conversion usually involves a character-by-character translation onto disk or tape media which can be read by a computer input device.

All four stages are extra steps which are necessary only because of computer processing; they cost time and money to achieve and inevitably add errors to the data, especially where the human element is involved. Data capture is therefore a costly and error-prone process, which adds delay to data processing and it would be desirable to minimize it, or avoid it altogether if possible.

The best way to avoid the costs, errors and delays of the data capture process is to eliminate as many stages as possible. This can be done by capturing data directly as closely as possible to the source, and there are several ways of achieving this. Firstly, methods have been developed for reading data source documents directly into the computer and thus avoiding altogether the data conversion stage. As the conversion stage is usually the most expensive, these methods, outlined below can produce significant time and cost savings.

OPTICAL MARK READING (OMR)

Specially designed forms are used with spaces which are filled in with pencil marks. The documents are read by a machine that detects the presence or absence of the marks (effectively a binary code). OMR is used where the amount of variable input data per form is very small (making the marks is quite laborious). It can be used to gather market survey data, job completion forms and other elementary information which can be presented as yes/no choices.

OMR is commonly used for student testing. A number of questions are provided with multiple-choice answers; each student marks his own form, and then the forms are gathered together for immediate computer input and processing. The Open University makes considerable use of OMR for teaching and assessment of its enormous student population which is scattered over the UK and elsewhere. The method eliminates the conversion stage of data capture (or rather, it forces that effort onto the person making out the form); the technology is very simple and machines to read OMR are inexpensive. The drawbacks centre around the laboriousness of making the marks, and the restricted amount of data which can be conveniently presented in elementary yes/no form; for these reasons OMR is only used under rather restricted circumstances.

MAGNETIC INK CHARACTER RECOGNITION (MICR)

Documents are pre-printed with characters in a special ink; a familiar application is the data printed on the bottom of cheques. These characters can be read directly by a MICR document reader attached as an input device to a computer. Unlike OMR, the MICR characters can represent the full range of numbers, letters and special characters.

Banks have been using MICR since the late 1950s to process the millions of cheques that pass through central clearing banks each day; a MICR device can read cheques at around 2400 per minute. The pre-printed MICR data on the cheque specifies bank, branch, cheque number and customer account number; all that is missing is the cheque amount. This is manually entered onto the cheque by a person operating a MICR device. The cheque is then ready to be machine processed. The MICR system therefore eliminates most of the data conversion process, with the exception of the cheque amount. Because of the costs and limitations of pre-printing the MICR codes, this data input method is restricted to very specialized situations.

OPTICAL CHARACTER RECOGNITION (OCR)

Very similar in principle to the MICR system, OCR documents are pre-printed with data which can be read by an optical scanning device attached to a computer. The OCR characters have a characteristic shape which the scanner can recognize, and special inks are not necessary. Information can therefore be printed by a computer printer fitted with an OCR font, on documents which can be re-input via a scanner. This gives rise to the turnaround document.

A typical application involves an organization with a large number of customers who are billed with predetermined amounts. An example would be an insurance company collecting standard premiums from its policy holders. The computer holds records on each customer and prints a turnaround document requesting payment of the amount due; data for this amount and the customer's account code and policy number are printed on the document in OCR font.

The document is sent to the customer who is asked to return it with his or her payment. The returned document is then read by the OCR document reader and input into the computer directly, the OCR data tells the computer which customer has paid and provides all the necessary details to update files. In this way, human processing is eliminated from the data creation stage and the data conversion stage is eliminated altogether. Compare this to the traditional process whereby the documents are entered by human keyboard data entry.

The turnaround document method can usefully be applied wherever predetermined information can be printed and re-input. Because of the relatively high capital costs of document readers, there is usually the need for large numbers of documents to be processed to make the method cost-effective compared to human keying. Gas and electricity supply billing systems come into this category, as do various governmental and big-business operations; in these circumstances where there may be millions of transactions to be processed, the method can be very cost-effective indeed.

TEXT AND HANDWRITING RECOGNITION

The next step from the specialized fonts of OCR and MICR is the development of devices which recognize any printed text, or even handwriting. Systems to achieve this have been under active research and development for many years, and it may seem surprising that such devices have not already replaced other input methods. But, in fact, the incredible ability of human perceptual systems to instantly recognize a variety of different written styles, both written and printed, is based upon extremely complex and subtle mechanisms in the brain, and duplicating the effects of these with electronic equipment has proved very difficult indeed. (See the chapter on artificial intelligence and the fifth generation (Chapter 20) for further discussion of these points.)

However, scanning devices have been built into commercial products which provide a limited capability to read printed text fonts. Current machines are either limited in scope and application, or are very expensive. Nevertheless, there may be certain data processing applications which require bulk input of data already printed in standard fonts, and then the specialized text scanner may be a cost-effective alternative to keyboard entry.

Commercial input devices which read handwriting have been built, based on various methods: one such device utilizes a special pad which senses movement of a pen upon it, and uses information about where the written character starts and stops, as well as its shape, in order to identify which character has been written.

VOICE RECOGNITION

Nothing would seem more natural than talking directly to a computer: consider the time and cost savings which would be achieved by eliminating all the unwelcome stages of data capture at a stroke! Research, both on machine recognition of human voice and the comprehension of language, has been undertaken by artifical intelligence researchers over many years (see the chapter on artificial intelligence, Chapter 20). As was the case for machine recognition of writing (and for similar reasons) it has proved extraordinarily difficult to achieve practical success.

The current state of the art in terms of commercially viable products in this area is that specialized machines utilizing pattern-recognition techniques can, under ideal conditions, accept simple voice input of single words spoken carefully. For example there is a TV set on the market which responds to verbal commands for 'on' and 'off' and single numbers for channel selection. More advanced devices have vocabularies of hundreds of words.

There are certainly many industrial circumstances where it is very useful to have machines which recognize simple voice commands, e.g. where machine operators have both hands in use; airline pilots are another example.

But these devices will certainly not solve the problem of the enormous data input needs of modern business and it remains to be seen whether future developments will achieve any real breakthrough in this area. In particular, machine comprehension of continuous speech, as it normally occurs in everyday life, seems to be very far away from realization.

BAR CODING AND POINT OF SALE (POS)

This recent and highly successful method of data capture utilizes a low-intensity laser beam to read code numbers represented by groups of solid lines. The width and spacing of the lines are used by the scanner to identify a code. The scanners which read the bar-coded labels can be in the form of fixed machines or hand-held wands.

One application of this method is to be found in the public library. The details of books bought, issued and returned are retained on computer file, as are details of borrowers. When a book is issued, a light-wand is passed over the bar-coded label inside the book and the book code is read and immediately transmitted to the computer. The wand is then passed over the borrower's ticket where it picks up the bar-coded borrower number. The computer has, thus, been given the codes for book and borrower and can record the transaction on file.

The point-of-sale (POS) terminal is now a familiar sight in many supermarkets and stores. Products are passed over the laser scanner at the check-out till, and the product code is transmitted to a central computer which accesses its product file to ascertain the price, description and other details. The price and description are transmitted back to the till which displays the information to the customer (as a check) and records it on the tally slip. The central computer also updates its stock records to show that the item has been sold, and the data thus generated can be used for stock re-ordering and for sales and stock analysis. This technique has very significant advantages over previous methods: it is quicker than manual entry and eliminates human transcription error, and there are many circumstances where use of the technique will prove to be cost-effective. Indeed, the system can be taken further by allowing the customer to pay for the goods by electronic funds transfer (EFTPOS). Here funds are automatically debited to the customer's bank account and credited to the vendor's account.

Output devices

The most popular output device is the visual display unit (VDU), usually called simply a 'screen'. A low-cost, low-resolution screen uses 80 × 24 screen elements, where each element represents one character, and this arrangement is called character-mapped. This can be used to display any business characters or graphic symbols needed, and in a variety of shades and colours. To achieve the fine detail of diagrams required in engineering and artistic design work, high-resolution graphics screens are available which have the electronics necessary to display the tens of thousands of picture elements, or pixels, required. A pixel is a tiny discrete area of the screen which is individually formatted by the computer. A standard high-resolution screen may display 400 × 640 pixels, and where the arrangement is that each pixel can be individually addressed by the computer, this is known as bit-mapped.

PRINTERS

Although the VDU screen is ideal for fast-changing, on-line communication between user and computer, there has always been the need for permanent output on paper and other media. The computer industry has developed a wide range of printers to cater for different needs. The main parameters which the user can vary in his or her choice of printer are price, speed and print quality. Print quality is usually described in terms of the similarity to top-quality typed materials: letter quality (LQ), near-letter-quality (NLQ) and draft (see Fig. 7.4). There are other considerations: the need for printing of graphics (shapes, diagrams and graphs rather than just letters and numbers), the amount of noise generated (impact printers can be very noisy), colour printing, and the need for multiple copies.

Fast printers are needed for the massive output requirements of big-business payroll, billing and customer mailing systems. The quality of these outputs may not be the first priority and in these cases the line printer is used. The line printer has an array of hammers, one for each character position across the complete width of a page. Each hammer will strike paper and inked ribbon against the embossed character on a moving chain or drum, when the approriate character is in position.

When the line of characters has been completed, the printer shifts the paper up one line and repeats the cycle (hence the name). Typical print speeds are 600–2000 lines per minute (lpm), depending on the price of the printer. Because

LASER PRINTER EXAMPLE OUTPUT   ABCDEFGHIJKLMNOPQRSTUVWXYZ

DOT MATRIX OUTPUT EXAMPLE   ABCDEFGHIJKLMNOPQRSTUVWXYZ

DAISY WHEEL EXAMPLE   ABCDEFGHIJKLMNOPQRSTUVWXYZ

Figure 7.4   Output from dot matrix, daisy wheel and laser

of the high speeds involved, print quality may not be perfect and the characters can wander slightly along the line. Characters printed are limited to the character set of the drum or chain in use, so graphics and colour are not possible. These printers are very expensive and are usually attached to mainframes and large minis.

Where sheer speed of output is not so important, character or serial printers are used. These print one character at a time (rather than a line at a time) and hence are much slower than line printers; the cost is very much less too. The print quality depends on the printing mechanism used.

The daisy wheel printer (Fig. 7.5) hits an embossed character against a ribbon. The relatively slow speed, around 40 characters per second (cps), equivalent to 30 lpm, and the individual positioning of the characters means that the print quality can be very high indeed, giving true letter quality. Because of the fixed

Figure 7.5   Daisy wheel and dot matrix printers

characters on the daisy wheel, graphics are not possible. But different fonts or typefaces are readily achievable, simply by changing the daisy wheel. Different colour ribbons can provide a limited colour capability. The characteristics of these printers make them ideal for word processing applications.

Slightly faster than the daisy wheel, dot matrix printers (Fig. 7.5) make up each character by firing pins in the approximate shape. Print speeds vary greatly, depending on the cost; 160 cps, equivalent to 120 lpm, would be typical. Because of the approximation of the dot matrix, the quality is usually not so good as the daisy wheel. Some matrix printers print draft quality at top speed, and then achieve NLQ by overprinting each character one or more times to give a clearer image, albeit at a slower overall speed. Dot matrix printers are the cheapest of all the printers and are usually found attached to micros and PCs where high speed and top quality are not important. Because the matrix can simulate any shape, graphics can be reproduced to a certain extent; with different ribbons, limited colour capability is also possible.

There is some overlap among these categories; for example, recent developments in dot matrix printing have expanded this printer's range into the very fast category, rivalling line printers, at one end, and into the high-quality range, rivalling daisy wheels, at the other.

The devices discussed so far are all impact printers; they rely on something hitting an inked ribbon against paper. A number of other serial printer technologies have been tried, including ink-jet and thermal printers. Ink-jet printers create a stream of ink which is deflected by a magnetic field to form characters; they are silent in operation and capable of very effective graphics and colour output. Thermal printers are similar to dot matrix types except that they use heated pins to make an impression on a special waxed ribbon; this can give good quality printed output.

Graph plotters have pens which are moved between coordinates on the paper to create line drawings of any shape or complexity; coloured pens can be used, and very high accuracies are possible. These devices are used mainly by engineers and designers to develop elaborate diagrams, charts, networks and other line drawings.

The laser printer represents a significant departure from the printer technologies discussed so far. It prints one whole page at a time, using techniques very similar to a photocopier process. The laser printer has a memory in which the image for a page of printing is built up as it arrives from the CPU of the computer. When the memory is full, a laser beam creates an image of the page on a photoconductive drum; special ink (called toner) is attracted to the drum and sticks to the surface where the laser has marked it. A blank sheet of paper is then brought into contact with the drum and the ink adheres to it; the printed sheet is then heated to fuse the ink to it permanently. The drum is then erased, ready for the next image to be drawn.

The laser printer has a number of advantages: it can be very fast indeed, faster than the fastest line printers with speeds of 600 pages per minute or more

Table 7.1 Printer types compared

Printer	Typical speed (lpm)	Print quality	Typical cost £000s	Application
daisy wheel	30	LQ	0.5	micro/PC
dot matrix	120	draft/NLQ	0.3	micro/PC
ink-jet (graphics)	120*	graphics and colour	2	micro/PC, mini
laser (desk-top)	500	LQ	3	micro/PC, mini
line printer	1 000	draft	10	mini, mainframe
laser	20 000	LQ	100	mainframe

LQ: letter quality, NLQ: near letter quality.
*Less than half this speed for graphics or colour printing.

(around 36 000 lpm); its printed image can be very high quality, as good as the best commercial publishing standards. Graphics are no problem, because the printing is laser generated and does not depend on predetermined shapes, in principle any image can be formed and printed. Laser printers contain a microprocessor as well as the image memory, and usually are programmed in a special printer programming language (POSTSCRIPT is one such language).

In practice, a major feature of laser printers is their ability to create virtually any typeface, character font or special printing effect. The situation is slightly complicated by the need for extensive and sophisticated software which can cope with print formatting and character definition in order to produce the effects of which the laser printer is capable. Nevertheless, the laser printer has made possible dramatic changes in the printing and publishing world, and has encouraged the development of desk-top publishing.

The main drawback of the laser printer has been its cost; very fast and sophisticated machines can cost hundreds of thousand of pounds. Such high-speed machines would be attached to large mainframes. However, recent developments have resulted in slower, desk-top versions becoming available which are priced at £2000–£5000. This cost is far higher than an equivalent serial printer, yet the laser printer has the advantages of speed, silence, a wide range of fonts and excellent print quality; this makes them very attractive, and businesses are increasingly connecting them to PCs and minis.

A desk-top laser printer is likely to print at a speed of eight pages per minute or so (equivalent to 480 lpm). The quality will be as good as, or better than, the best daisy wheel, and there will usually be a wide choice of fonts and special printing effects. Sophisticated software is needed to produce the laser printer's best characteristics, in terms of word processing or desk-top publishing software, together with an appropriate printer driver and printer programming language.

VOICE OUTPUT

Unlike the machine comprehension of voice input, computer generation of voice output, called speech synthesis, has been relatively successful. One elementary technique involves a computer program which examines the letters in the words or phrases given to it (they can be typed in on a keyboard, or provided from backing store) and reproduces elementary voice sounds (phonemes) to match; the result is crude, but recognizable, depending on the spelling of the words.

More sophisticated techniques involve the storing of a digital speech representation of a number of words in a vocabulary. These are matched against the input phrase and linked together to produce the final spoken output. The results here can be very acceptable, although the output does not have the usual human inflections and phrasing of everyday speech, and so the overall effect sounds rather mechanical. Most of the general-purpose software available for speech synthesis has been developed in the USA and has an accent to match.

Speech synthesizers are finding increasing uses in the business world. Cars which tell their owners to fasten seat-belts are commonplace (and there are many industrial applications where spoken messages may be the best means of communication); public telephone re-routing messages are spoken automatically when you dial a number which has been changed; some bank cash machines provide verbal instructions. As the technology develops and improves it is likely that voice output will play a far greater part in computer communications with the outside world.

COMPUTER OUTPUT ON MICROFILM (COM)

A relatively old technology, microfilm (a strip of film held in a cartridge) and microfiche (a 15 cm × 10 cm sheet) contain photographic images of pages of computer output which have been reduced by about 50:1. Because of this large reduction in image size, very large amounts of printed output can be stored in a small space; about 300 pages of computer output can be stored on one microfiche card. The usual method of creating the film is for a machine to photograph a VDU image of the data output, and then to reproduce a succession of these displays on the film material, together with titles and indexing codes. Most microfilm users send their data on disk or tape to a bureau which specializes in this work.

The costs of producing the output are relatively low, and it is a robust and very compact form of storage. The drawback of this method of output storage is that when a user wants to examine the stored data it must be scanned through special reading devices which magnify the image back to a readable size. These COM readers are not expensive, but using them is rather tiresome for the operator. In general, COM is suitable in situations where there are very large amounts of data to be retained for human access, but where the need to access any one part of it is small. For example, some organizations are required by law to retain details of their customer transactions for several years, the data being

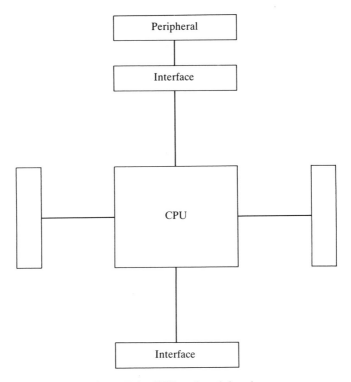

Figure 7.6   CPU and peripherals

rarely accessed. In these circumstances COM output is a cheap and space-saving solution.

Interfaces: communicating with the CPU

The input–output devices discussed in this chapter are all connected to the CPU via interfaces. An interface (Fig. 7.6) is a special package of electronics which acts as a go-between to enable the CPU and peripheral to exchange data.

The purpose of the interface is to match up two devices which may have very different electronic or data processing characteristics. There are several aspects of this electronic matching. For example, a daisy wheel printer can accept data for printing at 40 characters per second, but the CPU may be capable of delivering characters to the printer at the rate of 1 million characters per second. Clearly, if the CPU were allowed to run its course nothing intelligible could appear on the printer, which could accept only one character in every 25 000 or so.

So, the interface between these devices contains an electronic flag which tells the CPU when the printer is ready to accept another character. When the printer is busy the flag is set and the CPU waits (or turns to another task); when the printer has finished printing it resets the flag. Characters to be printed are usually stored in a buffer; this gives the printer time to cope with them and allows the CPU to continue with its program, rather than wait for the slow peripheral to finish its activity. Other flags signal if the printer has run out of paper, or if an operating switch has been set.

The interface also matches up different data characteristics between the CPU and peripheral. The CPU transmits data on a parallel data bus; some peripherals also accept data in parallel. However, the daisy wheel printer we have been discussing will probably be a serial device: it accepts characters one bit at a time which it assembles to form a complete character. The interface contains electronics which accept parallel data from the CPU and deliver serial data to the printer.

Generally speaking, when a peripheral data transfer is to take place, the control unit in the CPU will place data on the data bus and also place the address to which the data is intended on the address bus. The data could be destined for a printer or the VDU or an external memory device, depending on the value of the address. Each peripheral waits for 'its' address to appear on the address bus before accepting data from the data bus.

These considerations apply to all peripheral devices, and some devices need more complex arrangements than others. Data transfers between CPU and backing store devices such as disks occur at very high speeds, and usually are served by special interfacing methods. The electronic subsystem which handles data transfers between CPU and disk drive is called a disk controller and this is usually a very complex and sophisticated device.

It is quite commonplace to buy a computer from one supplier and peripherals from another. There are a number of manufacturers who specialize in one type (for example, Epson Corporation specialize in printers) so it is necessary to match up this firm's products with those of the computer supplier. Ensuring that the proper interfacing arrangements can be made between these products will be an important consideration for the purchaser. Some interface standards have emerged which are commonly used for certain devices: the RS232 interface converts from parallel to serial and is often used for serial devices and for telecommunication. The Centronics interface has become a standard for parallel devices, such as fast printers.

Summary

Peripherals, communicating with the central processor of the computer by interfaces, allow the CPU to communicate with the outside world. Peripherals may have a role as input devices, output devices or both; each was considered in detail.

KEY TERMS   Bar coding and point of sale (POS)   Bit-mapped   Character/ serial printer   Computer output on microfilm (COM)   Daisy wheel printer

Data conversion   Desk-top publishing (DTP)   Disk controller   Dot matrix printer   Electronic funds transfer (EFT)   Electronic funds transfer at point of sale (EFTPOS)   Graph-plotters   Hard copy   Impact printer   Interface Key verification   Key-to-disk   Key-to-tape   Laser printer   Letter quality Light-pen   Line printer   Machine-sensible   Magnetic ink character recognition (MICR)   Mouse   Off-line   Optical character recognition (OCR) Optical mark reading (OMR)   Peripheral device   Pixel   Point of sale (POS) Punch card   Source document   Speech synthesis   Text and handwriting recognition   Touch-screen   Turnaround document   Voice recognition   Voice synthesis.

Further reading

French C.S., *Computer Science*, DP Publications, Eastleigh, Hants, 1985.
French C.S., *Computer Studies*, DP Publications, Eastleigh, Hants, 1986.
Gandoff M., *Students Guide to Data Communications*, Heinemann, Oxford, 1990.
Sanders D.H., *Computers Today*, McGraw-Hill, New York, 1988.

8
Storing information, file structures and database

The storage and retrieval of information is fundamental to any information system. The speed and efficiency with which computers can manipulate data has resulted in far-reaching changes in the way that organizations can be managed. The methods by which data storage is achieved have important consequences in terms both of the costs of storage and also in the relative ease with which the information can be retrieved and used by managers.

Files and records: data entitites

Data items in the form of numbers, characters and symbols are stored in logical groups called fields; fields of logically related data are stored together as records; and groups of logically related records are stored together in files. In the payroll file example shown in Fig. 8.1 (obviously much simplified), there are four fields in each record. Each field contains a self-consistent piece of data: payroll number, employee name, department code and net pay to date.

The fields in this file are fixed length, that is, there are always four positions for the payroll number in each record and two positions for the department code. Every record is therefore the same length, too. If the need arose for a three-digit department code, then the file would have to be reorganized to allow for that. By the same token, if we allow thirty positions for the name field then this will suffice for most names, but many names will be much shorter than this and therefore there will be wasted space on the file.

An alternative is to allow for variable-length records. With this arrangement fields may be as long or as short as necessary, with much saving of space. We could also have some fields which were only present in some records and not in others. The drawback to variable-length records is that they add significantly to the complications of file handling. The computer must have a means of recog-

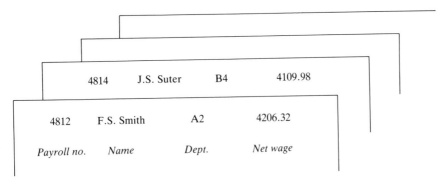

Payroll no.	Name	Dept.	Net wage
4812	F.S. Smith	A2	4206.32
4814	J.S. Suter	B4	4109.98

Figure 8.1   A file of payroll records

nizing where data items start and finish, and the software used in record storage and location must be very much more complicated to allow for the different record lengths. This all adds to processing time and cost, and so the choice of fixed- or variable-length records must depend on the circumstances of each application.

The position of the fields within each record is relatively unimportant; the position of the records within the file is very important indeed. The records in this file are positioned in sequence of payroll number, the lowest number first; payroll number is thus the key field. It may be desirable to have more than one key field. For example, the internal telephone directory for a university may be organized by department (primary key field) and then by name (secondary key), within department, and then by initials (secondary key). Files which have no particular sequence to begin with may be sorted in order to facilitate processing.

For the purposes of this discussion, it has not mattered whether the records are stored on paper, punch cards, magnetic tapes or disks. We can consider data storage independently of the medium on which it is stored: in this way we are talking about logical records and logical files. In the next section we shall consider the physical devices which are used to store the data.

Internal and external storage devices

The internal main store in the CPU of a computer is used to hold only the program(s) currently running, together with the data that are currently needed by the program at that instant in time. The large volumes of data which organizations hold about their operations are always stored on external or backing store in a form that can be retrieved when needed by the computer (may also be termed secondary storage). Magnetic disks are currently the most common form of external storage.

There are several reasons for this split in the roles of the two types of storage. Internal, main store, random-access memory (RAM) is usually made up of electronic semiconductor devices, in the form of memory chips. These chips are

Table 8.1   Data storage comparisons: internal vs. external memory

	Capacity (bytes)	Speed (accesses/second)	Cost* (bytes/£)	Volatility
Internal				
CPU registers	100	100 000 000	10	volatile
RAM	640 000	1 000 000	1 000	volatile
External				
hard disk	20 000 000	40	50 000	non-volatile
floppy disk	700 000	4	5 000	non-volatile

*Cost figures are relative and for comparison purposes only.

relatively expensive in terms of bytes of memory per £ cost (although the cost is coming down rapidly with advances in technology). Another drawback is that semiconductor memories are volatile. When the power is turned off (deliberately or as a result of power failure) the binary patterns stored in the memory are lost, and when power is resumed the memory assumes a random pattern.

There is, therefore, the need for a low-cost secondary storage device which retains binary patterns with or without power until the patterns are deliberately changed. This need has been fulfilled by a number of electromechanical devices over the years, ranging from magnetic drums to laser-accessed optical disks. Of course, the role of external storage is largely concerned with reproducing the characteristics of solid-state internal memories, but on a much larger scale and at much lower cost. If the technology of solid-state devices were to improve dramatically (and it is improving all the time), then external storage as it is currently perceived will no longer be necessary.

The prime advantage of the internal semiconductor RAM memory of course is its speed of operation. Being all-electronic there are no moving parts and the memory can operate as fast as the constraints of current electronic technology will allow, which is very fast indeed. The electromechanical devices used for external storage, on the other hand, depend upon physical movement of some kind: a spinning disk is read by a magnetically driven seek-arm, or a capstan-driven tape is wound past a read/write head. The result is that the secondary storage devices used today are many orders of magnitude slower than internal RAM. Table 8.1 illustrates comparable memory access speeds and other characteristics for a reasonably powerful business PC.

Magnetic tape and disk storage

MAGNETIC TAPE

Data storage on magnetic tape has a long history. The advent of very cheap, fast disk drives has meant that tape has been superseded for many traditional data storage applications. However, tapes are still a viable choice under certain

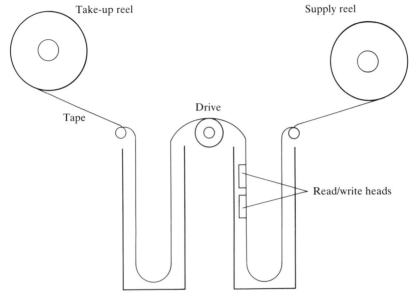

Take-up reel   Supply reel

Drive

Tape

Read/write heads

Figure 8.2 Tape drive

circumstances since magnetic tape is a physically robust medium which offers cost-effective storage where low hit-rate processing is involved.

The tape itself consists of a plastic base material coated with a magnetically sensitive substance and is kept wound on a plastic reel. When required for processing the reel is mounted on a tape drive (Fig. 8.2) which has the necessary electronics for reading the tape and transmitting the data to the CPU. The tape drive winds the tape from the supply reel past read/write heads onto a take-up reel. The data is read serially, byte by byte, as the tape moves past the head. Bytes of data are packed very closely together on the tape (1600 bytes per inch or more).

This dense packing means that a great deal of data can be stored on a tape, and the data transfer rate to the CPU can be very fast; it also requires special consideration in the construction of the tape drive and in the physical layout of the data on the tape. A typical tape may be 2400 ft long, giving a total data capacity (at 1600 bytes per inch) of 46 Mbytes of storage (2400 × 12 × 1600). The tape may be moved past the read/write heads at 200 inches per second giving a data transfer rate of 320 Kbytes per second between the tape drive unit and the CPU (200 × 1600). However, these 'ideal' figures must be modified in practice because of the need to have data-free areas on the tape.

The plastic tape is light and tough, but its weight is not zero. When some data has been read the CPU must then process it, and while CPU is busy (or perhaps another peripheral device, such as a printer, must perform its function) the tape drive must stop and wait until the CPU is ready to read some more data. The

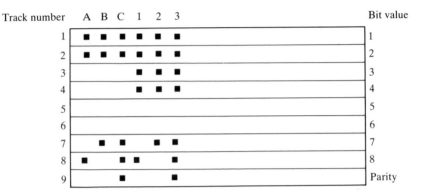

Figure 8.3   Tape layout

tape thus needs to stop and start quite frequently during normal data process-ing. To avoid stretching the tape, the drive is constructed with separate motors to power the reels and the tape itself; when the tape is drawn through the read/write heads, a sensor detects the loop of tape passing and causes the tape reel to move forward a little. When you see tape drives in action the reels often appear to be twitching round a bit at a time, although the tape is actually running past the heads smoothly.

Data recording is achieved by altering the magnetism in the material of the tape, and the recording principle is very similar to that of the home audio tape recorder. The difference is that home audio recording is usually analogue (although binary hi-fi systems are now becoming more common) and musical sounds are represented by a continuously varying signal; computer data is represented by discrete binary patterns and the setting on or off of individual bits.

Bytes of data are laid out vertically across the tape, using one of the standard data coding schemes: ASCII or EBCDIC (Fig. 8.3). In order to check that data has been written to the tape (and read from it) accurately, an extra bit is written to the tape for each byte giving nine horizontal tracks along the tape. The extra bit is known as the parity bit, and when the tape is written it is set so that the sum of the 'on'-bits for each byte is always an odd number. When the tape is read back later, the tape-drive electronics can check that each byte has correct parity. If any one bit on the tape has changed its magnetic character, or has been misread, then the sum of the on-bits including the parity bit will no longer be an odd number. Of course, if two bits were wrong then the parity check would not spot this; nevertheless, the chances of this happening consistently are remote and the parity check is a very efficient means of checking that the storage device is working properly.

During data processing, the tape must frequently stop and start in order to allow time for the CPU and/or peripherals to operate. Because the tape does not have zero mass it cannot be stopped absolutely dead in its tracks; therefore there

(a)

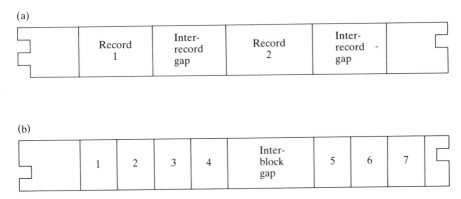

(b)

Figure 8.4 Tape records, blocks and inter-record gaps

must be a space on the tape in which no data is written to allow the tape to stop, or to gain speed when restarting. These spaces are known as inter-record gaps, because in its simplest arrangement the gaps will be kept between each individual record; thus the tape drive will read one entire record, then stop momentarily and wait until the CPU signals for the next record (see Fig. 8.4).

With the arrangement of Fig. 8.4(a) there will be a gap for each record, and clearly this will mean that a large proportion of the tape will consist of gaps, resulting in much wasted space and in a drastic reduction in the data transfer rate. The solution to this problem is to group the records together in blocks, so that the tape drive reads an entire block before stopping in the inter-block gap. Figure 8.4(b) shows records blocked in groups of four. The CPU usually processes only one record at a time, so arrangements must be made to hold the four records in a buffer store in main memory until their turn for processing comes.

Clearly the number of records chosen to put in a block, the blocking factor, must be chosen with some care: the higher the blocking factor the more efficient the tape drive in terms of storage and data transfer rates. On the other hand, the buffer store needed in main memory will occupy space that then cannot be used for other purposes. As memory space is usually at a premium, a blocking factor must be selected which exploits the tape drive speed as much as possible but within the constraints of program size.

An offshoot development of the tape drive is the cassette streamer. Physically similar to audio cassette technology, the streamer is used not to process data but to act solely as a back-up device. Because the device is designed only for the sole purpose of copying data regardless of records and formatting, it can be made to have a high capacity, work very fast and be relatively inexpensive. Capacities range from 60 Mbytes to 150 Mbytes or more. The streamer is usually found connected to micros and minis which have high-capacity Winchester-type (fixed) disks and hence there is the need for an inexpensive back-up medium.

Although floppy disks may be adequate back-up for stand-alone PCs, a streamer is essential for high-usage systems such as networked file-servers. An alternative high-capacity streaming device is the helical scan drive, a spin-off of video technology which packs 300 Mbytes of data onto an 8 mm video tape.

Processing data on traditional tape devices requires careful consideration. Records are stored serially, one after the other along the length of the tape. Imagine the file of payroll data from Fig. 8.1 stored on tape. Because the file is sequenced on payroll number, the computer must read the records in that sequence, one after the other, so a printout of the file must appear in that sequence. Suppose we needed a printout by department code sequence. Of course, we could arrange to sort the data on the tape but this takes time. Suppose we need a printout only of those people in department D5. The computer must physically read all of the tape, examining each record in turn to see if it should be printed or not. Suppose we need to print only the record for Mr Suter. The computer must still read every single record on the tape until it arrives at the right one.

If all of the file must be processed for an application then the process is said to have a high hit-rate on the file. If very few records need to be processed, then the application is described as having a low hit-rate on the file.

$$\text{Application hit-rate} = \frac{\text{number of records accessed} \times 100 \text{ per cent}}{\text{number of records in the file}}$$

Where applications have a low hit-rate, then processing data on tape will be very inefficient. Similarly, where data on a file is required to be processed in different sequences, then tape will be an inefficient medium.

Consider what happens when you use a bank automatic cash dispenser. The machine can tell you the balance of your current account, as can any of the bank's machines in the UK. The bank's computer will have a file of records for every customer with a cash card (perhaps a million or more) and this file is accessed when a customer uses the cash machine. But of course nobody knows which customer will access the data or when. The hit-rate is therefore very low indeed and tape-based storage is clearly inappropriate; it would be absurd to have a large file searched sequentially for just one record. Instead, we need a storage device which enables direct access to any record without serially reading the whole file, and for this we need a completely different physical structure: the magnetic disk.

MAGNETIC DISKS

Data storage on magnetic disk has been with us for as long as tapes; and high customer demand has ensured continual product improvement by manufacturers over many years. The result is a wide range of disk storage devices which offer different levels of performances at costs varying from a few hundred through to many thousands of pounds. Because of the rapidly decreasing costs, and increasing capacity and performance characteristics of disk storage, it is

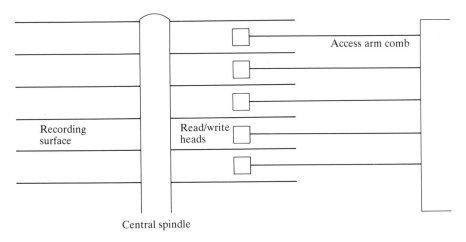

Central spindle

Figure 8.5 Disk drive and access arms

likely to remain the main medium for business data storage for some time to come.

Despite the wide range of products the principles of operation are similar for all of them. The disk consists of a double-sided platter of metal or plastic which is coated with a magnetically sensitive material, similar to that used on magnetic tapes. Smaller, cheaper disks use flexible plastic, hence the floppy disk.

One or more platters are mounted on a central spindle and the data is accessed by a comb of read/write heads which moves in and out of the platters (Fig. 8.5); one read/write head accesses the data on each recording surface. In the disk assembly there may be eleven platters; the top and bottom surfaces are not used for recording, leaving twenty surfaces accessed by the twenty heads.

Data is recorded on each active surface in the form of concentric rings of data called tracks. There could be 200 tracks, although high-capacity disks may have many more tracks. Data is recorded along each track bit by bit, byte by byte and record by record. The fact that the inner tracks are shorter than the outer tracks does not affect the amount of data stored on them.

Each track is divided into sectors where one sector is the minimum track length that the disk drive will read at one time. The disk drive can detect when a sector start is under the head, and can then commence reading or writing. Records are stored in each sector, and depending on the record size there may be many records in each sector; considerations regarding blocking factors also come into play in a similar manner to tapes.

The disk assembly described in Fig. 8.5 has a capacity of 1 Kbyte per sector, giving a total capacity of 32 Mbytes of storage ($1024 \times 8 \times 200 \times 20$). It spins as one unit, at speeds of 4000 rev min^{-1} or more and the read/write head assembly also moves as one unit, moving into position over one track in order to access data. Each head flies over the disk at a minute distance above the

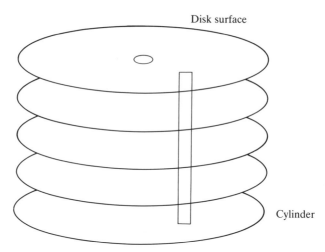

Disk surface

Cylinder

Figure 8.6   Cylinder disk storage

surface, but without actually touching; any trace of contamination, such as dust or smoke particles may cause contact to be made—a head crash—which can cause damage and loss of data. The flying disk head has been likened to a jumbo jet flying at 960 kph. 3 metres above the ground.

In order to avoid the possibility of contamination, most higher-capacity disks are kept in a clean-air environment, achieved either by sealing the disk permanently in an airtight enclosure or by ensuring that the computer environment is itself air-conditioned and filtered. Smoking is not allowed anywhere near disks!

Because the read/write mechanism moves as a unit, positioning the heads in order to read a certain track, say track number 36 on surface number one, will make available all the tracks vertically at position 36 on the other surfaces, simply by switching electronically between the heads. This section of tracks is called a cylinder, which is defined as all the vertical tracks that can be accessed by the head assembly without physical movement of the heads. This is most important because storing data serially in cylinders (Fig. 8.6), rather than serially in tracks on one surface, is an essential performance requirement.

The physical movement of the head assembly (seek time) is the major element in access times. If a file of 1000 records were to be written to the disk starting at surface 0, track 0 then moving to track 1 on the same surface, then track 2, then track 3 and so on, the head assembly must physically move for each track to be written. The physical movement is many orders of multiples slower than electronic switching.

A much more efficient method is to write the file 'down the cylinder'. The data is written to track 1 surface 0, then to the same track on surface 1, then to the same track on surface 2 and so on; the head assembly does not move at all until the cylinder is full of data. Similarly, when reading the file back for processing, the head assembly moves to the correct cylinder, then reads each track and switches electronically between the vertical tracks in the cylinder, so no head movement is needed.

Calculation of exact access times and transfer rates for disks is complicated by the fact that the disk drive must wait until a sector has spun round beneath the head (latency period), and this waiting time depends on the length of the last read/write operation and other factors. In general, a typical disk drive can deliver data to the CPU at rates of 300 000 bytes per second, or more; this is a similar rate to the tape drive discussed earlier. But high-speed, high-capacity drives connected to mainframe computers can provide transfer rates very much higher than this.

The principal feature of the disk drive is its ability to access individual records directly. Direct access is achieved because the read/write head assembly can move into any part of the disk assembly and read the data from any sector on any surface. This is a dramatic improvement over the tape drive, which must read the tape serially.

The difference between tapes and disks is comparable to that between the scrolls used by ancient civilizations and a spine-bound book. A scroll is retained on a baton of wood, and is wound onto another baton in order to read it. A lengthy scroll can only be accessed by unrolling it from one end until the desired material is reached; and this is what must be done with magnetic tapes. On the other hand, a book can be opened directly at the right page; and this is mirrored by the direct access disk. The 'technology' of the book is so superior to the scroll, in terms of ease of use, despite the extra difficulties and costs of binding the pages, that books replaced scrolls long ago.

Of course one can read a book serially, starting with page one, and 'process' it in the same way as a scroll. But if you need to access a particular topic in the book, you must first find out the page number in order to make the direct access action which takes you to the topic. Information about topic locations is contained at the front in a contents list, and at the back in an index.

Similar arrangements are used to access data on disk but, instead of a page number, disk locations are accessed by providing the cylinder number, the track number and the sector number. The location of files is retained in a special area of the disk, referred to as the volume table of contents (VTOC) or file directory; this list provides the details of exactly where a file is stored on the disk (it may be split into separate parts in different places), together with other information such as when the file was last updated, and so on. The location of records within a file may be given by a separate index for that file; the index gives the cylinder, track and sector reference for each record and enables true direct access to individual records to be accomplished. There are, it should be noted, other methods of arranging indexes, and achieving direct access.

Magnetic disks come in many varieties; some of these types are compared in Table 8.2. Cheaper, lower-capacity $5\frac{1}{4}''$ disks based on single-platter, flexible

Table 8.2 Comparison of storage types showing typical characteristics

Media	Media capacity (Mbytes)	Drive cost (£K)	Access type (serial/direct)	Applications
tape reel ($\frac{1}{2}''$)	40	5	s	mini and mainframe
tape cassette (streamer)	60–300	1	s	micro and PC
floppy disk ($5\frac{1}{4}''$)	0.3–1.0	0.2	s/d	micro and PC
diskette ($3\frac{1}{2}''$)	0.7–1.4	0.2	s/d	micro and PC
Winchester disk ($5\frac{1}{4}''$)	10–60	0.5	s/d	micro and PC
disk pack (removable) (14'')	50–500	20	s/d	mini and mainframe
optical disk (12'')	1000–5000	2	worm	micro and PC and mini
mass storage unit	20 000	100	d	mainframe

plastic (floppies) are common on PCs, although these are being superseded by the more robust $3\frac{1}{2}''$ micro diskettes (although these are still often called floppy disks!). Hard disks, based on rigid metal substrata, allow more accurate engineering and hence higher data capacity and performance, and single- or

Figure 8.7 Different disks, floppies and diskettes

double-platter hard disks are found on the more powerful business micros. Minis and mainframes, with their far greater data processing capabilities, have traditionally used the replaceable hard disk pack, with its multiple platters, high capacity and high performance.

Removable disks, including floppies and diskettes (Fig. 8.7), can be dismounted from their drives and stored until needed. This effectively provides an infinite storage capability; when the data on a particular disk is needed, it must be remounted and made on-line to the CPU for access. On-line is defined as being immediately available for access by (or to) the CPU; by the same token, off-line means that the device or file is not available to the CPU.

Fixed disks cannot be dismounted; however, because they remain undisturbed they can be sealed into a unit, avoiding the problems of dust and air contamination, therefore the engineering tolerances can be made much finer. Under these circumstances, significantly better performance can be achieved. A typical fixed-disk arrangement is the so-called Winchester-style disk, the $5\frac{1}{4}''$ hard disk unit increasingly found on PCs. Because of the vast demand for this unit, costs have been reduced dramatically, and capacities raised to 20–60 Mbytes and more.

Before they can be used for the first time, disks have to be formatted; that is they have to have the layout of the data and directory areas mapped out, and the sectors on each track marked electronically. This is done by running a special program which writes the necessary information onto the disk. Different manufacturers have different ways of formatting disks, so a disk for use on one machine must usually be formatted on that machine even if it has already been used on a different type. Formatting destroys any information stored on the disk.

Alternative storage devices

Because of the importance of secondary storage, many types and varieties of device have been developed over the years. Some of these have come and gone, such as magnetic drum storage (fast, but low capacity), micro-tapes (superseded by floppy disks) and many others. The technical development and cost reduction of the disk drive in recent years matches that of processors; for example, 20 years ago a 30 Mbyte capacity Model 2314 disk drive was marketed by IBM at around £45 000, equivalent to £250 000 today, and 1000 times more expensive than a drive of similar capacity today!

A device still used for very high on-line storage requirements is the mass storage unit. This employs multiple tape (or disk) cartridges arranged in a honeycomb; an individual cartridge is accessed and then the tape strip is read serially. With a data capacity up to 500 000 Mbytes or more this system provides a tremendous on-line access capability, albeit at the penalty of relatively slow access performance due to the mechanical movements involved in cartridge access and tape movement.

A new storage mechanism, based on laser technology, is the optical disk. The device looks and works rather like an audio compact disk. A laser beam is used to write a series of pits in the material on the disk, a pit changes the optical characteristics of the disk material. A pit or no-pit represents the binary 1 or 0 of digital data. The laser writes in a continuous spiral round the disk surface, rather like a gramophone record. Because of the laser technology data can be packed at very high densities indeed, with a single-surface 12″ disk holding 1000 Mbytes or more (1000 megabytes is referred to as a gigabyte). This technology is relatively recent, and it is likely that capacities will be enhanced even further.

The method of writing data to the disk is permanent. Data is written once by a high-power laser beam, and then can be read back by a low-power beam many times. The access characteristic is called WORM (write once, read many). WORM access means that the disk cannot be used for data processing in the usual way. Instead, it can be used for storage of unchanging data: archiving of permanent organizational records for example. A more likely use is for the accessing of large commerical databases; specialist firms hold and maintain these databases (on financial and stockmarket data for example), and their customers pay a fee for on-line access to the data. These large files can be stored on optical disk and the customer receives a disk for reading by his or her computer, thus obviating the need for costly on-line access to the information supplier's computer.

Demand for secondary storage devices with ever-greater capacities and faster performance has ensured that technology advances very rapidly indeed. For example, Winchester $5\frac{1}{4}″$ hard disks are now being built which provide 760 Mbytes of direct access capacity. By the time you read this book these high-capacity devices may be commercially available, and even higher capacities could be on the horizon.

Because of the relatively low cost and high capacity of the optical disk it is likely to be developed considerably in the future; if the optical disk could be made to read/write with the same ease as magnetic disk, there is little doubt it would quickly supersede other forms of storage for many purposes. Indeed, read/write versions are now coming onto the market, and one product already offers 1000 Mbytes of updatable storage. The drawback currently is that the data transfer and access rates are substantially slower than Winchester magnetic disks (about four times slower). Another problem is that the number of read/writes possible on one optical disk may be limited, i.e. the disk loses its changeable capacity after a certain number (albeit a very large number) of updates.

A new form of high-capacity, low-cost data storage is under development by ICI. This is called digital paper; it consists of a plastic base with optically sensitive coatings. The paper can be cut up and used on tags, cards or even reels of tape. The data storage density is very high indeed, and a 12″ reel of tape could hold 1 million Mbytes: a terabyte! (See Table 8.3.) Such capacities would indeed

Table 8.3 Storage size terms and values

		$base_2$	$base_{10}$
kilobyte	1024 bytes	2^{10} bytes	10^3 bytes
megabyte	1024 Kbytes	2^{20} bytes	10^6 bytes
gigabyte	1024 Mbytes	2^{30} bytes	10^9 bytes
terabyte	1024 Gbytes	2^{40} bytes	10^{12} bytes

revolutionize data storage. The drawback is that the new material currently has the same limitation as other forms of optical storage, i.e. it has only the WORM capability for access.

All the secondary storage devices we have examined have a major drawback: they all involve some physical movement in order to function, and therefore are truly secondary in speed and convenience to the computer's primary RAM memory. Ideally, we would like all data stored in main memory, permanently and securely and instantly accessible. It is surely only a matter of time before developments in the capacity and economics of solid-state, main-memory technology render secondary storage obsolete.

File structures and databases

A critical decision in any system is the type of file structure to be used. The principal conventional data structures are: serial, sequential, random and indexed-sequential. The main characteristics of each file structure can be seen most easily using as an example a set of student marks for an assignment, with one record for each student as follows:

John Smith	56
Fred Jones	85
Ann Storey	95
Nicky Martin	92
Alan Alder	42

If we wanted to find the average student mark for the group, we would get the computer to read all the records and add up the marks. The hit-rate is 100 per cent and the sequence of the records is immaterial. Serial organization, i.e. records in the file in no particular sequence, is fine for this purpose. Serial files can be stored on disks or tapes, and most other media too.

The next job might be to list all the students in alphabetic sequence. The hit-rate is again 100 per cent but this time the records must be sorted using surname as the key field. The resulting file is defined as sequential organization.

Alan Alder	42
Fred Jones	85
Nicky Martin	92
John Smith	56
Ann Storey	95

Sequential files can be held on disks or tapes, and most other media.

It is decided to provide a student result service, such that any student can come and ask for his or her mark, then we need to consider a file organization which enables us to access single records based on surname as the key field.

John Smith	56
Fred Jones	85
Ann Storey	95
Nicky Martin	92***
Alan Alder	42

For example, Nicky Martin may ask for her mark first; the computer must access this record, but only this one is needed. The hit-rate is now very low, i.e. one transaction per access, and the sequence in which students will request access is unknown. One of the fastest direct access methods uses random organization, where each record is located at an address defined by the key field. Only disk stores (and other direct access devices) can physically provide the direct addressing capability of random organization. Magnetic tapes cannot be used for this purpose, and this imposes a dramatic restriction on the processing capability of magnetic tapes.

Although random organization provides a very fast retrieval for each individual record accessed, it is not suitable for sequential access. If we need to list all the records in sequence from a random file, then the total access time is much greater than for sequential organization because of the great number of read/write head seeks involved. Suppose we wish to provide all three processing services from the same file. An indexed-sequential file organization could be used to provide a file in alphabetic sequence for lists and whole-file statistical processing, and at the same time provide a direct access capability for individual student enquiry. Only disk stores (and other direct access devices) provide the direct addressing capability needed for indexed-sequential file structures. Table 8.4 summarizes the choices available for traditional file structures.

The examples described here have been deliberately kept simple to illustrate the concepts. In practice, decisions about file structures for large systems can be very complex and usually require detailed knowledge of the file-handling

Table 8.4 Selecting file organization and media

File organization	Access method		Medium		Access requirement hit-rate	Example
	serial	direct	disk	tape		
serial	y	n	y	y	high hit-rate	average student marks
sequential	y	n	y	y	high hit-rate	alphabetic student list
random	slow	fast	y	n	low hit-rate	enquiry about a student
indexed-sequential	y	y	y	n	high and low hit-rate	student list and enquiries

characteristics of the hardware and software to be used, as well as knowledge of the characteristics of the data, the volumes involved and likely nature and frequency of access expected. These decisions can crucially affect the efficiency and performance of the system.

CHOOSING THE DATABASE APPROACH

The decision to select a full-scale database approach to data organization is not one to be taken lightly. Most organizations begin IS development with systems employing conventional file structures and perhaps convert these to database structures at a later date. In order to implement database fully, a substantial investment is required in database management system (DBMS) software, in the extra hardware needed to support it, and especially in the time required to organize and structure data into the necessary format. Because the database approach potentially affects systems across the entire breadth of the organization it is unlikely that the decision would be reached on the basis of the anlysis of a single system alone.

The rewards to the organization of a full database approach can include the following:

- improved data accessibility and availability,
- improved data control and security,
- improved data consistency and reliability,
- de-coupled programs and data,
- lower-cost application development,
- lower-cost system maintenance,
- application development design flexibility.

However, in order to realize these benefits there must be a systematic and fundamental appraisal of the data in the organization. Whereas traditional development involves developing data files for specific applications, where the application systems are de-coupled and independent of each other, the database

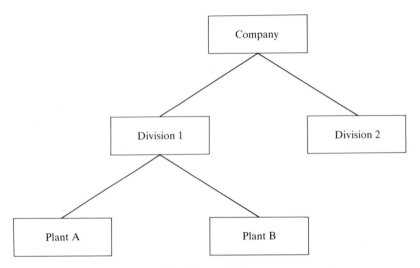

Figure 8.8   Hierarchical structure

approach involves analysing data access requirements, and then planning logical relationships, in respect of data across the whole organization.

Choosing a database involves selecting a suitable database management system (DBMS), the extensive software environment which will support the database application. There are three main types of DBMS; hierarchical, network and relational.

Hierarchical database structure

In this structure data elements are arranged in a tree, with pointers which relate data items together in chains; the main relationships are from parent data to child data, in one-to-many form (see Fig. 8.8). A commercial hierarchical DBMS is information management system (IMS) from IBM.

Network database structure

This is a variation on the hierarchical structure in which the one-to-many relationships are expanded to many-to-many relationships (see Fig. 8.9). A commercial system is IDMS from Cullinet Software.

Relational database structure

The relational structure presents data in the form of two-dimensional tables, although the tables are logical rather than physical (see Fig. 8.10). There are a number of commercial relational DBMS, among them DB2 from IBM for mainframe computers and dBase from Ashton Tate for micros and PCs.

Selecting a suitable DBMS involves weighing up the pros and cons of the DBMS types in the light of the data accessing needs of the organization.

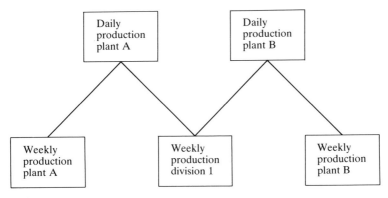

Figure 8.9 Network structure

Hierarchical and network structures can be very efficient and provide very fast access to large volumes of variable-length data. But the main data relationships must be specified in advance in order to gain these processing efficiencies. Changing data relationships is difficult and time-consuming, so accessing data in different ways to those pre-specified is not possible. These structures are therefore suitable where the applications are very well defined and where access efficiency is the key parameter. Airline booking systems traditionally utilize hierarchical DBMS, and personnel databases involving extensive employee–department relationships have made use of the network structure.

Relational databases offer flexibility. It is possible to add new records and create new relationships among data without extensive re-programming efforts; the access paths do not have to be specified in advance, and so creating new reports and *ad hoc* data analyses is straightforward. However, the price to be paid for developmental and access flexibility is poor access efficiency. Processing data involving multiple searches can be very time-consuming in a relational DBMS, although, to a certain extent, the database can be tuned to give greater access speed by developing indexes for frequently used data. Despite the slow processing, the advantages offered by flexibility of data access and application development means that relational databases are increasingly the choice for major business applications. Unexpected enquiries by management about data

	Field 1	Field 2	Field 3
	Name	Address	Phone no.
Record 1	Person A.	Anytown	0272-3666
Record 2	Smith J.	Othertown	0703-3324

Figure 8.10 Relational database structure

which does not yet exist, or which must be accessed in new ways, are not exactly unusual. In fact, they seem to be the rule rather than the exception.

Summary

Any computer system needs the ability to store and retrieve data in an efficient form. Storage can be primary, internal to the CPU, or secondary, external to the CPU. The data stored externally may be in magnetic format on tape, disk or drum; alternatively it may be in optical form.

KEY TERMS   Backing store   Blocking factor   Block   Bucket   Buffer   Cylinder Digital paper   Disk pack   External storage   Field, record, file   File directory Fixed-length record   Gigabyte   Hit-rate   Index   Inter-record gaps   Key field   Latency period   Logical record   Magnetic disk   Magnetic tape   Main store   Mass storage   Off-line   On-line   Optical disk   Parity bit   Physical record   Sector   Seek time   Sort   Tape streamer   Terabyte   Track   Variable-length record   Volatile   Volume table of contents (VTOC).

Further reading

Coles R., Death knell for disk drives?, *Practical Computing*, March, p. 102, 1989.
Ferris D., Streaming tape skips Sods Law, *Computer Weekly*, 10 Aug, p. 22, 1989.
Everest G.C., *Database Management*, McGraw-Hill, New York, 1986.
Goldstein R.C., *Database: Technology and Management*, Wiley, New York, 1985.
Zorkoczy P., *Information Technology: An Introduction*, Pitman, London, 1985.

9
Information systems communications

Information is not just processed by computer, it is also transmitted. From computer to computer, from device to device, between people in the same office and between computers in the same organization; across organizations, countries and continents, information is sent to wherever it can be utilized. An example would be the organization which has many branch offices taking sales at various points in the country. Cost-effective administration is achieved by linking minicomputers located at the branch offices to a host mainframe at head office, so that the minis can transmit local sales data to the mainframe for processing, and then access customer data held centrally at head office.

A common network application is the linking together of a number of PCs in one location so that users can communicate directly with each other, employing a system called electronic mail. Extending the PC network to take in connection to the mainframe allows the PC users access to central data files, and also then to remote sites and perhaps to external, commercial databases. An academic application involves the widespread linking of mainframe and minicomputers at UK universities and polytechnics in a network called JANET (joint academic network). This network is itself linked to similar networks in Europe, USA, Canada, Australia and elsewhere, so that academics in one institution can rapidly send messages, datafiles and programs to other academics in other institutions, and in other cities and other countries across the world. As well as sharing data, network users on JANET can share computer power too; super-computers are far too expensive for every institution to have one, but the network enables many different institutions to access large and powerful machines based at centres in London and Manchester.

Technology convergence

Over the last few years there has been a rapid shift in emphasis regarding telecommunications, such that this topic generally has become far more important in an information systems context than hitherto. There is now an awareness of the *convergence of technologies*, such that computer technology and telecommunications technology are increasingly being used together to complement and augment the benefits of each other. This new awareness is partly because there has been a revolution in the technology of communication: new, more efficient and cheaper electronic devices, new transmission techniques, including the use of microwave and infra-red transmissions, optical fibres and satellites as transmission media, cellular radio techniques for mobile car phones have all fuelled changes in the way that information is processed and disseminated. The rapid rise in PC usage has undoubtedly contributed to the phenomenon as well.

There are also other factors: the increasing availability and use of commercial information databases; structural changes in the way that business is carried out in multinational organizations; the splitting up of the Post Office telecommunications monopoly in the UK, and its private equivalent in the USA. Changes in world markets such as the European free trade agreement of 1992, and the dramatic lessening of international east–west tensions in general have also undoubtedly played a part in a massively booming telecommunications industry. It is possible that future developments in communications technology will have far-reaching effects on organizations and management, in the same way as the revolution in computer technology has done over the last decade. Telecommunications is clearly a tremendously wide-ranging and important topic but space precludes a detailed treatment in a book of this kind, and readers are recommended to specialist books for more details.

Technology of telecommunications

Telecommunications is simply the electronic linking of two physically separate devices. A *telecommunications network* is a set of components which have been linked together so as to achieve the transmission of data between two or more points.

In theory it is possible to connect almost any computer-based devices together. In practice, achieving effective telecommunications is not a straightforward matter. There are a number of technical difficulties which arise and these contribute to the costs and problems of widespread networking; there must be a careful matching of hardware components, and also operating system software and application software.

In order to transmit data between devices there must be a *transmitter*, a *receiver* and a *transmission medium*; the medium for a single transmission is called a *channel* (Fig. 9.1). These terms are often used interchangeably, although

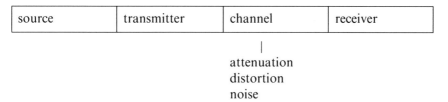

source	transmitter	channel	receiver

attenuation
distortion
noise

Figure 9.1   Conceptual diagram of communications channel

there could be several channels available in one mediun, for example a single co-axial cable can cope with about 200 telephone channels at once.

Data can be sent as a *parallel* stream of bits, one or more bytes wide. Within the computer itself, this is usually accomplished using a bus because of the speed required; transmitting data between CPU and fast peripherals is also usually performed in parallel. But each bit in the parallel transmission requires a separate carrier, and for most communication situations outside the computer itself serial transmission is used, i.e. data is transmitted one bit at a time.

There must be a means of *translating* data from a form intelligible by machines into a signal suitable for transmission. For example, digital electronic data from a PC acting as transmitter must be converted by a *modem* (*mod*-ulator–*dem*odulator) into analog signals for transmission down a voice-quality telephone line, and then converted back to a digital signal by another modem for input to a mainframe acting as receiver (Fig. 9.2). In order for the data transmitted to be intelligible to the different devices involved there must be a set of rules or protocols governing the way in which the data is transmitted.

The communication just described between the PC and the mainframe could be undertaken under different *transmission modes*.

SIMPLEX MODE   This involves transmission in one direction only. An analogy is one person speaking over a short-wave car radio transmitter to someone else who does not possess a transmitter, only a receiver. That person can hear what is said but cannot communicate back. Normally this is only used in a data context where computer-controlled equipment is switched on or off and there is no need for a response to a signal, or where information displays are shown with no interaction. Examples include travel information monitors seen at railway stations and airports, where information is shown on a screen and is updated

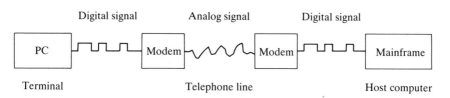

Figure 9.2   Communications over voice lines

at intervals; it is not possible for travellers to send information back to the computer.

HALF-DUPLEX MODE   This mode allows transmission in either direction, but in only one direction at one time. An example is the communication over a ship-to-shore radio: when one speaker has finished she says 'over' and the other party can speak: both parties thus take it in turns to communicate. CB radio operates on the same principle. When data is transmitted between computers over a telephone network, the transmitters and receivers in the modems are turned on and off depending on which way the transmission is going; the direction may turn round many times during the course of a transmission.

FULL-DUPLEX MODE   This involves transmission in both directions simul-taneously. An example would be two people chatting over a telephone: both may speak simultaneously which may be much faster than waiting for each person to stop talking! In a data context, full-duplex is used where large amounts of data need to be transmitted; the drawback is that extra line capacity and more complex equipment is required.

The terms half-duplex and full-duplex take on slightly different meanings when applied to the characteristics of devices acting as human-operated terminals. When a computer is acting in full-duplex mode it transmits back (echoes) every character it receives; if acting in half-duplex mode it does not do so. Conversely, if transmitting data in half-duplex mode the computer immediately displays the character it is transmitting to its own screen or teletype, but does not do so in full-duplex mode. Usually transmission parameters are set by software which controls the communication process. If the two computers are in different modes then characters will be echoed twice at one terminal, and not at all at the other.

The rate at which a transmission proceeds is measured in several different ways. *Bits per second* (bps) is the standard measure used to express the speed of a medium. Line speeds may be quoted as perhaps 9600 bps or 50 Kbps (using K as the computer person's 1000) or 48 Mbps (megabits per second). From this bps rate we can calculate how long it would take to transmit a certain amount of data. For example, given that a particular transmission channel is capable of 400 bps we would calculate that to send a file of 600 records, each of 20 bytes, would take 4 minutes ($600 \times 20 \times 8/400 \times 60$). In practice, the issue is more complicated because as well as data bits, the communicating devices send a number of control bits, used to activate the operations of the connected devices, and these reduce the capacity of the channel for data.

Another commonly quoted measure is the *Baud rate*; this measures the number of signal changes per second (e.g. when a digital signal changes from 0 to 1), and under some circumstances it can be the same as the bits per second rate for the channel. However, by using different frequencies and advanced

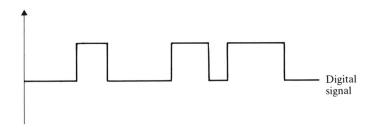

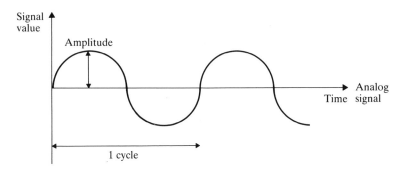

Frequency = number of waves/time interval

Hertz = 1 cycle/second

Figure 9.3 Carrier waves and frequencies

signal modulating techniques it is possible to send 2, 4 or more bits at the same time, so the actual bps rate may be far greater than the Baud rate.

Transmission speed is affected by many factors, including the types of terminal and computer in use, the type of modem or other device used, and the nature of the line discipline or protocol in force. *Bandwidth* is a measure of the range of frequencies which a channel can carry. *Narrowband* lines operate up to about 300 bps and are used for low-volume applications like low-speed terminals and teletypes; *voiceband* lines usually are telephone lines and operate up to about 9600 bps and are used for voice and data; *broadband* channels operate at higher rates and are used for high-speed transmission between computers or other high-speed devices (see Table 9.1). The 'lines' which carry communications channels can be copper wires, co-axial cable, fibre-optic light carriers, line-of-site microwave transmission, satellite transmissions and radio transmissions. The type of line is a key factor in transmission speed, and some representative line speeds are shown in Table 9.1.

The relative costs mentioned here relate to the intial cost of accessing the

Table 9.1   Communication channel speeds

Line type	Speed (bps)*	Relative costs
dial-up line	100–200	low cost
dedicated line	300–9600	∧
microwave (satellite link)	56 K–256 K	⋮
coaxial cable	256 K–480 M	∨
fibre-optic cable	500 K–500 M	high cost

*K: kilobits, M: megabits.

medium; the cost of sending data depends largely on how intensely the medium is utilized. For example, the dedicated line involves renting a line permanently from the telecommunications company and thus costs far more than simply paying for a phone call. However, if the line is used for high-speed transmission all the time, then the actual cost per bit of data sent may be far lower. These considerations apply with even greater force to the satellite link and fibre-optic cable which are capable of far greater data capacities.

Transmission techniques

Transmitting data requires a coding system for the data; in Chapter 6 we examined the two commonly used codes ASCII and EBCDIC. In practice, ASCII is the code most often used for data transmission; if a computer works in a different internal code, say EBCDIC, then a conversion process must be undertaken before the data is sent.

In order to send data between devices which may operate at widely different speeds (consider a human operator typing data on a terminal to a mainframe computer, or the computer sending data to a character printer), techniques have been developed which coordinate the transmitting and receiving devices. *Asynchronous transmission* involves sending one character at a time. Each character is framed by one or more start and stop bits which let the receiving device know that a character is to be sent and when the transmission has finished (see Fig. 9.4).

Asynchronous transmission is suitable where small amounts of data are sent at random intervals, with the transmission line idle in between characters; a human operator keying data will generate this kind of pattern.

Communication between automatic high-speed devices (say computer to computer) may demand a faster and more efficient method. *Synchronous transmission* involves sending blocks of characters, in a continuous stream, between devices which are synchronized together by clock mechanisms. Control bits flag the beginning and end of data blocks in a similar manner to asynchronous transmission (Fig. 9.5), but within the data block the devices can recognize each character byte using the coordinated timing pulses of the clocks. When a data

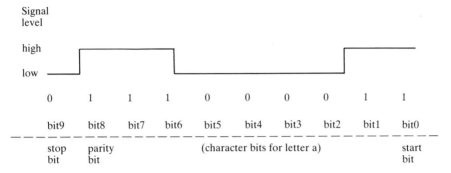

Figure 9.4   Asynchronous transmission

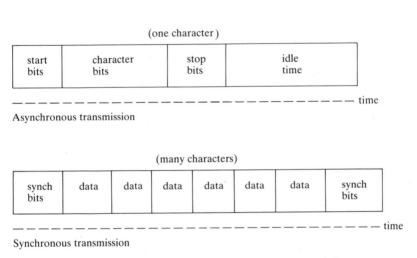

Figure 9.5   Asynchronous and synchronous transmission

block is finished, synchronizing characters are sent continuously to maintain line synchronization. The timing may be provided by a modem, or the computer itself, or another telecommunications device.

Synchronous transmission is normally used where transmission rates are greater than 2400 bps. Although the transmission rate is much faster than is possible with asynchronous transmission, the electronics needed are much more complex, involving the timing and synchronization circuitry and buffer stores to hold blocks of data.

Telecommunications devices

A number of special-purpose devices are used in data transmission networks. We have already met the modem; this device translates the signal from digital devices to analog signals and back again, it may also contain synchronizing clock circuitry, data checking components, and may possess the facility to alter data transmission speeds.

The modem is usually permanently connected between a communicating device and its communication channel. Used for the same purpose as the modem, *an acoustic coupler* is a device which is connected to a computer and then plugged onto an ordinary telephone handset. This is often used as a portable device which can be carried around and used to connect a computer to any telephone line. The acoustic coupler is a low-cost device which operates at very low speeds; it is designed to be plugged between devices temporarily, as and when needed, and is usually associated with portables and PCs.

When several terminals are required to share the same line, they may be connected using a *multiplexer*. This device was discussed before when we mentioned its use as a parallel data switch within the CPU (see Chapter 6). In a telecommunications context the multiplexer again acts as a 'clever switch' in that it combines data signals from several terminals and sends them over a single line, ensuring that the separate signals do not interfere with each other. This data combination can be achieved in different ways: *time-division multiplexing* involves taking fixed portions of transmission from each terminal and interleaving them into a single stream; *frequency-division multiplexing* involves sending several streams simultaneously, but using different frequencies for each stream. A similar device has to *de-multiplex* the data received from a single line and share it out to the appropriate receiving terminals.

To save line costs, a *concentrator* may be used. This device takes data from several low-speed terminals and stores it in a buffer until enough data has been gathered, at which point the device will transmit in a high-speed burst. Effectively, the device acts so as to optimize the line usage by making sure that the output from many low-speed devices occupies the capacity of a single high-speed line. A *front-end processor* is a mini- or microcomputer connected between a mainframe and an extensive telecommunications system. The front-end computer is dedicated to the housekeeping aspects of communications, and will perform all the translating, conversion, switching and error checking routines, leaving the mainframe free to process the assembled data.

Figure 9.6 shows a number of communications components linked to remote devices over data transmission lines. Such a network is called a *wide area network (WAN)* or *long haul network (LHN)* because of the distances and the technology involved. Such networks are often used to connect the separate segments of a large organization, and are designed to achieve a number of different objectives.

1. The sharing of data and management information between remote locations.
2. The facilitation of management communication between locations.
3. The sharing of computer resources (distributed processing), involving the sharing of computer power and costly peripherals, the sharing of skilled staff

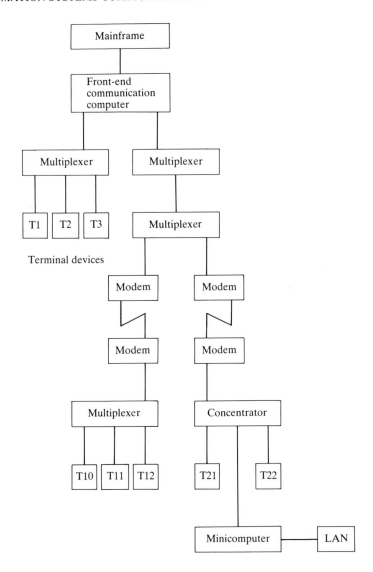

Figure 9.6 Communications components in a wide area network

and systems development capacity, the sharing of operating and data preparation workload over peaks and troughs in capacity.

4. The sharing of downtime risk due to component failure.

The configuration of the network may have a significant impact on the organization structure and locus of control. For example, the network may be devised so as to have a central mainframe and low-power terminals at remote locations; this provides some local computing power but retains control over information and resources at the centre: *centralized computing*. This centralized arrangement involves the bulk of the computer power and common data in one location, and the remote sites performing only local data processing tasks.

An alternative approach is through *distributed processing* whereby the data and the computer power are more evenly distributed around the network; here each location would have an equally sized computer facility, perform most of its own processing and share common data with other sites as necessary. The choice among network configurations may be influenced as much by management style as by technical considerations. Currently, it is fashionable to push management responsibility out to local centres and this is reflected by a trend towards distributed processing.

LOCAL AREA NETWORKS

The local area network (LAN) is a means of connecting a number of devices together over small distances, usually within the same building. The devices do not have to be computers and computer terminals: fax machines, telexes and other data devices may also be connected. Conversion to analog signals for voice-grade lines is not usually involved because of the short distances. A typical LAN consists of several PCs connected together, and sharing the services of a laser printer and fast disk drive; there may also be a connection to a mainframe, called a *gateway*. One of the PCs will control the communications within the system, and will act as the *network server*; it will have resident the software necessary to operate the communications protocols which enable the network to function.

The LAN can achieve a number of quite different objectives:

1. To enable direct communication between PC users on the net by sending messages to each other: *electronic mail*. Special software packages are available which facilitate this mailing application. Data files, programs and software can also be shared directly. In practice the multiple sharing of data files and programs raises a number of technical issues and the operating system software which controls this sharing becomes more complex.

2. To enable direct communication between individual PCs and the mainframe: to access large databases which could not be stored or maintained on the PC, and to have access to the mainframe's considerable computing power, perhaps to perform scientific calculations or extensive data search. Such a network may not require communication between the PCs, only between each PC and the mainframe. In this case a simple star topology can be used (see Fig. 9.7).

3. To share costly local facilities, such as a laser printer, or hard disk unit, which would be uneconomic if supplied to every PC. The costly device is connected to a PC that is part of the network and which then acts as a *server* to the other PCs; for example, the PC with a high-capacity hard disk becomes the *file-server* and can act as a large file-storage device for the other PCs that have

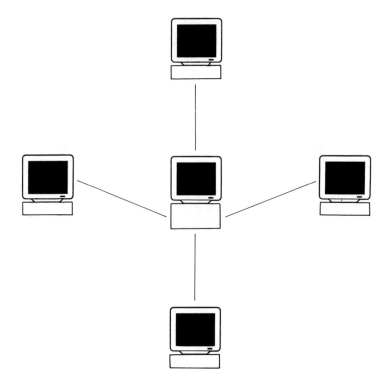

Figure 9.7   Network topologies: star network

the cheaper floppy drives. Similarly, a laser printer can be connected to one PC that acts as *printer-server*. As PC peripheral hardware costs fall, this purpose becomes less critical.

It is also possible to share application software, such as database or spreadsheet packages, in order to obtain a saving on the costs of acquiring and maintaining the software for the separate PCs. However, some commercial applications software cannot work in a networked environment because of the extra complexities.

4. To reduce the risk of system-downtime due to component failure. A LAN can consist of many components, many of which can carry on if one breaks down; a mini- or mainframe-based system must be out of service if the main unit fails.

In order for the LAN to function, it requires a set of telecommunications components in order to fulfil the communications requirements discussed earlier. There has to be a medium for the data to be sent and this usually consists of co-axial cable connected between each component so as to make a circle or ring (Fig. 9.8); each terminal or device on the ring is called a *node*. Also there has to be a set of rules, or *protocols*, which allow several different devices to

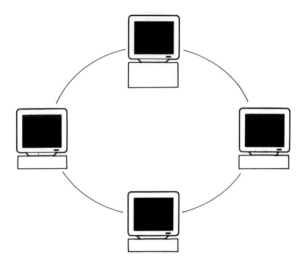

Figure 9.8 Network topologies: ring network

communicate with each other, and along the same channel, without confusion, collision or data loss.

This is extremely complex to arrange, and several competing systems have evolved. One solution which facilitates communication between all nodes in the network is called the *Cambridge ring*; and involves the sending of packets of data around the ring from node to node until the device for which the packet is intended removes the data. Empty packets are sent around the ring and a device that needs to send must wait for an empty packet; the packet is filled with data and is given a destination-device address; it travels around the ring and back to the sender, which checks that the packet is unaltered as an error-checking procedure. Every device on the ring checks the destination code of every full packet to see if there is a parcel of data for it. These activities occur at very rapid electronic speeds and the users may not be aware of any slowing of processing speeds unless the network is in extensive use.

Summary

In order to be useful, it is often necessary for data generated by computer systems to be transmitted. This may be locally, within one location (a local area network) or globally (via a wide area network). Transmission requires a coding system for the data and a mode of carrying the coded data to its destination.

KEY TERMS Acoustic coupler Asynchronous transmission Bandwidth Baud rate Bits per second (bps) rate Cambridge ring Centralized computing Channel Concentrator Control bits Convergence of technologies De-multiplexer Distributed processing Electronic mail (e-mail) File-server Front-end processor Full-duplex mode Gateway Half-duplex mode

Local area network (LAN) Long haul network (LHN) Modem Multiplexer
Node Printer-server Protocol Receiver Simplex mode Synchronous
transmission Telecommunications network Transmission medium Transmission mode Transmitter Wide area network (WAN).

Further reading

Chorofas D.N., *Designing and Implementing Local Area Networks*, McGraw-Hill, New
  York, 1982.
Fibre optics: the big move in communications—and beyond, *Business Week*, 25 October,
  1982.
Gandoff M., *Students Guide to Data Communications*, Heinemann, Oxford, 1990.
Held G., *Data Communications Networking Devices*, Wiley, Chichester, 1986.
Forester T. (Ed.), *The Information Technology Revolution*, Basil Blackwell, Oxford, 1985.
Wilkinson G.G. and Winterflood A.R., *Fundamentals of Information Technology*, Wiley,
  Chichester, 1987.
Zorkoczy P., *Information Technology*, Pitman, London, 1985.

Summary to Part Two

Part Two has been a bottom-up approach to information systems. It concentrated on the hardware aspects of information systems, demonstrating how
the physical parts of the computer system interact to acquire, process, store and
transmit data.

PART THREE

Software and its applications

10

Systems software and operating systems

If you can touch it, it must be hardware. Software is the universal term for the programs which instruct the hardware on how to behave. Part Two described the relationship between computer instructions and hardware components; software comprises the stored programs which make the computer uniquely valuable, and is the essence of information systems. Without software computers can do nothing, literally nothing. The hardware performs elementary functions directed by machine-language instructions held in main store, and it is only through these instructions that the machine can become useful. Software is a generic term that can be applied to any computer instructions, but in practice it is useful to consider two separate categories:

1. *System software* acts so as to manage and control the hardware and performs tasks associated with the computer system itself. This category includes operating systems, utility programs and language translators.
2. *Applications software* is designed to perform business tasks and provide direct support for user applications. This category includes user-written programs and various kinds of pre-written software package.

Operating system components

System software consists of a set of complex and sophisticated programs which are concerned with supporting the computer system. The first group of programs, the operating system, is concerned with the running of the computer system. Operating system software is developed either by the computer manufacturer or by a specialist software house. The operating system for a business micro or PC is usually bought ready installed on the machine.

Most operating systems contain these five elements:

- input/output routines,
- main store management,
- command processor,
- job control program,
- file management.

INPUT/OUTPUT ROUTINES

All programs which use the computer have to cope with input/output (I/O) devices. As we saw in Chapter 7 when looking at interfaces, fetching data from and delivering data to devices outside the CPU can be a very complex task indeed, involving the handling of data buses, channels, buffer stores, interfaces and devices which operate at vastly different speeds, and which therefore require complicated arrangements to work properly. In order to avoid involving application programmers or users in this very difficult programming task, the operating system has control over all the peripherals, and contains routines which handle all the I/O behaviour of the computer on behalf of the application programs.

MAIN STORE MANAGEMENT

Early computers ran one program at one time and it was usually necessary for main memory to be large enough to hold the entire program; main memory was then, and to a lesser extent still is today, very expensive. To overcome this problem software techniques have been evolved which allow a very large program to be run, even though main memory is not big enough to hold it all. A method called *overlaying* involves holding the main part of a program in memory and then swapping other lesser-used segments into memory from disk backing storage when necessary. Of course, overall running speed may be reduced considerably because the CPU must wait for disk transfers to occur when it needs a bit of program which is not in store, but with careful choice of program segments this may not be too troublesome. A drawback to this method is that the application programmer must specify the boundaries of the program segments.

A more sophisticated technique is called virtual memory. With this method, there is a notional or virtual storage which is very much larger than the real physical store available. Large and/or multiple programs co-exist in the virtual store, which is mainly retained on disk. Programs are automatically split by the operating system into small fixed-length segments called pages and these are swapped into the real main store as and when necessary; thus, at any one time, real memory contains only those pages of programs which are currently active. The application programmer need not be concerned at all with the details of the page splitting or swapping as these are performed automatically by the operating system. There is, of course, a penalty to be paid for the large virtual memory thus created: the machine must spend time shuttling program pages into main memory from backing store and this slows down machine performance. However, under carefully chosen circumstances, overall system performance may be considerably enhanced.

COMMAND PROCESSOR

This program resides in memory and accepts English-like commands typed by the operator onto the keyboard of a VDU or system console. The commands are addressed to the operating system and cause the computer to load and run programs, allocate disk space and perform many essential housekeeping tasks. The commands may be actioned immediately, or they can be grouped together and stored in files for automatic processing by a job control program. The latter method is very important because it means that sequences of operating instructions can be grouped together as 'jobs' and re-run whenever required.

JOB CONTROL PROGRAM

An important consideration is the operating efficiency of the computer system. Early mainframe computers were often run by a succession of different individuals, usually programmers, each of whom had a particular job to run on the machine. At the appointed time the programmer would step forward, mount a deck of cards in the card reader and activate the console switches which caused the program to be read into memory and executed. If something unexpected happened—which it often did—the programmer would ponder for a while, and perhaps study manuals or documentation while deciding what to do. He or she might re-run the program, perhaps single-stepping the machine instruction by instruction in order to see what was wrong. If all went well, he or she might mount magnetic tapes or disks carrying data to be processed, and, at the end of the program run, would expect to see printed output. At the end of the allotted time the programmer would collect his or her program cards, printed output and notes, and step away from the machine so that the next user could begin. In this kind of session, the following machine utilization figures might apply:

mainframe user session	30 minutes
computer running time	3 minutes
CPU active time	3 seconds

In other words, out of the total time for the session, the computer system would actually be running for only a small proportion of that time; and even then the CPU would be waiting for slow peripherals and so would only have worked to a fraction of its possible speed. As the machines were very expensive, the need to drastically improve the overall *system utilization* was realized at once and so software was developed which enabled the machine to control its own resources to a large extent.

   This was achieved in part by a *job control* program which automatically loaded and executed programs and made available the necessary data, and could be pre-programmed to handle error conditions. The operating system was also extended to improve the way in which the machine communicated with

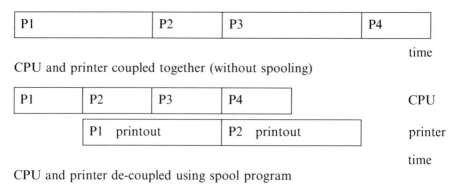

CPU and printer coupled together (without spooling)

CPU and printer de-coupled using spool program

Figure 10.1 Improved job processing using spooling

slow peripherals, and to increase utilization still further by allowing many activities to occur at the same time. This program resides in memory and loads and executes other programs, and their data, in a predetermined sequence called a *jobstream*. If unexpected situations occur, the job control program can handle them according to predefined instructions. For example, if one program in a jobstream hangs up, or fails, it may be very damaging to continue processing because other programs downstream may depend on the data output from it. The job control program is initially told what to do by the user through a special programming language called *job control language (JCL)*.

A sequence of job control commands is developed and stored in a special file, and then this file is automatically run as a jobstream. Another function of the job control program is *job accounting*: to provide data on how long jobs take to run, and to report on machine utilization generally. Data generated by the job accounting routines is used in assessing system performance and also in assigning computer department costs to user departments.

When a single jobstream is considered, it will probably be the case that some programs have poor CPU utilization simply because they depend on slow peripheral activity. (Remember that mechanical devices such as printers operate at speeds many orders of magnitude slower than the CPU.) For example, one program in a stream may print a line of sales analysis for each program cycle; the CPU has to wait for the printer to complete each line before it can continue with the program. One way of improving efficiency is called *spooling* (the word comes from the acronym s.p.o.o.l.: simultaneous peripheral operation on-line). Spooling involves a special program which intercepts data intended for a slow peripheral and writes it out to a disk file instead. The application program then runs much faster because the CPU does not have to wait for the printer, and the disk file can be transferred to the printer later (or simultaneously). Using the systemic language from Chapter 4, the two subsystems involving fast CPU and slow printer have been de-coupled to let each run at its own speed.

Figure 10.1 shows what happens for a jobstream with four programs where programs P1 and P3 use a printer extensively, and programs P2 and P4 do not. Without spooling the CPU is underutilized during the running of P1 and P3. With spooling, the CPU and the printer are de-coupled and P1 and P3 run in half the time because they do not wait for the printer; instead, printout is directed to a disk file, and from there simultaneously to the printer. In this example the spooled printer finishes at the same time as before, but the CPU finishes the stream much earlier and is free to run more jobs.

Although spooling can speed the overall running of streams of programs there is a penalty to be paid: the spooling software must occupy some main store which then cannot be used for other purposes, and the time taken by the system in writing printer output to disk (and then from disk to printer) is an extra due only to the spooling method. However, overall system performance can be considerably enhanced under the right circumstances, i.e. if the right mix of programs exists in the jobstream.

FILE MANAGEMENT

The file management system provides software which copes with the processing of files on disk and tape backing store. There must be a means of creating files on secondary storage; this involves finding a suitable space, writing the file to it and keeping a note of where the file is and what it is called. Large files may need to be split into several blocks, or *file extents*, in order to fit into the spaces between other files. There must also be a means of locating the files when access is required, and also of deleting them when they are no longer needed in order to free the storage space. Users do not want to be involved in the detailed management of exactly where on a disk a file is stored; it should be sufficient to refer to a file by its name in order to access it, and the file management system should do the rest. Above all, there must be a means of keeping track of files on disk; this is achieved by a file directory which is a list of data that relates each file name to its position on the storage medium, and provides other information about the file:

file name:	a unique identifier
file type:	serial, random, indexed-sequential
location:	physical disk address of start of file
file map:	addresses of separate file blocks
access mode:	e.g. read-only, password protected
date of change:	date file created or changed
current status:	whether currently open and in use

There must also be a means of copying files from one medium to another. These actions are usually provided by a series of utility programs which perform the required functions. (See, below, the section on Microsoft–disk operating system for details of the file processing functions for a PC.)

Multiprogramming and time-sharing

Thus far we have regarded the operating system as if it were coping with one program at one time but, in fact, the speed of modern computers relative to peripheral devices is such that it makes sense to run many programs at once, and several techniques have been developed to achieve this. Two common techniques are known as *multiprogramming* and *time-sharing*.

MULTIPROGRAMMING

Multiprogramming involves several separate jobstreams running concurrently in the same processor. From Chapter 6 we know that most computers are serial machines based on traditional von Neumann architecture; they process one instruction at one time. So how can they run several programs at once? The answer is that they do not, but with clever software, and some special hardware features, they can perform as if they do. The hardware feature involves the use of *interrupts*. Essentially, when a peripheral device requires some attention, say if a printer has completed printing a line, it will indicate its state by placing a signal on an interrupt line. This has the effect of stopping the CPU from performing its current task—hence the name interrupt—and causes it to start processing special *interrupt service routines*. These routines establish which peripheral caused the interrupt, and after resetting flags, cause the operating system to decide which process to continue with.

The effect is rather like that of a busy manager who is working on a report. On her desk there are five telephones, each with a light on top. After a while she finds she needs some information from another department, so she picks up a phone and asks for the information. It cannot be supplied at once so she asks for it to be rung through when ready. Now she can no longer work on her report, so she makes a note of where she is and puts the report to one side and turns to some other, lower priority work. When one of the phones rings, she stops working after making a small note as to where she is on her current task. She looks at the phones to see which one has rung (the light comes on when it rings and stays on until the receiver is replaced); picking it up she finds the caller has the information she asked for earlier, so she resumes working on her report.

In Fig. 10.2 there are three application programs resident in main store, together with the operating system. The CPU executes instructions in program 1 until the program requests a peripheral activity, say printer output. Under single program working the CPU would issue the output instruction and then wait until the peripheral activity had finished. But with multiprogramming the CPU issues the output command and then immediately begins processing program 2, having first saved the contents of key registers so that it can resume with program 1 later. The CPU processes program 2, and in this simplified example it comes to another peripheral instruction; the CPU issues the instruction and saves the registers as before and turns to work on program 3.

In this way the CPU has been continuously active and has processed perhaps

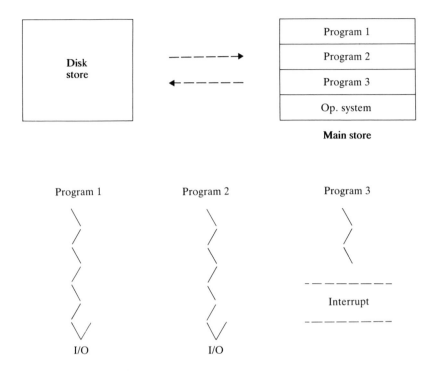

Figure 10.2   Multiprogramming operating system

many thousands of instructions during the time in which normally it would have had to sit and wait for a peripheral to finish its task. But what about the print output from program 2? What about the unfinished program fragments left hanging? Let us assume that during the processing of program 3, the printer now finishes its task set by program 1. The printer signals its changed state by asserting the interrupt line. The CPU then stops processing program 3 and saves registers, it establishes where the interrupt came from and performs various service tasks. It is then the task of the operating system to decide which program to process next. Most multiprogramming operating systems have a procedure for assigning prioritites on programs run concurrently, so that, other things being equal, programs higher on the list will be attended to first. In our simplified example, let us say that program 1 has the highest priority and program 3 the lowest; processing will then recommence with program 1. The operating system restores the registers with the data saved from the interrupt, and program 1 can proceed as if nothing had happened. Program 2 cannot be processed at this stage because it is waiting for a peripheral activity to finish.

  Where several programs are running concurrently and need the same peripherals (such as a printer), then a spooling program must be in operation to avoid programs sending interspersed data to the same peripheral. The spooler intercepts instructions to slow peripherals, and sends the data to a disk file instead. The spool program operates concurrently with the other jobstreams, and usually itself has a high priority. Because running many programs at once will take up more main store, a virtual memory system arrangement will be an advantage. Clearly, the operating system tasks of handling interrupts and allocating priorities are all extra work for the CPU, nevertheless, under the right circumstances significant improvements in overall efficiency can be achieved.

TIME-SHARING

Time-sharing involves many different interactive computer users sharing the same computer simultaneously. An example is the mainframe computer in a university which has hundreds of terminals (VDUs) located around the campus. (In fact there are many computers and networks, but for the sake of this example let us consider one mainframe computer and its associated network of terminals.)

Students and researchers can go to any free terminal, enter an identity code and password and gain access to the machine. A portion of disk backing store is allocated to each user, as is a small portion of main store. Once the user has gained access he or she can enter commands, run programs and process data just as if he or she had sole use of the computer. There may be many other users simultaneously doing a wide variety of very different work; each may be unaware of the others, apart from the times when the system is very busy and seems to run a little slowly. How does the computer handle these many simultaneous users?

The situation is different from the previous one where several jobstreams were running with different priorities. There, lower-priority jobs ran 'in the gaps' as it were, when higher-priority programs were waiting for peripheral activity. It is quite possible for a high-priority program with little I/O activity to hog the CPU at the expense of the other jobstreams.

With time-sharing the idea is that each user should have an equal priority, and no one should be kept waiting longer than anybody else. The operating system arranges to poll each terminal in turn and does this several times a second. (Polling means sending a signal to check whether the terminal requires attention.) When a terminal needs servicing, say because the user has pressed the return key since the last poll, the computer accepts the information from the terminal and the CPU processes that user's work for a fixed time interval, a *time-slice*. The time interval is only a tiny fraction of a second, nevertheless a modern mainframe running at several mips can of course do a lot of work in the small time.

When the time-slice is over, the computer stops working on that user's data and turns to the next user. In this way, all users have their 'crack of the whip' because each has the computer for the fixed-slice before relinquishing it to the next. Needless to say, the software which controls the concurrent processing of

Table 10.1 Contemporary operating systems

Operating system	Supplier	Application
MULTICS	Honeywell	mainframes
MVS	IBM	mainframes
VME	ICL	mainframes
VMS	DEC	mainframes/minis
Unix	AT&T	minis/micros
CP/M	Digital Research	micros/PCs
MS–DOS	Microsoft	micros/PCs
PC–DOS	IBM	micros/PCs
Windows	Microsoft	micros/PCs
OS/2	IBM	micros/PCs

data from hundreds of terminals, where users share computer time, disk space and slow peripherals, must be very complex indeed.

For many years, the only way in which users could gain access to low-cost computing resources was via a time-sharing arrangement through a central computer, and many businesses with small or infrequent processing needs utilized commercial time-sharing bureaux which specialized in this work. Now, the advent of very low-cost micros, together with the reduction in computer hardware costs at all levels, has all but removed the need for business-orientated time-sharing for this reason alone. But the time-sharing networks have not gone away; rather, the emphasis has changed to the sharing of data in the form of commercial databases, or sharing specialized software. Scientific and mathematical users still require time-shared access to large mainframes and supercomputers for mathematical computational work which is beyond the means of smaller machines.

Operating systems for PCs and micros

Micros and PCs need operating systems just as much as their larger counterparts, and, indeed, micro-operating systems perform very similar functions although generally they will be less sophisticated and offer fewer features. A popular operating system for IBM compatible PCs is MS–DOS (Microsoft–disk operating system), and it is useful to examine this system in a little detail. MS–DOS is similar in concept, and in much of the detail, to PC–DOS. MS–DOS has largely superseded CP/M, the popular PC operating system of the 1970s and early 1980s. Table 10.1 shows a selection of operating systems.

From a user's point of view, MS–DOS functions by obeying a number of commands which are entered from the PC keyboard. To load a program from disk and run it, it is sufficient to enter the name of the program only; MS–DOS assumes that any such name which is not one of its special command verbs is

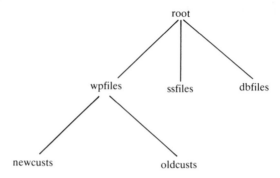

Figure 10.3   Three-tier directory structure

a program. Programs and data are stored as files which are named using a special convention: an up-to-eight character filename followed by an optional three-character extension. The extension names often have special significance for some packages. For example:

accounts.doc   *refers to a data file created by a word processing package*

program1.bas   *refers to a program file created by the BASIC interpreter*

In order to review the files stored on disk, the user enters a command to the operating system:

DIR

This has the effect of listing all the files in the current directory. Disk drives are referred to by a single letter and colon, thus 'C:' often refers to the hard disk, and 'A:' to a floppy drive. Combining file names with commands gives more control over the effects. For example:

DIR C:A*.DOC

This command lists only those files on drive C whose names begin with A and which have the extension .DOC. the asterisk acts as a *wildcard* and indicates that any characters to the right of 'A' are acceptable to the command.

Because there may be hundreds of files stored, MS–DOS offers a system of *multilevel directories* which allows compartmentalizing sets of files. These directories allow the grouping of related files together, spreadsheets in one directory, word processing in another and so on. This reduces clutter and confusion since files for one purpose need not be mixed up with other files. Directories allow the creation of data structures which represent the logic of tasks; a good file structure leads to more efficient computer use.

The main directory is called the root directory, and from this a number of subdirectories can be created which become the branches of a tree structure. In the example of Fig. 10.3 the PC user has created three new subdirectories which are entered from the root or standard directory. The three new directories will be used to store work from word processing, spreadsheets and database, respectively. The directory for word processing files is further subdivided into two separate workgroups.

As well as directory lists, MS–DOS provides a straightforward means of deleting and copying files, together with a range of other facilities. A brief extract from the 60 or so commands available shows some of the file and disk management facilities:

COPY	copy files
DELETE	delete files
DISKCOPY	copy entire disk
FORMAT	format disk
MD	make new directory
RD	remove directory
RENAME	change file name
SORT	sort directory list
TYPE	display contents of a file

As well as file handling, MS–DOS provides a means of running a sequence of commands automatically, rather like the job control language (JCL) facility of a mainframe operating system. This is achieved by storing a sequence of commands in a file with a .BAT extension. When this file name is entered at the keyboard, MS–DOS automatically runs the sequence of commands without any operator intervention. The command stream can be modified with IF and GOTO statements so that the operating system can take decisions and perform quite sophisticated tasks. The following brief sequence shows a simple decision–action routine:

```
CLS
ECHO OFF
ECHO This command sequence checks to see if files are
ECHO present before copying from drive C to drive A
IF EXIST A:SAMPLES*.* GOTO NOCOPY
COPY C:SAMPLES*.* A:
:NOCOPY
DIR C:S*.*
```

Although the system of commands in MS–DOS and PC–DOS has become something of a standard for micro-operating systems, this is by no means the only approach. The Apple Macintosh pioneered the WIMPS system which was intended to be much easier to use than the standard operating systems, and would therefore be more acceptable to managers and non-technical users. WIMPS is an acronym for windows, icons, mouse and pull-down menus. The *window* refers to the current activity of the PC; several activities may run concurrently and information about them can be displayed on the screen simultaneously in different windows. For example, it may be very useful to examine a word-processed document and modify a spreadsheet at the same time, or to examine two spreadsheets side by side.

Icons are simple shapes or symbols displayed by the operating system which refer to some activity or task. A wristwatch or clock appearing instead of the cursor means that the system is busy momentarily; a dustbin refers to the deleting of unwanted files; disk drives are indicated by a small symbol and so on. The idea is to minimize the necessity for memorizing and keying codes; the user points to an icon with the mouse in order to initiate an activity. Key words on the screen reveal menus when pointed to; these unfold to show choices and then disappear when the cursor is moved away. The WIMPS approach has been taken up by other vendors and is now available on IBM PCs and compatibles.

An operating system that is becoming more popular with minis and large micros is Unix. More powerful and sophisticated than the present generation of micro-operating systems, Unix falls somewhere between these and the very extensive systems for mainframes. In particular, it is designed to support multi-users and multi-tasking. These features will become more important as micros become more powerful, and as they change from stand-alone, one-person devices to become linked together in local nets which share data and tasks. For example, a micro user may wish to print one file while simultaneously editing another: during these activities the PC is constantly monitoring his or her electronic mailbox for incoming messages; later the user may wish to transmit data to a colleague's PC, send some graphic output via a fax copier and access a file held on the company mainframe. The present generation of small micro-operating systems do not fully support this level of interconnection. The latest micro-operating system from IBM is OS/2; intended for the more powerful PCs, it is designed to achieve multi-tasking and interconnectivity, particularly with mainframes, which previous micro-operating systems lacked. OS/2 uses virtual memory techniques and allows substantially more main memory to be used by application programs. Only time will tell whether Unix or one of its derivatives will become the new industry standard, or whether OS/2 will help IBM to retain its lead for business micro users.

Summary

Software can be considered as being of two categories: system software, to manage the computer system, and applications software, used to perform business tasks. Multiprogramming and time-sharing can be employed to run multiple programs simultaneously. The format of DOS, the most common operating system found on the majority of microcomputers, has been reviewed.

KEY TERMS   Applications software   Disk operating system (DOS)   File directory   Interrupts   Interrupt service routines   Job accounting   Job control language (JCL)   Jobstream   Multiprogramming   Multi-tasking

Overlaying   Pages   Spooling   System software   System utilization   Time-sharing   Time-slice   Virtual memory.

Further reading

French C.S., *Computer Science*, DP Publications, Eastleigh, Hants, 1984.

Janson P.A., *Operating Systems: Structure and Mechanisms*, Academic Press, New York, 1985.

Lister A.M., *Fundamentals of Operating Systems*, Macmillan, London, 1982.

MS–DOS User Guide, Microsoft Corporation, 1986.

QUE Corporation, *MS–DOS Quick Reference*, QUE Corporation, Carmel, Indiana, 1988.

Tanenbaum A.S., *Operating Systems: Design and Implementation*, Prentice-Hall, London, 1987.

11
Programming languages

The need for programming languages

Chapter 6 showed that computers work by obeying elementary instructions that are retained in main store. These instructions perform elementary arithmetic and logical functions, transfer data between store and registers and enable conditional branching to different parts of the program to occur. But how do we plan and put together the thousands of these instructions necessary to perform even the simplest business function? Computer scientists working on the very early machines would write down, and then transfer to main store, the instructions necessary to perform a task. They were writing programs in machine language.

Consider the fragment of machine code in Table 11.1. The machine language statements consist of the second column of numbers which must be entered into the store locations in the first column. The fragment uses the three instructions described in Chapter 6, plus a new instruction, code 099, which halts the machine (Table 11.2).

Every computer and microprocessor has its own distinctive set of instructions, and hence its own machine language. To write machine-code programs it is necessary not only to plan out in the minutest detail what the machine is to do, but also to specify the addresses of all instructions and data too. What are the chances of making mistakes in writing a program of 1000 instructions? How are these mistakes to be detected? Clearly, writing programs in this fashion is immensely difficult, time-consuming and error prone.

Further, suppose a change is needed in a program which has 5000 instructions. If the change involved adding more instructions in the middle of the program, then every single instruction thereafter must be changed to reflect the new store locations used. If software development had not advanced beyond the

Table 11.1 A machine language fragment

Location	Contents	Meaning
100	096	LOAD contents of 107 into accumulator
101	107	
102	092	ADD contents of 108 to accumulator
103	108	
104	098	STORE contents of accumulator to 109
105	109	
106	099	HALT
107	023	data
108	035	data
109	058	where result placed

machine-language stage, then computers could not possibly have achieved the role they currently play.

The first step towards making easier the task of program writing was to develop a computer program which would accept, as input data, computer instructions specified as mnemonics with symbolic addresses. This program would then automatically *translate* the input data into an executable machine language program. In addition, the program would look up a library of often-used routines (such as square root calculations and input/output peripheral routines) and combine these routines as necessary. Such a translator program came to be called an *assembler* because it brought together sequences of instructions into a complete program. A fragment of an assembler language is shown below.

```
;
;An assembler fragment
;
DAT1:      EQU 023
DAT2:      EQU 035
;
START      LDA DAT1
           ADD DAT2
           STA ANS
END        HLT
```

Table 11.2 Machine language instructions

Instruction	Op. code	Function
LOAD	096	move data from store to accumulator
STORE	098	move data from accumulator to store
ADD	092	add number in store to accumulator
HALT	099	stop machine

This program has the same effect as the machine language program of Table 11.2, but it has a number of important advantages. It is easier to write down and to refer to because the instructions are indicated by *mnemonics* rather than by numbers; the assembler program automatically translates the mnemonic into machine instruction operation codes. Store locations are not referred to directly by the programmer; instead the assembler allocates memory usage automatically. Key points in the program can be referred to by *labels* (START and END are labels in the program fragment above). Decision statements can direct control to any line in the program by referring to its label. Finding errors in the program and correcting them is much easier than would be the case in a machine language program. If new instructions are to be added, these can be readily inserted into the source program which is retranslated and the assembler automatically reallocates the instructions into new locations.

Assembler language represents a marked improvement on writing programs in machine language, but still calls for detailed knowledge of the computer and considerable technical programming skill. The assembler language for any one computer is unique to that particular machine because it is very close to the actual machine language instructions used; but the assembler statements across a family of related computers may be similar.

Machine code and assembler are referred to as *low-level languages* because they operate at the machine level and require a one-for-one statement for each computer instruction. This requires considerable programming effort for even an elementary application.

High-level languages

The correspondence between distinct generations of software is not nearly so clear cut as with hardware, nevertheless it is useful to consider five phases of software, as shown in Table 11.3. The character of the fifth generation of software is not at all certain; unlike the fifth generation of hardware, the objectives of a completely new departure in software have not even been specified.

One of the first attempts to overcome the problems of low-level languages was the development of FORTRAN in 1954. This language was created by John

Table 11.3 The evolution of programming languages

Generation	First appearance	Language	Examples
first	1949	machine code	UNIVAC
second	1950s	assembler	IBM 1400 assembler
third	1960s	high-level	BASIC, COBOL, RPG
fourth	1970s	very high-level; non-procedural	Query-by-Example, THEMIS, LOTUS 1-2-3
fifth	1990s?	natural?	none as yet

Backus, working for IBM, to help mathematicians, scientists and engineers. It was designed to enable the user to write mathematical formulae which were translated into machine instructions, hence FORmula TRANslation. See, for example, the following mathematical statement and its FORTRAN equivalent:

$$\text{Equation 1} \quad x = \frac{y(a - b)^2}{3n} \quad \text{(mathematical form)}$$

line 100   X   =   (Y*(A − B)**2)/3*N (FORTRAN statement)

The structure of FORTRAN influenced many other programming languages which followed it, particularly BASIC.

Statements written in FORTRAN are processed by a special program called a *compiler* which translates them into machine language. The machine language program is then loaded into store and run with any necessary data. The language is called *high level* because each FORTRAN statement may generate many machine-code instructions when compiled.

FORTRAN was the first of many high-level languages. The benefits of such languages are many. Firstly, the program is written in a form close to the problem: in this case the language of mathematics; secondly, it is very much easier to look at, to change, and to find errors, than a low-level language; thirdly, the programmer does not have to think about computer instructions or about store locations, instead he or she can concentrate on the application problem that has to be solved.

Programs written in high-level language are usually not unique to any one particular machine, that is, they can be run on any machine for which a compiler exists, although they will need to be recompiled. Thus they are *portable*. This is a vital point: organizations may invest hundreds or even thousands of person-years of effort in creating software. If this exists only in the form of low-level language programs then the programs must be re-written for a different machine, at vast trouble and expense. Many firms were caught out by this when they tried to move to new machines in the 1960s. The costs of conversion were very high and this experience helped the rise of third generation languages. Learning to program in a high-level language is very much easier than for a low-level language; once learnt, programs can be written for any machine for which a compiler exists, so the language skills are portable as well as the programs.

High-level languages all have a potentially significant drawback. The object programs they create are of necessity 'generalized' sets of machine instructions which reflect the input source code statements. The machine language programs produced will not be as efficient, in terms of running speed and memory usage, as low-level code created by a skilled programmer specifically for the task. Compiled programs may run very much more slowly, and use far more memory, than programs written in a low-level language. As computer hardware is constantly becoming cheaper and faster this drawback is far less important than at earlier times; also, the high-level compilers have been improved and enhanced over the years to produce more efficient code. Nevertheless, there will still be occasions when it is necessary to go all out for efficiency, and then a low-level language may be the best answer.

In the late 1950s, European and American academic teams joined forces to create a new language called ALGOL (algorithmic language), which was intended to compete with the IBM-linked FORTRAN. After much discussion (including a row over the representation of the decimal point by a stop (American usage) or a comma (European usage)) versions of the language were published in 1958 and 1960. Although ALGOL was favoured in Europe, it did not catch on in the USA, mainly because the IBM-preferred FORTRAN (provided free with the computer) was already too well established.

Until 1960, computer languages favoured the mathematical user; they were designed primarily to ease the manipulation of numbers using algebra. This made sense because many early computer users were scientists and engineers. But business use was increasing and a special language designed for commercial users was needed. The answer was COBOL (common business oriented language), developed on behalf of the US Department of Defense by a team which utilized the work of Grace Hopper. The essence of COBOL was not the manipulation of numbers since business mathematics are usually straightforward but, rather, the handling, storage and retrieval of alphabetic and numeric data. In addition to offering simplified data and especially file-handling, the language is structured to provide logical groups of English-like statements that are intended to be self-explanatory to a large extent. (Whether COBOL programs achieve this in practice is another matter.) COBOL became extremely popular with business users, and there are probably more lines of business application code written in COBOL than in any other computer language (see Fig. 11.1).

Another business-oriented language is RPG (report program generator). This was originally developed in 1964 to reflect the working of punched-card machines, and includes an underlying input–calculate–output program cycle which reflects the data processing tasks that are common to many basic business applications. Not nearly so verbose as COBOL, it is self-documenting to some extent and later versions have good facilities for file handling, printing and VDU output. The language has been considerably extended and is now in its third version, RPG III; in this version it is still much used on small mainframes and minis.

In the early 1960s software development had polarized into three separate groups: scientific, business and systems programming, each of which utilized one of the specialist languages available. IBM then sponsored the development of a new language which would replace all the others; the new language was eventually called PL/1 (programming language 1). The advantages of such a universal computer language were clear to all; the problem was to develop one

```
00265   00250   PROCEDURE DIVISION.
00266   00251       OPEN  INPUT  SALES-FILE
00267   00252                    FIN-PRINT
00268   00253                    AGPROF
00269   00254             OUTPUT PRINT-FILE

00271   00256       SORT SORT-FILE ON ASCENDING KEY ST-CODE
00272   00257                         DESCENDING KEY ST-PREM
00273   00258             INPUT PROCEDURE IS BEGIN-INPUT
00274   00259             OUTPUT PROCEDURE IS SORT-RETN-010
00275   00260       CLOSE SALES-FILE
00276   00261             FIN-PRINT
00277   00262             AGPROF
00278   00263             PRINT-FILE
00279   00264       STOP RUN.
00280   00265   BEGIN-INPUT SECTION.
00281   00266   INPUT-ROUTINE-002
00282   00267       PERFORM READ-FILE-005 UNTIL
00283   00268             END-OF-FILE-SW EQUAL 'YES'.
00284   00269       PERFORM DIVISION-PRO-009.
00285   00270       GO TO INPUT-EXIT.
00286   00271   READ-FILE-005.
00287   00272       READ SALES-FILE AT END
00288   00273             MOVE 'YES' TO END-OF-FILE-SW.
00289   00274       MOVE REP-NO TO REP-RED.
00290   00275       IF END-OF-FILE-SW EQUAL 'NO'
00291   00276             PERFORM PROCESS-RECORDS-007.
00292   00277   PROCESS-RECORDS-007.
00293   00278       IF REG-DIST GREATER THAN 99 AND
00294   00279             REG-DIST LESS THAN 500
00295   00280             PERFORM PROCESS-ITEM1-020
```

Figure 11.1 Fragment of COBOL program

with all the right characteristics. PL/1 combined the attributes of FORTRAN, ALGOL and COBOL and became a large and complex language.

But PL/1 has not been generally adopted by the world's programmers. It has not replaced either COBOL or FORTRAN; indeed, if it had not been for the patronage of IBM it might well have died an early death. Nevertheless, it is in use in a number of (mainly IBM) installations. The reasons for its failure to attract more users may include the fact that in an attempt to be 'all things to all people' it became too complex and unwieldy; perhaps also it suffered from the natural intertia which people feel towards replacing something familiar with something new.

None of the languages discussed so far can be described as particularly easy to learn; and nearly all programs written in the early days were developed by professional programmers or researchers. BASIC (beginners all-purpose symbolic instruction code) was created at Dartmouth college, USA, by John Kemeny and Thomas Kurtz in 1964; its primary purpose was to facilitate the learning of programming by novices and computer trainees.

BASIC is similar in concept and function to FORTRAN; it is oriented to mathematical use and is awkward for input and output, especially using disk files. Nevertheless, it has become probably the most-used computer language of all time, and for very many non-professional computer users it is the only computer language they know (see Fig. 11.2).

The other high-level languages discussed so far generate compiled program output, that is, a *source program* is written and submitted to the compiler as a batch of data. The compiler reports on any errors it can detect and then, if all

```
2300 PRINT : PRINT "PLEASE NAME THESE OUTCOMES :-" : PRINT : FOR I = W TO QU(NC
: PRINT " OUTCOME " ;I; "IS ";: INPUT Q$(I,NO):
2305 NEXT I
2310 NEXT NO: GOTO 20
2690 FOR I = W TO N2
2700 GOSUB 1200: PRINT "EXAMPLE NO. ";I;" ON NODE"; NO:PRINT :PRINT
2710 FOR J = W TO VA(NO)
2720 PRINT "VARIABLE ";J;" (";V$(J,NO);") IS;: INPUT E(J,I +EZ(NO),NO)
2730 NEXT J
2740 PRINT : PRINT "AND THE OUTCOME IS ?" : FOR J = W TO QU(NO):PRINT J;"."; Q
J,NO): NEXT J: INPUT "ANSWER BY NUMBER:"; E(VA(NO)+W,I + EZ(NO),NO)
2750 NEXT I
2760 EZ(NO) = EZ(NO) + N2
2770 NEXT NO : GOTO 20
```

Figure 11.2   Fragment of BASIC program

is well, it produces a machine-code *object program* as output. The object program can then be loaded and run at will.

In practice, it may take several attempts to get a program to work properly and this requires changing source code and recompiling. This has its drawbacks for learners because they must wait until the entire program has been compiled before finding out the effects of their work. BASIC is intended to be more immediate. It is designed for interactive use, which for many students originally meant using the large time-sharing computers on college campuses, but now more often means using a PC. To achieve this, BASIC uses an *interpreter* instead of a compiler.

Statements in BASIC are not translated in a batch; instead, each statement is entered and stored. When the program is run, the interpreter translates a statement into machine language, checks it syntactically and then executes it if it can. This provides immediate feedback on errors, and makes program development 'at the screen' faster. The drawback is that the statements must be reinterpreted every time the computer executes them, so run-time speed may be very much slower than a compiled program. Some systems offer BASIC compilers as well as interpreters, and for some users the answer is to develop their programs using the interpreter, but then to compile them when finished in order to gain the superior run-time speed.

In the decades since the 1960s many new languages have been devised. Among the more important ones are:

- ADA: named after Lady Ada Augusta Byron, Countess of Lovelace, Babbage's collaborator. This was commissioned by the US Department of Defense and appeared in 1983. It was designed to develop programs where real-time applications are crucial, for example in the computers used in a guided missile or plane.
- APL: a programming language. Designed by Kenneth Iverson and Adin

Falkoff in the 1960s, the language was intended for data processing applications, but statements are expressed in a mathematically elegant style as distinct from the verbose English of COBOL.

- C: name derived from a language called B, a variant of BCPL. This was developed as a general-purpose language by Dennis Ritchie in 1972. Intended for professional programmers, it has been used to develop system software where operating efficiency is very important; for example the operating system Unix was written in C.
- FORTH: name derived from fourth. Devised by Charles Moore in 1971, it was intended to be a fourth-generation language and includes a number of unique features. Used mainly in astronomy, robotics and graphics applications it remains the tool of the skilled programmer. Now, the term 'fourth generation' usually refers to the many business-oriented, data-query systems available.
- LISP: list processor. This was created by John McCarthy and appeared in the early 1960s. It was developed to handle symbolic information, i.e. items that represent ideas and concepts, and their relationships. It has been used extensively to develop expert systems and other knowledge-based programs (see PROLOG).
- PASCAL: named after the seventeenth-century French mathematician. Devised by Niklaus Wirth in 1970, it is oriented towards mathematical applications and was designed to teach good programming practice. In some organizations it has replaced FORTRAN and BASIC.
- PROLOG: programming in logic. This was devised in 1972 to handle the predicate calculus relationships used in developing expert systems and artificial intelligence programs generally. It is used extensively by AI researchers, and its main rival in this respect is LISP. Significantly, the Japanese chose PROLOG as the basis for their fifth-generation project and this decision may have far-reaching consequences for the language. A scaled-down version called MICRO-PROLOG is available for micros.

Fourth-generation languages (4GLs)

There is no absolute definition of a fourth-generation category of languages, although the essence of it is the move away from traditional procedural languages which tell the computer what to do, to *non-procedural* programming tools which describe what is wanted. The idea is that the new tools can easily be learnt and used by computer-inexperienced staff, or, alternatively, that they can make programming much faster for the professional.

There are two distinct strands of development. First is the idea of serving the needs of business users who wish to access data held on computer files, but who have no desire to learn a conventional language like COBOL or to spend time writing lengthy programs. Such people are often referred to as *end-users*, and include managers, professionals and information workers generally. The second idea concerns the *productivity* of programmers and system developers in the information systems department who are involved in application software development. While hardware costs have consistently fallen in the decades since the first machines appeared, staff costs have consistently risen so that personnel costs form an increasingly significant proportion of information system budgets.

Along with the costs, there is the parallel and acute problem of staff shortage in a constantly expanding industry. At the same time, increased demand for new systems and more information has led to extended backlogs of development work in the IS departments of many organizations; this has resulted in users 'doing their own thing' rather than waiting for the IS specialists.

The result of these considerations has been the development of a plethora of software tools which go some way towards eliminating the need for traditional programming. The availability of terminal access to databases, and especially the widespread use of PCs, has hastened the spread of these tools and affected their design.

The distinction between some very high-level software tools and application packages is rather a fine one, and the categories are in any case somewhat blurred; nevertheless three distinct functions can be discerned:

1. *Query languages.* These are very high-level languages intended for examining data already held in files or databases. Some of them allow for updating information as well as retrieving it. Examples include query-by-example (QBE) from IBM, FILETALK, FOCUS, MAPPER and SEQUEL. Some of the languages require programming-like statements such as the following:

   > PRINT CUSTOMER_NAME IF TURNOVER < £10 000

   But working with QBE, and others like it, involves inserting information into a visual format on screen. This makes the tool very easy to learn and use.

2. *Report and graphics generators.* These contain facilities for extracting data from existing files, and creating printed reports or displaying the output in graphs and bar charts. Some of these generators are part of packages like Lotus 1-2-3 and dBase III; others are more complex and powerful, and include features that make them more like traditional programming languages. (In fact, the language RPG could be described as a very early 4GL.)

3. *Application generators.* These are used to create complete systems, and usually include modular facilities to generate databases, file querying, reports, graphics and data modelling. One way of working is for the system to ask questions about the application which the user answers, and so the system is built interactively. Where specific application needs cannot be met by generalized routines, programming tools are provided to customize the final system.

The current trend in software development is very much towards increasing the use of the 4GLs at the expense of conventional programming languages because of the potential for very substantial improvements in programmer productivity, and also towards increasing the involvement of end-users in the development of their own systems.

Choosing a programming language

In a business context there are many programming languages to choose from. The criteria for choice could include two sets of characteristics:

1. *Characteristics of the language*
   ease of learning
   language availability and portability
   application development efficiency
   system efficiency
   degree of self-documentation
   power and flexibility
   ease of change
   popularity with other users
   degree of supplier support

2. *Characteristics of the situation*
   type of application
   type of computer system
   degree of programming expertise available

In practice, many of these characteristics lead to criteria that are in conflict with each other: powerful and efficient languages, by their very nature, tend to be complex and difficult to learn and result in low programmer productivity. Characteristics such as self-documentation and ease of use tend to be so important that for many organizations they are the prime deciding factors.

However, most large organizations have existed for some time and will already have a well-developed information systems capability, including programming expertise. This usually implies an extensive investment in business software which has been developed over the years, often in COBOL or another high-level language. A move to a different language would involve substantial retraining and redevelopment costs. However, the continuing development of 4GLs is encouraging organizations to move towards systems development utilizing these software tools, in order to achieve improved programming productivity gains.

A smaller-sized company wishing rapidly to develop straightforward but specialized business systems might consider RPG III because of its relative ease of use and speed of development. It would probably also examine application packages and general-purpose software. A small business, with a computer facility consisting of a few PCs, might consider acquiring specific application packages for its main business systems, and perhaps general-purpose packages (word processing, spreadsheets and database) which would provide a significant data processing capability. For specialized programs involving small-scale original development work, BASIC has proved popular because it is so easy to learn.

Summary

A number of levels of programming languages have been identified: machine code and assembler language at the lowest level; high-level languages; and fourth-generation languages. Within these broad categories there are a number of variations, mostly designed with a specific task in mind. Clearly, information systems users will have very little contact with low-level languages; indeed, their intention may be restricted to the use of packages which are discussed in Chapter 12.

KEY TERMS ALGOL   Assembler   BASIC   COBOL   Compiler
FORTRAN   High-level language   Interpreter   Labels   LISP   Low-level
language   Machine language   Object program   PL/1   Portable   PROLOG
RPG   Source program   Translator   4GL.

Further reading

Baron N.S., *Computer Languages*, Pelican Books, London, 1988.
Christoff K.A., Building a fourth generation environment, *Datamation*, September 1985.
Harel E.C. and McLean E.R., The effects of using a nonprocedural computer language on programmer productivity, *MIS Quarterly*, June 1985.
Wilson L.B. and Clark R.G., *Comparative Programming Languages*, Addison-Wesley, Wokingham, England, 1988.

12
Software packages, applications and management support

The need for packages

Developing software is a major cost item for any organization. High-level programming languages enable computer programming without the difficulties of machine language, and fourth-generation languages make programming much easier and faster. But software packages are intended to remove the need for programming altogether; they are programs designed and written by specialists for customers who buy them 'off the shelf' and ready to use. Some users have highly specialized requirements and may commission a specialist software house to develop a package for them. But many organizations share similar computing needs, for example to process payroll data and basic accounts, and to type letters. The package suppliers have therefore moved in to supply an enormous market for standard software. Because the software vendor usually hopes to sell the same software product to many customers, the price for each unit can be very much less than the total cost of designing and producing the software. Some packages, such as the more popular word processing and spreadsheet packages, have sold hundreds of thousands of copies world wide. Micros and PCs are often used by people who do not have programming skills, or do not wish to spend time developing their own programs; thus the market for micro packages is truly enormous, and represents a major growth area. To a large extent, software packages have removed the need for specialist programming staff for micros and have opened the way to the very wide range of applications for which they are now used. Because of the breadth of software available, there is now less of a demand for software houses to create bespoke software for individual organizations; instead the trend is increasingly towards standardized, commercial packages.

Packages and applications

Software packages can be considered to fall into two main groups: dedicated and general purpose. General-purpose packages include word processors, spreadsheets and databases. They can be used for a wide range of different applications and are very popular on PCs and small business machines. *Dedicated packages* address one particular business application. There are dedicated packages available to do just about any business function; the following list shows some of the enormous range of business-orientated topics now covered.

airline reservations	linear and integer programming
banking	management science techniques
basic accounting: sales, purchases	mathematical modelling
and nominal ledger	market research
budgeting	operational research techniques
computer aided design (CAD)	payroll
computer aided learning (CAL)	pension planning
computer aided manufacture (CAM)	personnel records
decision analysis	production scheduling and
decision support systems (DSS)	control
desk-top publishing (DTP)	sales analysis
executive information systems (EIS)	sales order processing
expert system shells	simulation
financial analysis and management	statistics
forecasting	stock control
investment appraisal	systems modelling

These dedicated packages range in price from one to two hundred pounds for an elementary payroll system through to hundreds of thousands of pounds for a sophisticated DSS package. In addition to the more usual business functions, there are business-specific packages designed for the specialized work of doctors, dentists, solicitors, stockbrokers, estate agents, insurance agents and travel agents.

The three most popular application areas for dedicated business packages are payroll, basic ledger accounting and stock control. Payroll was one of the first business applications to be computerized in the early 1950s; payroll calculations are intricate and repetitive and it is hardly surprising that it is the most popular package for the business micro. A typical payroll package suitable for a small business costs somewhere around £300, plus annual maintenance charges.

The functions of the payroll package include:

- calculation of gross and net pay for employees including hourly, weekly and monthly paid staff;
- incorporating PAYE deductions, national insurance and pension contributions, and any other special amounts;

- printing pay-slips, cheque lists and/or bank giros, and coin analysis;
- maintaining constant, current and cumulative data on each employee, and updating these records;
- printing information for end-of-year, periodic and special tax forms, such as P60, P11 and P45;
- providing postings to the nominal ledger for PAYE, insurance, cash and wages accounts;
- producing organizational and divisional summaries of payments made on a current and year-to-date basis for management.

Payroll packages are provided by a number of vendors. More than perhaps with any other package, it is important that the user can count on ongoing vendor support. While computer problems which cause system failure may be a nuisance on some systems, failure to pay employees correctly and on time would be a disaster. The support takes two forms. Firstly, answering queries by telephone in emergency, which helps to overcome any unexpected difficulties that might arise. Secondly, the automatic provision of changes and amendments to the software to cope with legislative changes which affect tax rates and other items. The support is usually provided as part of an annual contract which attracts a fee.

ACCOUNTING APPLICATIONS

Accounting packages are designed to cope with records for the principal account ledgers: sales, purchases and nominal. Although these can be acquired as separate packages, most users buy them as an *integrated accounts package*. The package is usually designed to facilitate entries between the purchase and sales ledgers, and the nominal ledger.

The sales ledger has the following functions:

- invoicing customers for goods or services, including allowing discounts and calculating appropriate VAT charges (although invoicing is not strictly part of the sales ledger, most integrated packages include this facility);
- crediting customers for returns or errors;
- accepting payments received from customers;
- maintaining sales ledger accounts for each customer: file maintenance such as adding new customer records, deleting unwanted records if zero balance, updating records for changed names and addresses and other constant data;
- printing statements of each customer's account;
- management information: sales day book, aged debt analysis, monthly sales analysis.

Most packages allow coding of customer and product transactions to facilitate later analysis. The better packages maintain open-item accounts, whereby transactions are retained on file until fully allocated against cash or credit. Simpler balance-forward systems transfer summarized balances at the end of each period.

The purchase ledger operates in much the same way as the sales ledger, except that the accounts refer to suppliers and not customers, and the purchases statement which is sent out to the supplier is usually accompanied by a cheque rather than a demand for payment! In other respects the functions and operations of the packages are very similar.

The nominal ledger holds those nominal accounts specified by the user as being necessary for analysing the financial transactions of the firm. Most firms have the following nominal accounts: fixed assets, current assets, current liabilities, long-term liabilities, revenue, expenditure and trading accounts. These accounts may be further divided or detailed to show specific groups of sales or puchases for example. In order to achieve the automatic posting of entries from the other ledgers (sales and purchases) transactions entered onto these ledgers must be coded with the corresponding nominal account codes. As well as receiving entries from the other ledgers, journal entries are made directly within the nominal ledger for other financial transactions, such as heating and lighting, rent and rates, and depreciation. The nominal system produces a trial balance, listings of the nominal accounts, a profit and loss statement and a balance sheet.

Last, but by no means least, the accounts package has to provide system controls, an acceptable audit trail, and back-up security routines to provide a means of recovery in the event of failure or other disaster. System controls are calculated by the package to check that the data held is internally consistent; for example, the sales ledger total debt should equal the debtor's balance in the nominal ledger. These internal checks should 'prove' that the system is functioning correctly and that records and files are in a valid state. Control totals are printed which can be checked against the system's output, and can be used to check that all input data has been successfully processed and that each system run is consistent with the next.

An *audit trail* is essentially a means whereby the auditor can follow the progress of a transaction throughout the system. One problem with computerized systems, from the auditor's point of view, is that data is held invisibly on magnetic media and cannot be readily examined. Another is that the system operates according to a complex set of rules embodied in a computer program, the details of which are almost certainly incomprehensible to the auditor. The audit trail consists of printouts which identify the origin and progress of all transactions through the system, and shows how they make up balances and control totals in the various parts of the system.

There are many reasons why a system can fail. These range from physical disasters such as fire and flood, through human error and deliberate fraud, and include hardware and software failures. The purpose of back-up is to retain one or more complete copies of the system and its files so that there is a recovery route in the event of disaster, whether it be of a major or minor degree. (The very important question of security is covered in more detail in Chapter 16.) The integrated package should provide a straightforward means of taking regular security copies of key files. This usually consists of routine copying of files onto floppy disks which can be stored securely and reused as part of a back-up cycle.

STOCK CONTROL

Recording accurate stock levels is an essential business activity, and vitally affects many other functions, including accounting, sales, purchasing and production. Computerized stock recording essentially involves receiving data on all stock movements in and out and maintaining a balance for each product item. The physical stock level quantity is often a more useful piece of information to sales staff when reduced by known customer demand, giving the *free stock level*, i.e. the amount that can be allocated for sales from stock. When the stock balance has reduced to some predetermined level, a replenishment order must be produced. Monitoring stock levels in order to trigger replenishment is a normal feautre of stock control systems. Some packages also provide routines for the supply side of the systems, in the form of orders on suppliers' schedules and suppliers' records.

It is an accepted maximum of stock control that 80 per cent of the total stock value is usually made up of only 20 per cent of the products, and it is to this important 20 per cent that most management attention should be given. A more elaborate scheme is known as Pareto analysis, or ABC analysis, which indicates three groups to which different levels of management attention should be directed. The stock control package will produce a listing of products in each category. Such an analysis might yield the following groups of products:

Class A items: 80 per cent of value; 20 per cent of items; review constantly

Class B items: 15 per cent of value; 30 per cent of items; review less frequently

Class C items: 5 per cent of value;   50 per cent of items; review rarely

The maintenance of stock holdings at an optimum level which balances stock holding costs against the risks of stock-out (and hence lost sales) is a crucial management problem. Mathematically, the optimum stock reorder level, the *economic order quantity (EOQ)* is given by

$$\sqrt{2Co * D/Cs},$$

where Co is the ordering cost, D is the demand and Cs is the stockholding cost. Management science techniques have been developed which can forecast future demand from past sales. One technique is *exponential smoothing*, a mathematical forecasting procedure which can take into account seasonal and random fluctuations in order to provide estimates of likely future demand based on past history. By taking into account physical stock, customer demand (actual and forecast), together with orders on suppliers, the stock controller can calculate when and how much stock to order from a supplier or from the production department. Clearly, the calculations involved are lengthy and tedious and made an ideal computer application.

Many firms manufacture items from several components or subassemblies. Calculating stockholding requirements requires analysing demand for finished products in terms of their component parts. Enumerating the components and their subcomponents and their sub-subcomponents results in a parts explosion exercise which becomes immensely complex. Computer-based techniques for handling the extensive calculations involved are known as *material requirements planning (MRP)*, or *bill of materials processing (BOMP)* systems. Routines to handle MRP or BOMP are available either as part of a stock or production control package, or as a separate system.

COMPLETE BUSINESS PACKAGES

Several packages are currently marketed which aim to provide many general business functions. Pegasus has modules which include payroll, accounts, order processing and invoicing, stock control, job costing and bill of materials. Another popular package called Tetraplan contains payroll, accounts, cash book, order entry, invoicing and sales analysis, purchase order scheduling, bill of materials, job costing and fixed assets. The Sage business package contains payroll and accounts, word processing, spreadsheet and database, communications software, and a 'desk-top organizer' with automatic telephone, alarm and diary features. The modules of these packages can usually be bought individually, depending on the requirements of the business; but the linkages between the modules should be more straightforward than if the user had bought separate packages from separate suppliers, and the advantages of similarity of format and consequent ease of use may offset problems due to parts of the package not matching user needs exactly.

Advantages and disadvantages of applications packages

Make or buy: which is the best choice? Because the availability of a software package removes the necessity for costly and time-consuming programming, it might be thought that there is little point in ever developing software in-house if a suitable commercial package is available. Indeed for many small businesses who lack any internal systems development capability, packaged software may represent the only way of implementing computer systems. But, in practice, packages can have their drawbacks and it is worth considering with some care the advantages and disadvantages when compared with purpose-built software.

ADVANTAGES OF PACKAGED SOFTWARE

Reduced costs

A package should cost less, overall, than the real cost of developing the software in-house. A commercial programmer may command a salary of £20K p.a. or more, with overheads on top, and a typical system may take the equivalent of 6 months to develop; a package to do the same job may cost only £1000 or so.

In practice it may be hard to measure the real costs of an internal programming project; also, commercial software often comes with annual licence and maintenance fees which make direct cost comparisons awkward. Packages often need modifying and updating, and certainly need reviewing and understanding, and users will need training. A key point is that the full costs of implementation are always greater than just the initial cost of the software.

Reduced time for implementation

In theory a package should be ready to run; there is no need to wait for the in-house development cycle of systems design, programming and testing to occur. (But there is still the problem of evaluating and choosing the package.) Where the organizational IS development team is tied up for months or years ahead with priority projects, then packaged software may be the only way to proceed.

Inbuilt expertise

Hopefully the package has been developed by experts in the topic, be it stock control, sales forecasting or a system for airline seat reservations. This enables the built-in expertise in the package to be tapped by the user, and reduces the need to develop technical application expertise in-house. For example, acquiring a stock control package with a demand-forecasting option provides the forecasting without the need for the user to become expert in the mathematics of exponential smoothing.

Error-free package

Hopefully the package has been fully tested. If it is one of the more popular commercial packages, then many thousands of other clients will have already run the software and most of the bugs should have been found (by somebody else) and disposed of. The moral here seems to be: 'first in gets the worst deal'. In practice, no software can ever be regarded as entirely bug-free.

DISADVANTAGES OF PACKAGED SOFTWARE

Inexact fit on user requirements

Rarely will a package do everything in exactly the way required by the users. Sometimes packages can be tailored to user requirements, by the vendor or internally; either way this adds greatly to the costs and time involvement, and if extensive modifications are needed then the point of using a package may be obviated. Some organizations are prepared to change their procedures to fit the package. More usually a compromise is arrived at, with changes made to procedures and to the package.

Dependence on the software supplier

Some organizations will not be prepared to delegate crucial information systems to an outside organization; the systems may be especially sensitive, or with high security requirements such as those associated with national defence. In these circumstances system development by outsiders represents an additional security risk. Even without these factors some organizations will prefer to do crucial systems development themselves in order to ensure that they have full control.

Ongoing maintenance and support

Information systems never stand still; changes in legislation and trade practices require changes in operational procedures. Also, organizations are forever changing in response to internal and external pressures, and user needs are therefore changing too. Maintaining internally produced software is bad enough; maintaining packaged software can be a major problem area. The larger software vendors can provide training, support and the modifications that are needed for all their clients, and this facility is often built into an annual maintenance charge. But where a client requires special modifications, the vendor may decline to undertake the work or may charge enormous fees. A very real problem arises with the smaller software houses; as with any small business, the risk of ceasing to trade is large and if this occurs clients are left high and dry with no sure way of getting help or of changing their systems. In these circumstances, companies may be forced to abandon their systems and start afresh with a new software house.

General-purpose packages

These packages include word processing, spreadsheet and database. They are highly flexible and can each perform a wide variety of different business functions. Because of this they are used very extensively on business PCs and we will consider them in detail.

WORD PROCESSING

Word processing is one of the most popular of business micro applications. The ability to manipulate text and to store, print and modify it at will represents a crucial advantage not only for professional typists and secretaries but increasingly for managers, professionals and information workers generally. (This book was written on a word processor; it was typed directly by the authors and the output sent to the publisher for typesetting.) A complete word-processing system essentially consists of a CPU, VDU display, keyboard, printer and disk storage, together with one or more software packages. The software can be very basic, giving typewriter-like effects such as bold, italic and underline, or it can be very sophisticated indeed with a wide range of fonts and special effects and can include automatic spelling check and thesaurus, automatic section numbering and indexing facilities, context-sensitive help, plus much, much more.

The basic characteristics of word processors include the facility to type text freely on the keyboard, an immediate display on the VDU screen, and automatic adjustment of end-of-line and word-wrap. Errors can be seen and corrected easily on-screen, and sections of text can be moved about or copied or deleted. Most packages have the ability to search for chunks of text and to replace sections with new text automatically. The more sophisticated packages tend towards the detailed control of printing associated with desk-top publishing (DTP). Achieving different fonts and special effects requires not only the software but also the printer which can physically reproduce the effects, such as a laser or ink-jet type (see Chapter 7).

One of the crucial features of a word-processing system is its ability to present WYSIWYG (pronounced Wizzywig) which stands for 'what you see is what you get'. This means that the screen display shows how the typing will appear on the printed page, including font size, italic, bold and any special effects. This is very difficult to achieve in an absolute sense, and requires exceptional computing power on a PC, together with an expensive screen and associated electronics. The more recent and sophisticated word-processing packages, running on powerful 16- or 32-bit PCs, can produce something approaching WYSIWYG. If it is necessary to manipulate the print layout in absolute detail, then a desk-top publishing package may be more suitable. The Apple MAC is ideally suited to this kind of work and for a long time has been the main contender for sophisticated text creation.

Context-sensitive help is a facility found on some of the more sophisticated packages. For example, using WORD to print a report involves selecting the print menu and making suitable selections about pagination, number of copies and so on. If the user does not understand or has forgotten what the commands mean he can enter a special function code—Alt H—and look at a display of help information which relates directly to the command he is considering. This saves considerable time looking through manuals, searching indexes and so on, and provides a relatively painless way of learning more about the package. It also means that help information does not clutter up the working display or slow down the experienced user who does not need it. Context-sensitive help is not restricted to word processing and is found on other types of package too.

An important facility for a business is the ability to reproduce standard letters which have been personalized with a customer name or other special insert, for marketing or other purposes. The standard part of the text is called 'boilerplate', and the technique has become so common with junk mailers that not many of us are impressed with these so-called 'personal' letters any more. Some packages offer this feature as a special facility called *mailmerge*; the technique involves the user producing a file of names which the package automatically merges with the boilerplate text to produce complete letters. Similar techniques are used to produce address labels and self-addressed envelopes.

No one commercial word-processing package has captured a lion's share of the enormous market recently; instead, the market is currently shared widely among many contenders. In terms of the installed customer base, Wordstar (in its several different versions) is the leader. Some of the other popular packages are: Wordperfect, Multimate, Wordcraft, Displaywrite and Word.

DESK-TOP PUBLISHING (DTP)

Packages for DTP take word-processed textual materials and combine them with graphics, artwork and other non-textual materials to produce a complete, printed document, the format and layout of which can be controlled in great detail. The professional publishing world has already been revolutionized by the advent of computer-based publishing systems. DTP places the facilities of the professional publisher on the desk of any businessman or professional.

DTP gives business the opportunity of developing printed materials to a high standard in-house without the need to send out to professional printers. This can represent substantial savings in time and costs; effectively the sequence of author's drafts, proofing, checking and correcting can be reduced or eliminated. Examples of the kind of work which can be done include advertising materials and brochures, headed notepaper and notices, newsletters and internal reports, books and pamphlets. Figure 12.1 is a typical example.

A DTP system consists of similar elements to a word-processing system, except that in order to achieve the more sophisticated effects of professional printers, more powerful software and equipment are needed. A reasonably sophisticated system might consist of the following components:

- Apple MAC or IBM PC/AT compatible PC
- 20 MB (or larger) hard disk
- Laser printer with Postscript printer-driver
- PageMaker DTP software

The market for DTP packages is much more recent than for word processing, and two products—Ventura and Pagemaker—currently lead the market. Other popular packages include: Fleet St Editor, Fontasy and MacAuthor. A DTP software package will offer similar facilities to the more sophisticated word-processing packages, but in addition to this there are some special features which can distinguish the two types. These extra features include the following:

- Multi-column and block-text presentation: this is seen in newspapers and journals, it is usually difficult to achieve with ordinary word processors;
- Fonts: additional, and special fonts and print sizes; some common fonts are:
  Courier abcdefghijklmnopqrstuvwxyz
  Dutch Roman abcdefghijklmnopqrstuvwxyz
  Swiss Roman abcdefghijklmnopqrstuvwxyz
  Bookman abcdefghijklmnopqrstuvwxyz

Widget World News

Views and News of Widget Manufacturing in the 80s

142 Guitrep Pkwy.   *Detroit, MI 98987*   *(413) 567-9888*

Software Salaries: How do you stack up?

by Joe Smith

How much your software professionals are paid is a function of many variables, and a subject of considerable interest to your organization.

Software salary pay scales
Because of the dynamic growth of the software industry over the last decade, the demand for experienced, qualified programmers has greatly increased, thus leading to a spiraling of salaries.

But what causes managers to pay one programmer more than another?

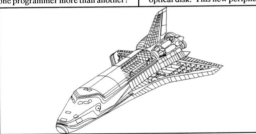

Figure 1   Columbian

Does the type of organization, its size, or location make a difference? What career path or programming specialty leads to the most remuneration?

To answer these questions, Acme Magazine recently conducted its third annual compensation survey for software professionals. This newsletter article presents the results of this study and explores what the findings may mean to you.

Acme Magazine asked Joe Smith, a compensation consulting specialist for the software industry, to design and conduct the survey. Twenty-four positions, representing four pro-

grammer job families plus management, were included.

Data was collected for base pay, bonus and incentive payments, and whether nor not incumbents received stock options or other forms of equity.

Questionnaires were sent to the data processing heads of 2,400 organizations throughout the United States.

CD-ROM Breaks New Ground

Compact Disk Read Only Memory (CD-ROM) is a rapidly emerging new technology for the retrieval of vast amounts of information from an optical disk. This new peripheral device allows a totally new level of functionality in the use of microcomputers.

Physically, the CD-ROM device has a laser disk drive (or "player") the same size as a traditional 5 1/4" drive. The removable disk is 4 3/4", and has a capacity of 550M bytes (equivalent to 1500 360K floppy disks).

Theory of Operation
Information stored on a CD-ROM can be loaded into memory (RAM), displayed and printed, as with other media. While that data in RAM may be altered and stored to a conventional magnetic disk, the orig-

inal information on the CD-ROM is unalterable, always ensuring the original copy is intact, making archiving easy.

The storage capacity, low cost, and read only feature of CD-ROM bring an enormous new capability to microcomputer users — that is, information retrieval of very large reference publications. How people receive and use information in the immediate and long term future will be dramatically changed by CD-ROM.

In addition to the huge capacity of raw information storage, specialized software for the search of that information is currently being introduced. This software allows searching the information in areas, methods and speeds not previously feasible.

It now becomes possible to electronically publish reference material more economically than to print the same material in book form. That cost benefit, coupled with search and retrieval software, make an astonishing price/performance ratio.

Table of Contents

Figure 12.1   Widget World News
Source: Ventura Publisher Software Reference Guide. © 1987 Ventura Software Inc. Reproduced with permission.

Palatino abcdefghijklmnopqrstuvwxyz
Avant garde abcdefghijklmnopqrstuvwxyz
- Special effects such as {☒} and {☐};
- Kerning: the closing up of printed letters proportionally so that they appear more pleasing to the eye; this has always been a manual craft skill and even now automatic kerning by DTP software may not be as good as that done by a skilled typesetter;
- Material assembly: text, graphics, line artwork and materials from other packages are merged together on the page;
- WYSIWYG: fully accurate display, with zoom control over magnification, or several levels of magnification available.

Although the facilities available in DTP packages make page layout and design technically easy and place a wide range of special effects at the user's disposal, it is still by no means certain that the end result will be pleasing to the eye, or more effective as a means of communication. It is still necessary to supply artistic and creative skills in order to create pleasing results. This was dramatically demonstrated recently in a university department, where the internal news-sheet was first produced using an advanced word processor. The new news-sheet appeared in a plethora of type styles and special effects, which had clearly been chosen 'because they were there'. The result looked amateurish and was not at all pleasant to read. After a time, some discipline returned and a more restrained approach resulted in an improved effect.

SPREADSHEETS

The electronic spreadsheet has become the standard working tool for many managers, accountants and professionals. The essential, and very simple, concept behind the spreadsheet is the *data matrix*. This consists of an area marked out by numbered rows and columns, and in which the user enters numbers. The junction of each row and column is referred to as a *cell*, and cells can be filled with numbers (values), text (labels) or formulae. The part of the matrix shown on the screen is not the limit of the spreadsheet; most modern packages allow hundreds of rows and columns to be addressed, giving many thousands of cells. The spreadsheet effectively continues to the right and below the visible portion; to see these parts the user moves the cursor, and the spreadsheet automatically scrolls sideways or up and down to bring the new parts of the sheet into view. The screen can be thought of as a window onto the much larger electronic piece of paper lying behind it.

Initially the spreadsheet is empty and shows only the row and column headings. The user then moves the cursor to a cell and enters data (in the form of numbers, text or formulae). In Fig. 12.2 the word 'Sales' has been entered into cell B2 and the number 3208 into cell B3. Cells C2 and C3 and D2 have also been filled. No number is entered into cell D3, where we want to see the profit figure appearing. Here, we can command the spreadsheet to calculate the answer for

	A	B	C	D	E
1	[cursor]				
2		Sales	Costs	Profits	
3		3208	2943	(B3 − C3)	
4					
5					

Figure 12.2   Spreadsheet data matrix

us by entering a simple *cell formula* which tells the spreadsheet what to do. In this case we want it to subtract the figure in C3 from that in B3 and put the answer in D3, so we enter the formula (B3 − C3). The brackets tell the system that this is a formula rather than ordinary text or label. The formula disappears from view and is instantly replaced by the answer which the spreadsheet calculates for us. The formula has not been lost; it sits invisibly 'behind' the cell and guides the contents of that cell continually until the formula is changed or deleted. So changing the data in cells B3 or C3 results in a new answer appearing in D3 with no effort from us. It is important to grasp the difference between the background of the spreadsheet, into which the formulae are placed, and the foreground which displays the results. Good spreadsheet model building requires the modeller to think primarily in terms of the background.

In this way the spreadsheet performs elementary calculations on columns and rows of data. There are few limits on the complexity of the formulae which can be used. For example, a command such as (F2 * G2 + E2/26% + SUM(Z3..Z10)) has the symbols *, / and % which act as multiply, divide and per cent, respectively, and SUM is a function code which tells the package to add up all the cells between Z3 and Z10 inclusive. Most spreadsheets also have a range of inbuilt special functions including financial, mathematical and statistical operations. So the calculations performed can be very complex and sophisticated indeed.

A key point is that once data and formulae have been entered it is very easy to change one figure and see what effect this has on all the others. For example, Fig. 12.3 shows a slightly extended version of the previous spreadsheet; in this

	A	B	C	D	E
1		John Smith's Ltd	Sales in £000s		
2		Sales	Costs	Profits	
3	Product A	3208	2943	| 265	
4	Product B	2209	1307	| 902	
5	Product C	4966	4998	| − 32	

6	Totals	10383	9248	1135	

Figure 12.3   Spreadsheet matrix

latter version the spreadsheet will calculate all the figures below and to the right of the dotted line. Now suppose we ask: what if costs for one product change? Let us say we want to see the effect on the totals if the costs for product B go up. To do this we simply alter the figure in cell C4, and all the affected totals will change immediately and automatically as the spreadsheet recalculates its formulae. This *what if* capability is a very powerful and effective feature of spreadsheets and enables an enormous range of business problems to be studied quickly and easily.

The spreadsheet example (Fig. 12.3) is both simple and short; but supposing there were 100 products to be evaluated, would this not represent a lot of keying-in of formulae? In practice, spreadsheets offer clever ways of speeding the process of entering formulae. In the above example the profit formula would be entered once only in cell D3; this cell would then be reproduced in the other 99 cells with a single *replicate* command: the spreadsheet itself calculates the relative formula values required for each cell. In this way quite large and complex spreadsheets can be developed and evaluated very rapidly.

The first spreadsheet packages were Visicalc and Supercalc, developed in the late 1970s. Since that time hundreds of packages have appeared on the market, each based on the original concept but offering more in the way of features and enhancements. Currently the market is led by Lotus 1-2-3 and Supercalc, which hold about 80 per cent of the market between them. These two packages represent the industry standard for business users. Both offer an extensive range of facilities, including extensive graphics capabilities (Fig. 12.4) in addition to the ordinary spreadsheet features (the 1-2-3 of the Lotus title refers to the three features of spreadsheet, graphics and database). Other popular packages include: Multiplan, Excel, Quattro and VP Planner.

The graphics capability of the modern spreadsheet is most important and enables columns of figures to be displayed by histograms, pie charts or line graphs. Choosing the right sort of graphical presentation is not always straightforward, and the following guidelines may be helpful.

1. *Time series*: showing data which changes over time. Use bar charts or line graphs (Figs 2.5 and 12.7). Multiple data sets require careful labelling and/or colour differentiation.
2. *Proportions*: showing data as a part or percentage of the whole. Use a pie charge (Fig. 12.6(a)). Significant portions can be shown very effectively as exploded segments. Where several data sets are involved, stacked bar charts (Fig. 12.6(b)) can be an effective alternative.
3. *Comparing values*. Use bar charts, either horizontal or vertical (Fig. 12.5).
4. *Relationships between variables*. Use line graphs (Fig. 12.7) with sample data points which can make an effective display, as can bar charts.

The use of colour, both in the highlighting of negative numbers in tables and in differentiating variables in graphs, is a powerful display technique which enhances the role of the spreadsheet as a very effective means of communicating

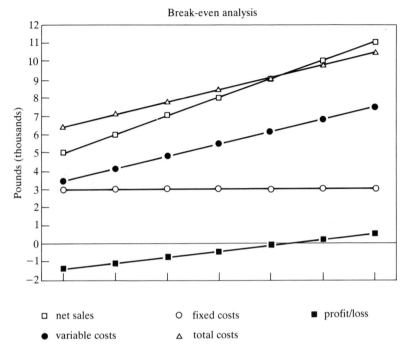

Figure 12.4 Spreadsheet graphic

ideas. The use of the spreadsheet as a method of presentation highlights its key potential role in management decision-making.

DATABASE

The database package is the last of the 'big three' general packages for the PC or small business micro. It performs the crucial task of organizing and storing large amounts of data in such a way that information can be retrieved easily in different ways. Most organizations generate huge amounts of data; the computer has, above all else, the vital ability to store information securely and then reclaim selected parts of it rapidly and flexibly. The database package is the software which enables these functions to be achieved. Some typical database applications are as follows:

- personnel records
- customer mailing lists
- consultant's client records
- club membership records
- plant and machinery records
- equipment maintenance records

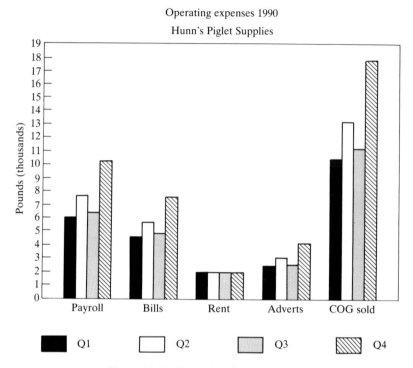

Figure 12.5   Example of mini graph

- computer dating agency records
- books and journals on loan from a company library

Before database software became readily available, data storage and retrieval involved writing programs to accept the data onto disk, then choosing disk access methods (see Part Two) and writing more programs which selected and analysed the information required. Often a file structure would be chosen and programs written, only to find that changing user needs meant more data being added to records in the file or required that data to be retrieved in new ways. This usually meant costly and time-consuming reprogramming in order to accommodate the changes.

The database package significantly reduces the design and programming effort involved in file creation and processing. The package provides a ready-made file structure which is 'empty'; it needs only to be defined in a simple way and then it can be filled with the user's data. Thereafter, the data can be sorted and retrieved in a number of ways using the package's flexible search and selection facilities. When new data has to be added, this can be appended to the end of the file and sorted, or inserted into the correct sequence. If new data must be added to each record then the records can easily be modified to allow this.

(a)

Operating expenses 1990
Hunn's Piglet Supplies

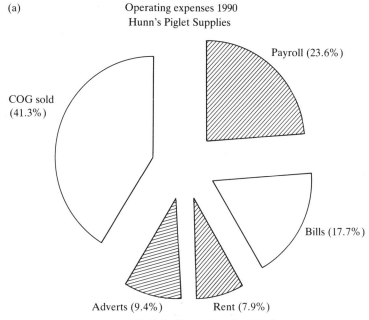

Figure 12.6(a) Example of mini pie

(b)

Operating expenses 1990
Hunn's Piglet Supplies

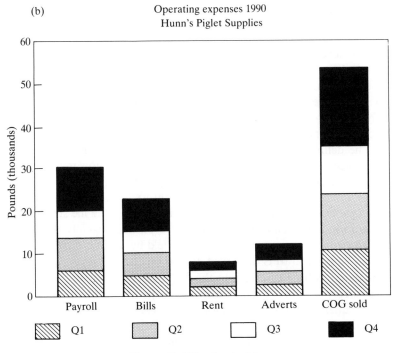

Figure 12.6(b) Stacked bars

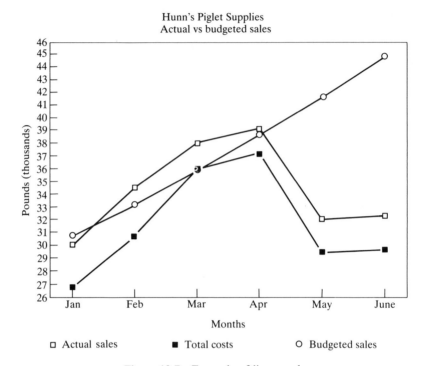

Figure 12.7   Example of line graph

In order to achieve this simplicity from the user's point of view, the file structures employed are highly sophisticated and are usually based on *relational
database* techniques.

Most packages are menu-driven and are quite straightforward to operate; the
more sophisticated ones also provide a means of entering commands directly
which speeds up work for experienced users. Some packages offer context-sensitive help. The definition of the file structure is achieved in different ways by
different packages; usually a record is defined by specifying how many fields are
required, the size of each field, the content type of each field (for example,
numeric and alphanumerics are handled differently) and then a field label (by
which each field can be referred to later). Having defined the file structure, the
next step is normally to enter data into it. The package usually displays the
empty record structure on screen. This is filled field by field until complete, and
then the next empty record is displayed and so on.

Once the data has been entered into the file, it can be listed and processed in
various ways. Key features of the database package are the ability to sort data
into various sequences and select data for listing or further processing. Data can
be initially entered into the file in any sequence, or 'as it comes'; it can then be
sorted and resorted as the need arises by defining a suitable list of fields for the

sorting key. The package can sort the file directly by physically rearranging the file into a new sequence. A different method, which can be more efficient, involves creating an index for the file and then sorting that.

Retrieving data from the file can be handled in several different ways. The entire file can be listed in several different sequences, for example. More usually, it is useful to select records or groups of records for review, or to list them as part of a report. Selecting records is done by choosing fields and conditions, for example:

$$\text{list for year} \; = \; 1990$$

where YEAR is a numeric field in the record. The effect of this command is to list only the records with that year number. More complex criteria can be set up using $\langle$ and $\rangle$ and also the Boolean operators and, or and not. For example:

$$\text{list for YEAR} > 1857 \text{ .AND. AUTHOR\_1} \; = \; \text{'Dickens C'}$$

This command selects only those records where the year is greater than 1857 and author name is Dickens. It does not show records with either of the two conditions, this would require an .OR. setting instead of the .AND.

Some numerical work can be done on records. For example, numeric fields can have calculations performed and results entered into a spare field of the record. Also, totals can be made of specified fields for a selection of the file. In this way quite complex calculations and file processing can be carried out. In practice, defining sophisticated calculations may be more dificult to do than on a spreadsheet.

As well as the file structure, sorting and retrieval facilities, some database packages have more advanced features. The first of these is a *report writer*, which helps to structure the printed or displayed output from the package into well-presented reports. The report formats can be stored in a separate file and reused with the appropriate data file whenever needed. The report writer in dBase 4 is a menu-driven function which allows the user to build up a report column by column, specifying which fields are to be shown and how they should appear. Report titles and column headings can then be chosen. The report can also be specified with control breaks and subtotals, and elementary arithmetic can be performed on numeric fields.

For more advanced applications that require complicated record retrieval and processing, a *command language* is used together with an *automatic command processor*. The command language consists of statements similar to a high-level programming language which enable complex comparing and processing steps to be undertaken. A sequence of statements can be prepared and stored, and these are executed automatically by the command processor. The effect is to offer similar design and programming flexibility to that of a bespoke programmed system. A simple automatic command sequence using dBase 4 is shown in Fig. 12.8.

This command sequence accesses a file called bookfile stored on a floppy disk;

```
*
* a command sequence which lists a file and then lists a
* selection of records in a new sequence
*
use a:bookfile
list author_1,cost,year
sort on cost to c:bookwork
use c:bookwork
list author_1,cost,year for year = 1990
use
erase c:bookwork
*
* end of command sequence
*
```

Figure 12.8   An elementary command sequence in dBase 4

the file is listed in its current sequence showing only three fields: author_1, cost and year. The file is then sorted, with the new sorted file being output temporarily to the hard disk under a new filename: *bookwork*. The sorted file is then listed, but only those records for books published in 1990. Finally the files are disconnected from the system and the temporary sorted work file is deleted.

There are several database packages on the market; of these, dBase from Ashton Tate holds the dominant market position and represents the industry standard. The first database package to appear was dBase 2; this has been replaced over the years by dBase 3, dBase 3+ and dBase 4, each version being more sophisticated than the last, although each is based on the same basic principles. The dominance of this package is rather surprising as it is not the easiest one to use, and it retains a fixed record length which makes some applications a little awkward to design. However, its sophisticated facilities and powerful command language make it the preferred tool of many professional system developers. Other popular database packages include: Dataease, Reflex, Delta 4, Cardbox Plus and Archive.

Choosing between the main package types

The applications which database packages lend themselves to are very varied, and there may be some degree of overlap with spreadsheets, and even with word-processing packages. Lotus 1-2-3 has its own database routines built in, although these are rudimentary compared to a full-blown database package. It is quite easy to maintain simple lists on a word processor provided that not too much processing is expected. Some word processors, such as WORD have built-in sorting and macro routines which make data storage quite straightforward. Which package is suitable for your work? Often, it is clear enough that

Data volumes

	low	high
low	word processor	database
high	spreadsheet	specialist/ dedicated

Processing complexity

Figure 12.9   Choosing a general package for data storage

a certain type of application is directly suited to a certain package type. Sometimes it is not so obvious because the nature of the work is such that two or three package types may be suitable. A rule of thumb is that where there is a large amount of data with not too much data manipulation involved, then a database may be suitable; where there is a relatively small amount of data with substantial manipulation or calculation involved then a spreadsheet may be the first choice. If there is only a small amount of data which does not require much manipulation then a word processor may be best. If the requirement is to process large amounts of data using highly complex selection and processing techniques, then it may be best to look for a dedicated package or even to create software especially for the application. Figure 12.9 summarizes the choices.

Apart from processing involved, there is the nature of the output to be considered. A straightforward tabular report can be achieved on any of the package types. Incorporating substantial text elements and producing awkward or complicated formats is best done on a word processor; spreadsheets are best for producing bar and pie charts and other forms of graphical display. See Chapter 21 for discussion on an expert system which helps to make the choice between packages. Often the user will want the best of all worlds and would like to pass information from one package to another for further processing. Unfortunately this is not always possible and is rarely a straightforward operation because of the lack of compatibility between packages. This problem has given rise to the integrated package.

Integrated general packages

Most users have one or more of the three general packages: spreadsheet, word processor and database. Each package is very good at its own particular job but may not be so good at the other functions. If the user wants to take output from one package and use it as input to another, for example, selecting data from the database and inputting it to the spreadsheet for some calculations, then usually severe problems arise from incompatibility between packages. In an attempt to overcome this problem, Lotus 1-2-3 contains a limited database capability in addition to its spreadsheet and graphics components. This might be regarded as

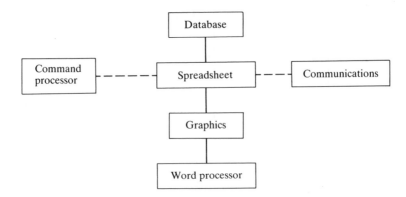

Figure 12.10   Main elements of the integrated general package

the forerunner of the *integrated general package*, which attempts to combine all the general package facilities in one united set. In addition, some packages also integrate other elements such as electronic diary, communications and e-mail facilities; and there may be a command processor in order to build the complex systems of which these packages are capable. A modern integrated package thus combines several facilities in one as shown in Fig. 12.10.

The idea of the integrated package is that the user selects one and buys only one package for all her needs. The user can then easily transfer data from one facility to another, e.g. from the spreadsheet to the word processor, without the compatibility problems inherent in the separate packages. Thus a totally integrated business application might involve the following stages:

1. selecting data from the database;
2. passing it to the spreadsheet to perform what-if calculations
3. graphing the results;
4. building graphed and tabulated results into a report using the word processor;
   and possibly
5. e-mailing the entire report across the world to a colleague in another division of the organization.

A further potential advantage of the integrated package is that command structure, help facilities and documentation can all be of the same format. This can reduce the user's learning time and help to speed application development. Leaders in the market place for integrated packages are Symphony and Framework; other popular packages include Smart, Open Access, Ability and Gem Collection.

Advanced financial modelling packages

One of the great strengths of the spreadsheet is its conceptual simplicity. The format of the spreadsheet closely follows traditional methods of developing financial plans; the matrix of cells clearly defined by rows and columns and the formula directing each cell supply a direct and powerful means of manipulating data. However, although spreadsheets are ideal for developing all kinds of straightforward application, they have limitations for the serious financial modeller. For example, in the input and manipulation of large and complex data structures there are insufficient advanced features, and some types of evaluation such as *sensitivity analysis* are not fully provided. In order to expand his or her scope, the serious financial modeller must look to more comprehensive packages. Because of their extensive storage and computer processing demands financial modelling packages have traditionally been based on mainframes rather than micros, but the increasing memory and power of modern PCs has resulted in some of the recent packages being offered in limited versions for the PC.

A number of advanced packages are currently on the market which are aimed at the specialist financial modeller and offer more advanced features. These advanced packages can be grouped into three broad categories: multidimensional spreadsheets, language processing systems and database financial systems.

MULTIDIMENSIONAL SPREADSHEETS

The standard spreadsheet offers a two-dimensional matrix in which to place data. This is adequate for many applications. In financial modelling it is common to develop a two-dimensional model with time along the top axis (columns) and financial variables along the horizontal axis (rows). The model then needs to be developed for several products or divisions. This can be achieved by copying the matrix several times down the spreadsheets, or by having several different data files; but this is not altogether satisfactory because the manipulation of each matrix must be done separately. The solution is a three-dimensional matrix in which the items in the third dimension can be compared to the leaves of a book. The package provides data input and manipulation facilities which cater specifically for this kind of situation and which make model development much easier. Examples of three-dimensional packages include ReportManager and Boeingcalc and the latest verisions of Lotus. Packages offering even more dimensions are available; for example VP Planner offers five dimensions.

LANGUAGE PROCESSING SYSTEMS

These packages are based around a similar matrix data structure to the spreadsheet, but the processing logic is not confined to formulae that define individual cells. Instead, a high-level programming language is provided which enables far more complex and sophisticated manipulation to be defined than is possible using a spreadsheet. The user develops a program in the language which refers to the matrix of data. The program is then run against the data in the matrix.

The programming logic is completely separate from the data, so that several data sets may be run against the same program, and vice versa. These packages usually offer many more financial and modelling functions than usually found in spreadsheets, including perhaps some of the more exotic operations such as sensitivity and targeting analysis, risk analysis and fuzzy logic. In addition to the data manipulation and analysis features the package may also offer advanced graphics and report building. There are many packages in this general category, examples include: Reveal, FCS, Javelin and Mastermodeller. As a corollary to the extra features these packages have to offer, it must be said that learning to use them and using them effectively is altogether a different matter to using a simple spreadsheet; a substantial time is required to learn how to use them and some knowledge of modelling is required. In addition, most packages in this cateogory cost much more, running into tens of thousands of pounds in some cases.

DATABASE FINANCIAL SYSTEMS

These packages are based on a different type of modelling concept. Instead of specifying the precise form of the model to be developed, it is necessary only to outline its main features: the dimensions, the main data elements and the logic which connects the variables. The logic can usually be specified in a *non-procedural* manner, i.e. the sequence in which the processing logic is specified is not important. Although the data may appear to be held in multidimensional matrix form, the inherent database structure allows any relations among the data to be explored readily. They tend to require specialist systems experts to develop models and, because of the wide range of facilities provided, they are very expensive. These packages are generally suitable for very large corporate users who have massive and complex data sets for analysis. Examples include System W, Express and FCS-Multi.

To some extent, all computer-based information systems provide some assistance to decision-makers. In some systems, particularly of the transactions processing type, the primary focus is not managerial. However, the final part of this chapter considers a family of computer-based systems designed specifically for management use.

Management support

DECISION SUPPORT SYSTEMS

In Chapter 10 we reviewed the range of decision types faced by managers. We highlighted the fact that most managerial decisions, especially those faced by higher-level management, are not amenable to programming. Some of the characteristics of non-programmable decisions are that they are unstructured, uncertain and rely on judgement. This makes computer support more problematic and certainly means that decision-taking is with the computer not

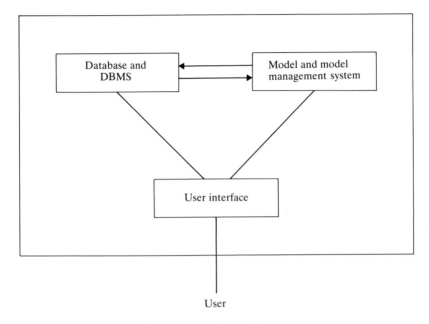

Figure 12.11   Components of a decision support system

by the computer. Thus, while the manager will use the computer-based decision model to assist him or her in completing tasks, no attempt is made to replace the decision-maker. These systems are termed decision support systems (DSS).

Decision support systems have a history of less than 20 years. This recency reflects a number of things: a recognition of the range of managerial tasks, including unstructured ones; that computer support or automation is easier, and the return greater, for high volume transactions processing systems, hence these received first priority; and that the interactive nature of decision support, problem solving with the computer, requires a flexible, user-friendly system. Thus, construction of decision support systems is highly dependent on the technology available. Sprague and Carlson (1982) see decision support systems as 'evolving from the congruence of information technology and interactive modelling'.

COMPONENTS OF A DECISION SUPPORT SYSTEM

Every decision support system has three essential components. These are a database, a model-base (decision model), and a user interface (see Fig. 12.11). The user interface is particularly important given the system's nature. The interface will need to take account of the relative skills of the user and system. The concept of complementary intelligence is apposite here: both the system and the user have skills, the system in data-intensive activities, the user in the creative, wider decision activities. There is little to be gained from trying to make either participant perform functions better performed by the other. The user is likely to be the decision-taker. In traditional computer-based systems operators will interact with the system and provide the decision-taker with filtered information; seldom does the decision-taker actually use the computer him- or herself. The reverse is true for DSS. This necessitates a user-friendly interface. Often this is achieved by the use of what has been termed dialogue generation management system (DGMS). According to Turban (1990), the DGMS provides the following characteristics: it can receive and present data in an assortment of formats, using a variety of input devices; it will allow easy access to the database and model-base and facilitate communication between different users.

The database associated with the DSS will be derived primarily from the firm's internal transaction processing and management information system data. However, higher management will need access to information external to the firm. This may be data on competitors, the economy, legal aspects or whatever. The DSS will have to have the ability to integrate both internal and external data in order to make strategic decisions. The database will have, as a front-end, a database management system (DBMS) which provides it with the same types of facilities as the DGMS does for the user interface. It will allow flexible access, manipulation and query of the data, while maintaining the integrity of the database.

The heart of the decision support system is the model-base. This allows analysis of the database to give forecasts and insights into future scenarios. The model may be relatively simple, perhaps a rolling cash flow forecast with what-if capability, or it may be extremely complex, consisting of a large optimization financial model. Whatever engine drives the DSS, it needs to be usable by the manager, often in decision situations which require rapid analysis and action. In such a case a simple, highly aggregated overview of the organization may be necessary, rather than a detailed analysis, product-line by product-line, or unit by unit.

These two roles for DSS—supporting one-off decisions and frequently made decisions—have been termed *ad hoc* and institutional. Institutional problems are those that reoccur (hence, are, to some extent, programmable). Given that they reoccur, they can be anticipated and it is worth building a model to address them. *Ad hoc* problems, as the name implies, cannot be anticipated and they do not reoccur sufficiently frequently to be modelled. *Ad hoc* problems test the DSS and user abilities much more than institutional ones. The ease of construction and use is vital here if they are going to be built rapidly, often by a user who has poor computing skills. Institutional DSS, on the other hand, can be built by professional DSS staff, utilizing a tried and tested method (perhaps, the systems development life cycle approach or rapid prototyping).

GROUP DECISION SUPPORT SYSTEMS

Very recently the idea of supporting group decision processes rather than individual decision-taking has been seriously addressed. Management is often team-based: task groups are assembled to tackle major issues. Even if this is not the case, the ultimate decision-taker will usually have subordinates, from whom he or she will get advice and inputs, and superiors, to whom he or she will have to 'sell' the decision. This will constitute an informal group. Early DSS were constructed with an individual decision-taker in mind; support of group processes may not be achieved with the same type of system.

Groups taking decisions differ from individuals in a number of respects. The group will have more, and more varied, knowledge and information. It will have more points of view, opinions and a wider range of self-interests. Group decision-taking may have to rely on negotiation and discussion to reach a consensus on what action to take. A group decision support system will need to allow all members of the group to interact with the models and data available, to see what other users are doing, to integrate multiple viewpoints and to try to aggregate these in order to present outputs. There may need to be procedures for resolving conflict by comparing alternatives put forward or by allowing participants to vote.

Group DSS have tended to consist of a physical location in which all group members have the facilities mentioned above. However, there is no reason why, with suitable communications facilities, participants cannot be in different physical locations and even different time zones. By sharing members' thoughts and proposals, the participants can be involved frequently, over a long time period. Essentially this will become a sort of Delphi solution where participants iteratively solve a problem by successively incorporating their own and others' ideas and information into their solutions.

EXECUTIVE INFORMATION SYSTEMS

Most recent in technology to support managerial tasks are executive information systems (EIS). It is not clear if these offer managers anything new, or if it is just that the technology is now available to give executives the facilities always promised by management information systems. EIS are a computer-based means by which information can be accessed, created and delivered for use by senior executives who have little computing experience. The information will be available on-demand, at whatever level of detail is deemed appropriate by the user. This latter aspect is known as drilling-down. The user can review data at increasing levels of detail to locate problem areas within the business. For example, an executive may review data at company level and identify a potential problem with one division. Reviewing that division reveals problems at one factory, but not at the other three; further analysis of that factory may reveal problems only in one product line or even one substantial order.

The information can be displayed in a variety of formats reflecting the users' cognitive preferences. As we saw in Part One, people favour information of different types; some may prefer coloured, graphical exhibits, other textual, or indeed, a mix of the two. The EIS should have the capability to deliver information in the form most useful to the decision-taker. As with decision support systems, executive information systems allow access to external data sources in addition to the internal database.

A number of reasons have been put forward for the lack of computer use by senior management. These include: time pressure, the tendency for executives to have subordinates whose job it is to seek information, and the development of managers' interpersonal networks of contracts which are an information source and means of dissemination. These networks may rely more on informal rather than formal information systems within the organization. According to Long (1987), the emphasis and benefit of EIS is in problem-finding not problem-solving. EIS are the latest in a long line of decision technology, which has sought to emphasize the managerial rather than the technical aspects. The extent to which the case is true for EIS is not proven. Too few working systems exist, and those that do have no real track record. It should also be borne in mind that the costs of providing executive information systems is high: figures of up to £500 000 are not atypical.

Most companies using executive information systems have developed them in-house, but there are a number of commercial vendors offering essentially EIS shells. The products available include Commander-EIS, Resolve and EIS-Epic. One role that EIS may fulfil is as the front-end to a decision support system.

Decision support systems, group decision support systems and executive information systems should all be thought of as a family of tools, designed to help higher level management tackle unstructured decisions. Increasingly, these systems together with expert systems (discussed in Chapter 21) will tend to merge into a single management support tool, utilizing whatever facilities are needed for the decision in hand.

Summary

Software packages largely remove the need for computer users to become familiar with programming languages. These packages proliferate, being available for almost every mainstream business function. There may, however, be occasions when packaged software is not the best choice. The three major pieces of general purpose software are word processors, spreadsheets and databases; most businesses would have at least two of these products. More sophisticated business might need advanced financial modelling tools. For tackling non-programmable tasks, managers may need to use decision support systems, or executive information systems.

KEY TERMS   Audit trail   Automatic command processor   Bill of materials processing (BOMP)   Boilerplate   Cell formula   Command language   Context-sensitive help   Data matrix   Database financial systems   Decision support system   Dedicated packages   Desk-top publishing (DTP)   Economic

order quantity (EOQ) Executive information system Exponential smoothing
Free stock level Fuzzy logic General-purpose packages Group decision
support systems Integrated accounts package Integrated general package
Kerning Language processing systems Mailmerge Material requirements
planning (MRP) Multidimensional spreadsheets Non-procedural programming Pareto or ABC analysis Relational database Replication Report
writer Risk analysis Sensitivity and target analysis Spreadsheet What-if
analysis WYSIWYG Vendor support.

Further reading

Bryant J.W., *Financial Modelling in Corporate Management*, 2nd edition, Wiley, New
    York, 1987.
Cretien P.D., Ball S.E. and Brigham E.F., *Financial Management with LOTUS 1-2-3*,
    Dryden Press, New York, 1987.
Lewis C., *Managing With Micros*, Basil Blackwell, Oxford, 1988.
Long R., *New Office Technology: Human and Managerial Implications*, Croom Helm,
    London, 1987.
Liskin M., *dBase IV Made Easy*, Osborne/McGraw-Hill, Berkeley, California, 1989.
Martin J. and McClure C., Buying software off the rack, *Harvard Business Review*,
    Nov.–Dec., pp. 32–60, 1983.
Sprague R.H. and Carlson E., *Building Effective Decision Support Systems*, Prentice Hall,
    Englewood Cliffs, N.J., 1982.
Turban E., *Decision Support and Expert Systems: Managerial Perspectives*, Macmillan,
    New York, 1988.

Summary to Part Three

Part Three has looked at the software side of information systems. This,
together with the hardware aspects considered in Part Two, form the non-
human side of information systems. Software has been analysed on three levels:
systems software, programming languages and applications software. Nearly all
business computer systems will consist of software of all three types. It is
important to recognize how the software categories overlay and interact with
each other.

PART FOUR

Systems development

13

Background to systems development

Systems development involves analysing information needs and deciding what kind of computer system is needed, creating a detailed design of how the system is to work and agreeing this with user departments, developing and testing software and then implementing the new system in an organizational setting. To be truly successful, the approach adopted must do far more than simply develop or buy in software. The successful development and implementation of computer-based information systems is one of the most challenging jobs management can undertake. Success often eludes even the most experienced and skilful of systems practitioners, and the history of business computing is littered with projects which have overrun on costs, on time, or have failed to achieve their design objectives.

Systems design and programming are essentially craft skills, carried out by individuals who usually work to predefined specifications. Where the system under development is a large one, many people with different specialisms will be working in teams and the problems are even further compounded. At the end of the day, a new system has to be incorporated into the working fabric of an organization; this may demand that complex social changes occur. Problems with computer-based systems arise because of the need to predefine objectives, the time-lag between system definition and implementation and because of the inherent inflexibility of computer systems once a design has been implemented. In contrast, manual systems can be quickly and easily developed and altered because people can readily adapt to changing circumstances, and can 'make do and mend' in order to make systems work.

Experience in managing the complexity of large-scale systems development has resulted in the development of methods for overcoming these difficulties; over the years a number of principles, practices and techniques have been evolved which are used to manage and control the systems development process.

People involved in systems development

Ideas for new systems can come from several sources. Most often, functional departments detect situations where computers may help the operations of the firm, or where improved management information could help in decision-making. The IS department itself may suggest new systems, perhaps to take advantage of opportunities arising from new technology. Senior management may also initiate new systems as a result of strategic decisions about new business activities or in response to perceived competitive pressures.

Traditional systems development is usually undertaken by the organization's IS department, acting on behalf of the functional group who will eventually take over and use the new system. Other approaches are also evident; for example, end-user computing (EUC), whereby non-specialists design and implement their own systems independently, is playing an increasing role. But most large development projects follow a traditional pattern involving professional specialists. *Systems analysts* from the IS department will discuss information needs with potential users of the new system, and will design in outline a computer-based system with them. Detailed *system specifications* will be passed to *applications programmers* who turn the specifications into working software which can be tested. See Chapter 17 for a list of information systems people and their roles. Management from the IS department allocate people resources and coordinate systems and programming effort; managers from user departments discuss and agree objectives and liaise with the IS department. Senior management also are involved in agreeing objectives and deciding on the allocation of IS resources. At various times, other people and groups may be involved. For example, staff union representatives are consulted about any changes which affect staff jobs, and various professional and technical experts may be consulted.

The detailed work involved in analysing, designing and programming computer-based solutions is often undertaken by a project team made up of IS staff (systems analysts and programmers) together with user staff from the relevant business areas. The mix of skills required in the team will vary depending on the project. With large projects there may be several teams working simultaneously on different aspects of the same project.

Managing a systems development project: the steering committee

Because systems development involves many people, and people from different backgrounds and disciplines, there is great scope for problems to occur due to a lack of communication and coordination. One common solution is to form a *steering committee*, whose task is to agree overall objectives for the project and to oversee and monitor progress. The steering committee will consist of representatives from interested groups, and will be chaired by a senior manager who has overall responsibility for the success of the project. The steering committee is not involved in detailed, day-to-day management of the project but in overall objective setting and task coordination. It reviews overall progress and decides whether the project should proceed to the next phase; formal approval to proceed is given at various key stages of the project. One of the first tasks of the steering committee is to specify *terms of reference* for the project. The terms of reference document acts as a concise statement of the agreed intentions of the project. The document contains an outline of the principal objectives and scope of the project, the main benefits and costs expected, and an overall time plan for completion.

KEY TERMS   Applications programmers   Steering committee   System specifications   Systems analysts   Terms of reference.

Further reading

Senn J.A., Essential principles of systems development, *MIS Quarterly*, **2**(2), 17–26, 1978.

14
The systems development life cycle

Information systems proceed through several distinct phases, from initiation through development to implementation and review. There are distinct go or no-go decisions to be made at the end of each stage, when the steering committee formally approves progression to the next step. Large-scale projects usually go through several discrete phases; smaller projects may be run less formally, and some phases may be combined, or shortened. The activities in each stage (and the terminology used) differ slightly from organization to organization, and from one textbook to another; but the essential features and sequence of events are the same. New software tools and system development methods offer alternatives to the traditional systems life cycle. Nevertheless, most medium- to large-scale systems projects are still developed along classical lines and show the stages outlined.

The principal phases of the systems life cycle, together with the outputs from each phase, are shown in Fig. 14.1.

Key events during the development life cycle:

1. terms of reference issued by steering committee;
2. feasibility report findings agreed, and approval for system study;
3. statement of system requirements agreed;
4. testing complete and implementation timing agreed;
5. post-implementation review undertaken.

Feasibility study

The first stage of any major project is to undertake a brief, but careful, analysis of the situation, sometimes referred to as a 'quick and dirty' study in order to determine whether it is worth while to proceed. This study is intended to help management decide whether it is worth committing organizational resources to

Life cycle phase	Phase output
feasibility study	feasibility report
systems study	requirements analysis
systems design	system specifications
system development	tested software
implementation	working system
review	evaluation report

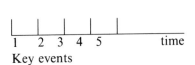

1 2 3 4 5   time

Key events

Figure 14.1 Systems development life cycle

this project, or whether the resources might be employed more usefully elsewhere. Large development projects may take up many person-years of specialist effort, to say nothing of general management and user time, and this may represent a very substantial cost to the organization. On the other hand, the costs of not proceeding (and perhaps losing competitive advantage) or of proceeding on the wrong basis can also prove massively costly. The feasibility study is undertaken precisely in order to avoid these dangers. The study is usually performed by a small team of experienced analysts who have proven skills and judgement in the field of business systems analysis.

The main object is to estimate, to a reasonable degree of accuracy, the principal costs and benefits that would be incurred if the main project were to proceed. *Cost/benefit analysis* shows relevant, feasible alternatives in terms of the major costs that will be incurred during the development and running of the system, together with the major benefits that are expected to accrue (Table 14.1). The feasibility study will look only at the major costs and benefits, and at the principal alternatives. More detailed analyses are performed in the main systems study phase.

There are a number of assumptions behind cost/benefit analysis:

1. that all feasible alternatives have been examined;
2. that all costs and benefits can be identified and measured;
3. that the costs and benefits can be expressed in common (usually financial) units.

In practice, these assumptions will rarely hold good and managerial judgement is required in order to incorporate varying elements of the analysis into the decision process. Comparisons between costs and benefits and between feasible alternatives which show benefits over time are usually made using *discounted cash flow (DCF)* or *internal rate of return (IRR)* methods. It is impossible to

Table 14.1 Cost/benefit analysis: examples of categories that might be considered

System costs	System benefits
Costs of implementation: development staff time user staff time staff training hire of additional staff data conversion equipment upgrade/purchase packaged software consultancy charges	*Data processing cost reduction:* reduced staff wage costs reduced staff overheads consumables savings (stationery)
Costs of system operation: data preparation consumables computer time software maintenance equipment maintenance operations staff internal program maintenance	*Decision enhancement/automation:* reduced stock wastage/losses reduced stockholding costs improved sales improved profitability reduced production costs improved cash flow

do every thing at once; choosing between several potential IS applications is a challenging management decision.

Apart from the financial variables there will be a number of intangibles: these are costs or benefits that may be very important, but that are difficult or impossible to quantify accurately. Examples are listed below. Customer satisfaction may be a very real and important benefit, but it can be very difficult to measure satisfactorily in the context of an information systems study. Many of the *benefits* of information systems are intangibles (and often the benefits are realized only over lengthy time-scales) and this makes evaluating information systems proposals very difficult. Examples are:

- improved planning
- improved operations
- improved information flow
- improved decision-making
- improved employee relations
- improved employee morale
- improved customer relations
- improved corporate image

On the other hand, the *costs* of the new systems in terms of equipment and staff training may be highly tangible and obvious, and may occur as 'up-front' charges which have to be borne before the systems can commence operation.

The output of the study will be a *feasibility report* which will contain an outline of the present system and information requirements, an outline of the proposed new system highlighting costs and benefits to be expected in terms of tangibles and intangibles, and an analysis of the likely time-scale of the project. At this point the steering committee, in conjuction with senior management, decide whether or not to proceed with the next phase of the project. This is a vital decision because the next phase involves investing substantial effort in a major investigation.

The systems study

The systems study is the major investigatory phase of the systems life cycle. It is usually undertaken by a team of systems analysts, often acting with representatives from user departments. The study is trying to establish answers to two basic questions about the operations of that part of the organization defined in the terms of reference: what exactly is happening now, and what should be done in future? The detailed questions that must be asked include the following:

- What are the objectives of the present system(s), and what are the results?
- What are the present inputs and outputs?
- What information is currently produced, and how is it used?
- What are the present weaknesses, problems and drawbacks (and strengths)?
- How *should* the system(s) perform?
- What information should be produced, and who should use it?

The results of this study are detailed in a report which includes the *statement of requirements*. This document describes the present situation in detail, then analyses the objectives for the new system and develops a detailed specification of *what* the new system is to do (although it may not at this stage specify in detail exactly *how* things are to be done). Since the systems study provides the basis for the design work that follows, the success of the entire project will depend crucially on the skill with which the study is completed. Also, at this stage, it is possible to produce a cost/benefit analysis which shows more detail than that produced in the feasibility study. The completion of this phase represents another major decision point, and the steering committee will review the resulting documents with great care.

The essence of the systems study is to achieve a thorough and insightful understanding of the existing organization and systems. In order to perform the systems study successfully, the study team must undertake a significant information-gathering effort. The results must be documented accurately (and in detail) in order to provide a sound basis for creative and successful systems design. A number of traditional information-gathering methods are employed which can include the following:

1. consulting existing documentation, paperwork and records,
2. questionnaire surveys,
3. interviews,
4. observation.

1. EXISTING DOCUMENTATION

Existing documentation provides a useful starting point in systems analysis. Organization charts, job descriptions and specifications give indications on organizational structures and the personnel roles involved in the present system. Procedure manuals, transaction data, reports, files and memos provide detail on how tasks are performed. Operating statistics, cost data and performance reports give information about current system volumes and costs. Studying existing records is straightforward, but unfortunately the information is often incomplete, out-of-date and inaccurate. This is an unfortunate, but inevitable aspect of systems investigation. Often, crucial information exists only in people's heads and must be discovered by other methods.

2. QUESTIONNAIRES

Questionnaires represent an efficient means of gathering information from a large number of people. Indeed, it may be the only feasible method if hundreds of people are involved, or they are geographically remote. For questionnaires to be effective they must be very carefully planned; questions need to be straightforward and unambiguous, and it is surprisingly easy to ask biased, misleading or confusing questions which are misunderstood by respondents or are answered in different ways. Designing and testing a suitable questionnaire demands expertise, and can be very time-consuming. Another problem concerns response rates. Unless there is a real incentive to respond, the analyst may find that only a small proportion of his or her survey population returns the questionnaire; in this case the sample may be biased, and not representative of the population as a whole. A compromise method involves researchers visiting respondents in order to ask the questions contained in the questionnaire; this overcomes some of the difficulties mentioned, but obviously increases the costs enormously. Where the pitfalls can be avoided, the standardized responses from a questionnaire are usually very suitable for computer processing and analysis, and evaluating the results of the survey can be quite straightforward compared to other methods.

3. INTERVIEWS

The personal interview is a major source of information for systems studies. Unlike methods 1 and 2, the interview enables open-ended questions to be discussed, and permits problems and difficulties to be resolved at once. The interview can address subtle issues and can provide in-depth materials on all aspects of the system and its environment. Interviews are often the main source for key insights into the working practices of an organization, and allow differing, perhaps conflicting, viewpoints to emerge. The main drawback with the interview technique is the time involved. Interviews usually last between half an hour and an hour, and there is also the set-up time and subsequent data analysis to be considered. There are different formats for interviewing: structured and semi-structured techniques may be employed, and to a large extent the success of the technique may depend on the individual skill of the interviewer (and also on how articulate the respondent is). Unless the interview is fully structured, in which case it may be just a convenient way of administering a questionnaire, the interviewer must either take a detailed set of notes or use a tape recorder. Analysing the interviewee's statements afterwards is time-consuming and may prove difficult. Clearly, interviewing is far more costly per capita than methods 1 and 2. The method is best employed where crucial, in-depth information is required from a few key personnel; it is obviously essential where information for management decision-making is a required output from the system.

4. OBSERVATION

Observation provides a different perspective on organizational systems. However knowledgeable and articulate respondents may be, they are providing their own unique perception of the state of affairs in a certain set of circumstances. There are a number of reasons why people may distort reported reality, whether this is done unwittingly or not. Actual observation of the situation by the systems analyst can provide vital insights on what happens, and often on those events about which it is hard to acquire information: mistakes, bottlenecks, interruptions and peaks and troughs in workload may be hard to describe, or may not be mentioned in interviews. Direct observation can show a system operating in normal circumstances, warts and all. There are drawbacks to direct observation, just as with any research method. Firstly, observation can be time-consuming and hence costly. Secondly, people behave differently when they know they are being observed; as with research methods in other areas of science, the observer affects the situation being observed. Finally, people may resent being watched; however carefully the situation is explained, some people may regard it as 'spying' and be antagonized.

Although the four methods described above are traditionally employed to elicit information about current systems and future needs, it has been recognized that there are limitations to these straightforward information-gathering strategies. The traditional methods are appropriate where there is a high degree of structure in the system under investigation, i.e. where the system objectives are clear cut and well understood, and where the operation of the system follows some well-defined framework. But not all systems can be so clearly defined.

In order to involve people more actively in design considerations and in order to stimulate broader and less inhibited thinking about information system solutions, group discussions with users can be useful. Discussion groups, or forums, need to be carefully planned and led by people who have skills in group work and who can gain the respect and trust of group members. Techniques which have been found successful include open discussions, brainstorming, group consensus and Delphi methods. The idea is to liberate opinions and encourage different, and perhaps outlandish, suggestions in order to achieve new and creative solutions to organizational problems. Apart from encouraging idea generation, the participation of users at the design phase of the system project is usually a vital precondition of successful system implementation.

The information derived from the fact-finding phase forms a detailed description of the current system. Recording this information calls for standardized methods. A *narrative* description is used to outline the main elements of a system, and discuss complex issues which arise during its operation. Several shorthand techniques can be used to record information accurately in a standardized way and this helps with later analysis. *Organization charts, job description forms* and *staff utilization documents* are used to record details of people and their roles in the system. *File description* and *record description* documents can be used to describe the use of paperwork in the system. *Data analysis* is a systems design technique which focuses closely on the movements and usage of data as it moves around the organization; this technique is best employed on operational-level systems such as accounting and order processing. A convenient and accurate method of recording the behaviour of the system in terms of its procedures is the *system flowchart* (Fig. 14.2). The essence of the flowchart is that the symbols represent processes, decisions and information media; and the connecting lines mark the *flow of information* between processes.

Where multiple and complex decisions occur during the processing steps of a system, then these can be recorded conveniently using *decision tables*; an example is shown in Fig. 14.3. The top half of the decision table identifies the conditions and the values of each condition, while the lower half identifies possible actions and the actions to be taken under the conditions given above.

Not all systems development is concerned with the operational level of the organization. An increasingly important sector of systems development is concerned with decision-making at higher management levels, and recent developments in executive information systems (EIS) indicate that even the most senior managers can make use of interactive computer-based information. Analysing information requirements for these higher levels involves skilful discussions with the managers involved, together with an assessment of the organization's *critical success factors* to establish key information categories.

As a result of the system investigation, an accurate picture of the current system can be built up and documented. The objective of the system study is to develop a *statement of requirements* which details what the new system should do, in terms of what information should be produced, who needs it, in what form, and when. This is a crucial phase of the systems development project; errors here will result in the subsequent systems development effort being expended in the wrong direction. The statement of requirements is developed partly as a result of the detailed analysis of the existing systems, partly by analysis of agreed objectives for the system and partly by discussions with people about their information needs. To some extent this analysis occurs as the

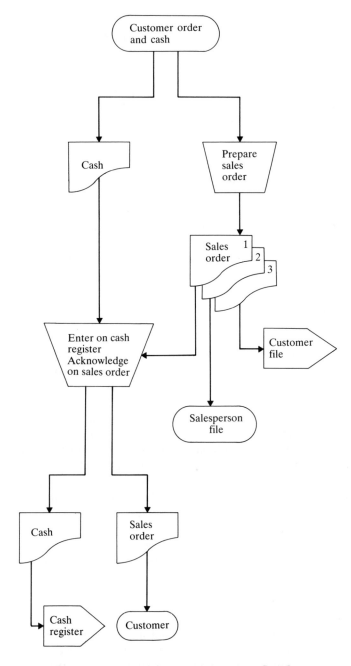

Figure 14.2   Manual order entry system flowchart

PRINTER SELECTION

CONDITIONS	DECISION RULES			
	1	2	3	4
WIDE CARRIAGE	Y	Y	N	N
PRINTS NLQ	Y	Y	N	Y
PORTABLE	Y	N	N	Y
BUY PRINTER	X	X		
DON'T BUY			X	X

Figure 14.3   Part of a decision table

old system is being investigated; also to a certain degree there will be discussion and negotiation with people as to the extent of their needs.

System analysis and design is not yet a science (and perhaps it may never become one), instead it is at least partly a matter of experience and judgement. There is no doubt that experienced and skilled systems analysts produce better systems, no matter how advanced the systems techniques employed, and that possessing a facility for interacting with people successfully may be at least as important a qualification for a systems analyst as detailed technical knowledge. Systems analysis must consider not only the goals to be achieved, but also the inevitable economic, technical and human constraints that exist.

Human and organizational issues must be very carefully considered. Often, organizational goals are unclear and there may be groups of people, and individuals, who disagree about methods and conclusions. Reconciliation of conflicting viewpoints and interests is an essential part of the development process. It is often the case that the analysis and design of a new system is an opportunity to review organizational objectives and to improve and alter the way in which the organization operates. Imaginative and clear-sighted solutions that cut across existing views are often called for. Clearly, the tasks involved in systems development are not merely technical ones, and the skills of the systems analyst must be as much human as technological.

Once the statement of requirements has been agreed by system users, managers and other interested parties, it can be formally reviewed by the steering committee; this stage represents another crucial go or no-go decision point in the development cycle.

Systems design

Systems design is the process of planning and specifying how the new system is to achieve the functions, outputs and operational performance described in the statement of requirements. It involves devising in detail the methods and solutions which deliver the required functions and outputs to the users. Whereas the preceding analysis phase concentrated on what the system should do, the design phase concentrates on how the system should work and what methods should be employed. The results of this phase include a detailed *systems specification* which will form the basis for programming; it also includes detailed specifications for database design, any necessary hardware enhancements, telecommunications requirements, and security and control methods.

The factors that should be taken into account in system design choices are wide ranging including the following:

- information requirements and preferences of users;
- system performance and reliability requirements;
- implementation time-scale;
- system flexibility and maintenance characteristics;
- management style and organizational culture.

It is unlikely that there will be only one way of achieving the purposes set out in the statement of requirements. Instead, systems analysts provide outline designs for several feasible system alternatives in order to evaluate these for decision. Cost/benefit analyses are performed on likely options and it is then a managerial decision as to what option shows the best mix of costs, benefits, advantages, disadvantages and preferred time-scale.

Involvement of system users in system design has long been called for. It has been shown in a number of studies that where users participate fully and realistically in systems design, then the resulting systems are far more likely to reflect users' real needs and priorities and system implementation is far more likely to be successful. The classic non-participative approach has been called the 'hit and run' method. According to this model, the analyst appears in front of the user, asks mysterious questions about the user's job and takes notes; the analyst then disappears back to his or her office and designs the system alone. Some time later a completed system is presented to the user as a *fait accompli*, on a 'take it or leave it' basis. Clearly in these circumstances the user has had no chance to ask questions, to understand what the new system means, or to improve his or her knowledge about how the new system will work. Most importantly, the user has not been able to contribute to the design from his or her own knowledge and experience of the real workings of the system. The issue of 'system ownership' is important; if users feel that they have made key choices and that the new system contains their ideas, then the system is truly 'theirs' and there is an increased commitment to implement it and run it successfully. Inevitably there are additional costs and drawbacks in a fully participative approach, for example, involving more people in systems design involves much more discussion, communication and education and all this takes time and involves extra costs. Achieving a successful balance between these factors is another key management task.

The basic technical components of system design include the following items:

1. selection of system type,
2. design of outputs,

3. design of files and database,
4. design of processing operations,
5. design of inputs.

It is, of course, necessary to specify the outputs in some detail *before* considering the data and file structures that must produce them; the data structures must be determined before the processing methods can be defined, and only then can the system inputs be defined. The sequence of events shown below is deliberately ordered back-to-front to reflect the natural sequence.

SELECTION OF SYSTEM TYPE: BATCH OR REAL-TIME MODE

Some systems can operate most efficiently when data is collected together in bulk and processed in one computer run. These systems are referred to as *batch systems* because the input data volumes are split into batches for easier control. Typically, these systems are run at regular intervals, perhaps weekly or monthly; examples include payroll, monthly accounting routines and regular management information reporting. Because data is collected together and processed at a certain time, these systems are called *time-driven systems*.

Alternatively, some systems receive data inputs which are instantly processed against master-files to give immediate response to users. These are called *real-time systems*, because the system responds immediately to events as and when they occur. Since these systems are available to process a transaction whenever it might occur, they are referred to as *event-driven systems*.

In order for a system to respond in real-time it is necessary for the master-files to be available (i.e. on-line to the computer) continuously in order to process input data whenever it occurs (Fig. 14.4). Examples of real-time systems include flight booking systems, automatic bank cash point machines, customer order processing and enquiry systems, and many other systems designed to provide instant information.

An *interactive system* is one in which the user can undertake a genuine dialogue with the system. Word processing is truly interactive because the user

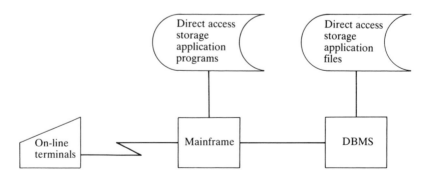

Figure 14.4 Components of a real-time processing system

enters data, the computer responds directly and immediately, and the user is able to monitor the response and amend the result with a great deal of flexibility. Most on-line business systems are interactive to some extent, but the amount of true interaction possible is usually strictly limited because of the processing burden involved. For example, an on-line order processing system may be installed on a mini-computer with twenty terminals providing on-line enquiry and order entry. The nature of the system requires that the terminals access the same master-files (customer records and stock levels, for example) simultaneously. In order for the computer to cope with the hundreds of transactions that may occur in a minute, complex software is required which can allow multiple file processing to occur without contention or error. In these circumstances, the system responses must be kept simple in order not to overburden the processor and cause unacceptable response delays.

There is usually not a straightforward dichotomy between batch and on-line systems; these represent types at either end of a continuum, and systems often possess elements of both. For example, a sales ledger system may process input transactions on a daily batch basis but enable on-line enquiry to customer account details throughout the day. Batch systems are generally suitable where there are large volumes of data to be processed, and where processing efficiency is more important than immediate output timing. On-line systems are usually employed where transaction volumes are not too great and where immediate reponse is desirable.

The choice of whether to process data in real-time or batch mode often involves deciding how important it is that an immediate computer response is really necessary. An on-line system will be far more expensive than an equivalent batch system in terms both of computer capacity and development costs. This is because all the data files must be continually on-line at all times, and because the software required to handle the transactions is far more complex than that associated with batch systems.

However, the continuing reduction in the real costs of computing owing to improvements in hardware technology, together with the advent of improved software packages, means that the on-line option is more and more likely to be chosen. There can be little doubt that interactive systems can offer far more processing capability than batch systems, and it is likely that in the future batch systems will tend to be used only where the efficient processing of very large data volumes is the prime consideration.

DESIGN OF OUTPUTS

Output design involves choosing an appropriate output medium, be it tabulated report, graph, microfilm or interactive display (see Chapter 7), and then planning the contents and formats so that it is suitable for the recipient. The statement of requirements should already indicate the *information* content needed; now, the analyst, in consultation with users, must plan the detail of how that information should be presented. Should the information be presented in the form of a report? If so, how often is it to be produced, and when? Should it be produced on an exceptional basis? Exactly which data items should be included, and what sequence should they have? The layout of the output can be a crucial factor in the usefulness of the information produced. Studies of human information processing indicate that individuals have preferences towards certain styles of information display, and these should be catered for where possible.

The following items must be considered in detail:

- output medium,
- output frequency and timing,
- exception reporting,
- output contents and sequence,
- output format and presentation.

The output from interactive systems is intricately bound up with the input from the user, because both occur at the same time; in this case, design considerations are discussed in terms of *dialogue design*.

DESIGN OF FILES AND DATABASES

Accurate decisions on file structures and processing methods have a crucial bearing on the efficiency and operation of the resulting system. File design aspects which must be considered in detail include the following:

- conventional or database files,
- file media,
- addressing methods,
- file size,
- file structure,
- fixed/variable record formats,
- hit-rate,
- record layout and blocking factors,
- back-up and security arrangements.

Decisions about the files and record layouts will be arrived at after carefully considering the way that the data is to be processed, the type of access required and the frequency, and expected data volumes.

DESIGN OF PROCESSING OPERATIONS

There are a number of steps which are required for most data processing systems to function properly. The vast majority of basic batch data processing systems can be resolved into a sequence of steps as follows:

- data input validation,
- sorting,
- summarizing,

- file updating,
- output processing.

Firstly, input data has to be *validated*. This involves checking input data for errors, inconsistencies and missing data and shedding any error transactions so that they can be corrected and resubmitted. It makes sense to remove all suspect data as early as possible in the processing cycle, so that programs and processes downstream are not affected by it. The computer can be programmed to check for:

1. *Data presence.* Some data must be present, e.g. employee number for payroll data.
2. *Data format.* Numeric fields, such as cash values, must contain numeric data, not alphameric or special characters.
3. *Size and range.* An account number always has a certain number of characters; range checks look for obviously invalid data, such as employee age under 16 or over 65, or overtime hours greater than, say, 50.
4. *Check-digit codes.* Reference numbers such as account numbers, personnel numbers and product codes can be designed to be self-checking, in that the computer calculates what the check-digit should be for the input reference number and checks this with the number input. Check-digits guard against digit transposition (a very common human error) and other errors.
5. *Master-file presence.* Data on products, customers and employees can be verified against the appropriate master-file to ensure that the transaction refers to a current, valid master-file entry.

Input data documents for batch systems are split into baches of 50 or so transactions to make control and management more easy. It is essential that all data is accounted for, so that it can be proved that all data has been correctly processed. A common way of doing this is to manually add up the key field on each input transaction document—say hours worked for payroll data—to give a total for each batch of data. Any numeric fields can be used for control purposes, such as customer account numbers or document reference numbers; in this case, where the total has no intrinsic meaning, the control figure is called a *hash total*. The data validation program adds up the same data and gives its total for each batch. Where the batch totals agree, then the data within those batches has correctly entered the system. Where the batch totals disagree, the entire batch of data is excluded from the remainder of the processing run while the discrepancy is being investigated.

Input data usually arrives serially, i.e. in no useful sequence. It must be sequenced by sorting into the correct sequence for each stage. The data sorts are usually performed on disk files by proprietary sort software supplied by the computer manufacturer or software supplier.

Perhaps the most common data processing task is that of summarizing data. This involves summing or aggregating data from specified fields for all records within a certain sort category; for example, adding sales values for all records with the same product code to give a product sales analysis. Summarizing within several different levels involves accumulating totals within control breaks defined by the sorting data fields. Summarized results may be printed or stored on new records for onward processing.

File updating involves processing transaction data against a master-file and replacing the contents of update fields with new data based upon the old entry plus the new transaction data. The flowchart example in Fig. 14.5 shows a master-file update for an elementary batch payroll system.

Designing output processing requires designing the calculations and data formatting necessary to present the selected data for output to the chosen medium. It is sometimes possible to merge this function with the file-update part of the system. This will save processing time because files will not have to be reread for the output process alone; however, there is much to be said for keeping these logically separate stages of data processing physically separate in two different programs in order to simplify system changes or updating.

DESIGN OF INPUTS

Designing the input side of the system depends largely on decisions that have already been made about outputs required, files needed and processing steps. Decisions must be made about the following aspects of the system:

- data capture methods and devices,
- frequency and timing,
- optimizing data and preparation,
- input forms and screens,
- on-line dialogues,
- data code design.

The first stage of input design involves choosing suitable data capture methods and devices. Devices and methods were covered in detail in Chapter 7; commonly used methods include: key-to-disk, on-line keyboard entry, optical character recognition and bar coding (Table 14.2). The decision on method revolves around the suitability of the method and its cost in relation to the nature of the data input expected and, in particular, its expected volume. For example, key-to-disk is a flexible method which can be used for many different input purposes; however, it depends upon people manually keying data and is thus error prone and expensive. Key verification may be required, which effectively doubles the preparation time and cost. Some form of optical character recognition, perhaps involving a turnaround document, would eliminate data preparation, but the reading devices are expensive and are therefore economic only where large volumes are expected. The above methods are all essentially off-line methods, which are low on computer resource usage but involve delays before the data is processed. Systems that require immediate reponse to events require on-line input and real-time response; this usually involves a VDU and keyboard, together with mouse, light-pen or other device.

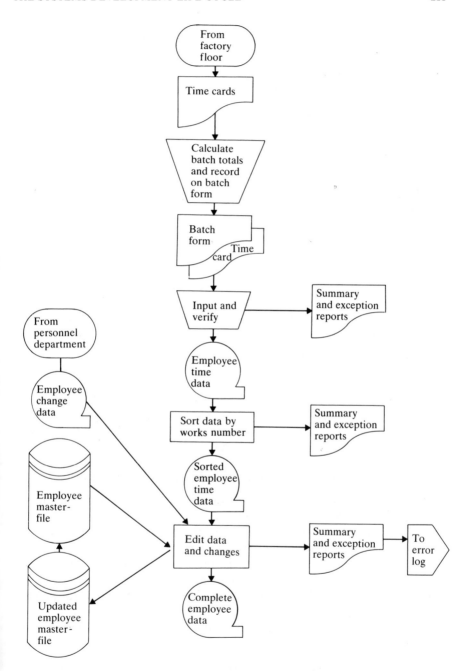

Figure 14.5 Batch payroll system

Table 14.2   Input design: examples of input methods

Application	Data volume	Real-time requirement	Method
payroll hours	high	no	key-to-disk station
insurance premium collection (fixed)	high	no	OCR reader (turnaround)
stock level changes	low	no	key-to-disk station
customer enquiries	low	yes	on-line VDU
stock count	high	no	portable bar code reader

Designing effective input forms and screens which people are to use comfortably and effectively requires considerable care. Forms should be self-instructing (rather than requiring a separate manual or training) and designed so that entering information is straightforward and efficient. The sequence and layout of the form should be carefully chosen for ease of use, and checked with users to ensure that the form achieves its objectives. Specialist software is available that can be used with a PC and laser printer combination to create and manage form designs.

Many information system applications require the creation of codes to identify products, people and events. Customer account numbers, personal ID numbers and payroll numbers, finished goods product codes and supplier references are all examples of reference codes. Codes can serve several different purposes.

Coding systems can be designed to provide the following benefits:

1. *A unique identifier.* There are lots of John Smiths, so distinguishing among them by name alone is not enough.
2. *A shorthand reference.* This avoids having to input a potentially wasteful and inaccurate lengthy description each time a particular product is referred to.
3. *An analysis framework.* Allocating specific groups of codes in a meaningful way provides a means of summarizing data in reports.
4. *A security check.* ID and password codes can be used to prevent unauthorized knowledge of the entities to which the codes refer.
5. *An accuracy check.* Check digits can be added to codes to avoid transcription errors.

There are a number of different coding schemes available. Some commonly used ones include the following:

Sequence codes

Numbers are allocated to entities starting with 0001 and working up; there is no relationship between code and entity to which it refers.

examples:

0001 pencil
0002 ball-point
0003 roller ball

Such a scheme provides no obvious link between a code and the entity; the codes are simply allocated sequentially as new entities occur. The anonymity can be turned to advantage when used as a payroll number, so that pay-slips showing the code only can be printed, and issued to employees so that unauthorized personnel cannot gain knowledge about an individual's pay details.

Group codes

One or more digits are allocated to groups of entities so that the code is meaningful and provides an analysis framework when entities are sorted together on the code sequence.

code structure:

1nn – Northern region salesmen
2nn – Southern region salesmen
3nn – Western region salesmen

examples:

123 – Fred Smith (Northern region)
238 – John Jones (Southern region)

Codes can be made to serve more complex purposes by utilizing significant digits to represent different aspects of the entity. In order to assist interpretation of codes, digits can also be used which directly represent some particular property.

examples:

G3-1500-X refers to a car with a 1500 cc engine
G3-1990-Y refers to a car with a 1990 cc engine

Faceted codes

Each digit or group of digits refers to a class of entity; this makes it possible to identify an item from the code alone. The following example is the code for a clothing item from a West End of London tailor:

SU-M-B-40-12
SU – suit
M – male
B – black
40 – size
12 – fashion line

Of course, mixed numeric and character digits can make codes difficult to memorize and the size of a code and the number of digits or groups also has a direct cognitive link. Human short-term memory can cope with a maximum of seven 'chunks' for a few seconds before the information must be processed and codes which have more than 5 or 6 digits (or short groups) may be difficult to use. LE11 3TU is a postal code; each group is significant and the entire code refers uniquely to an area.

There are many other types of coding system, most of which are combinations of types already discussed. A more specialized system is the Dewey decimal system used in library book cataloguing:

658.4 Henry Mintzberg – The Nature of Managerial Work

In this system the position of the digits is significant, and each digit refers to a classification within a hierarchy, as follows:

600   Technology
650   Business Administration
658   Management
658.4   Executive management

The usefulness of this system to most library users is somewhat doubtful (even librarians make little use of the structure of the code) and it is possible that a straightforward group code would be easier to use and more efficient.

Check digits

These are usually added to the end of the code, which can be of any format. The check digit for any one code is calculated from the code itself.

customer account number: 51934

In this example, 5193 is the basic code and 4 is the calculated check digit. There are many ways of creating check digits; one simple method is called the modulus 11 check digit. Using this method, each digit has a weight as follows:

code: 5193

weights   5432

Each digit is multiplied by its weight and the answers are summed. The sum is divided by 11, and the remainder is subtracted from 11 to give the check digit (the dividend is ignored):

multiply weights and sum: $(5 \times 5) + (1 \times 4) + (9 \times 3) + (3 \times 2) = 62$

divide sum by 11 and take remainder: $62/11 = 5$ remainder 7

subtract remainder from 11: $11 - 7 = 4$

When the code is written down, the check digit is written with it as part of the code; on input to the computer the code is re-calculated, and the calculated check digit compared with the one received. Any discrepancy points to an error in the code. The check digit is useful as a guard against human transposition and transcription errors (research indicates that these two account for a large proportion of input errors in codes). Taking the account number 51934 and accidentally transposing two digits might give:

customer account number: 59134

Calculating the check digit for this code gives 7, which shows that the code is wrong; the computer can report this, and human intervention is then necessary to examine the error and correct the transposition. There is only a one-in-ten chance that an error in one digit will result in a valid check digit.

DEVELOPING ON-LINE SYSTEMS

Real-time systems require an altogether different design from batch systems, although the approach is much the same. A batch system allows for data to be passed in bulk sequentially from one process to another, until the data has passed through all stages. Real-time systems may have similar data processing requirements but necessitate immediate response to individual input transactions whenever these occur. The emphasis is therefore on speed of response. A response time of more than a few seconds is usually too great and causes user dissatisfaction. Fast response times require suitable hardware and suitable software techniques acting in harmony. Figure 14.6 overleaf shows a flowchart for an elementary on-line system.

The flowchart shows a system which handles on-line entry of customer orders. The operator takes the order over the phone and enters data which he or she prompts from the customer. Customer details are entered and these are checked immediately against the customer master-file. As each product line is entered, the system checks the stock master-file for sufficient stock and updates the balance; if the product is not in stock the operator suggests alternatives to the customer. After the product lines have been entered, the operator keys an order-complete code and the system produces a delivery note at once which acts as a trigger for the despatch of goods. The program which achieves these activities is clearly far more complex than those for the corresponding batch system, requires far more main storage and calls for faster processing times to provide a speedy response time.

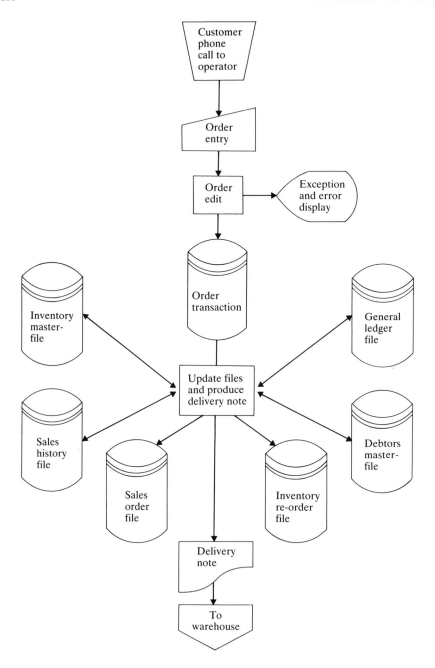

Figure 14.6   On-line order entry system

Summary

This chapter has introduced the systems development life cycle: a structured method for building and implementing new systems. The life cycle breaks such development into discrete stages which are addressed sequentially. The feasibility study establishes the desirability or not to proceed with the project. The systems study investigates the requirements of the proposed system and the abilities of the current system, if any. Systems design plans and specifies how the proposed system will perform in order to meet requirements.

KEY TERMS   Batch systems   Cost/benefit analysis   Decision tables   Dialogue design   Discounted cash flow (DCF)   Event-driven system   Feasibility report   Hash total   Interactive system   Internal rate of return (IRR) Modulus 11 check digit   Real-time systems   Statement of requirements System flowchart   System maintenance   Time-driven systems.

Further reading

Beizer B., *Software System Testing and Quality Assurance*, Reinhold, New York, 1984.
Connor D., *Information System Specification and Design Road Map*, Prentice-Hall International, Englewood Cliffs, New Jersey, 1985.
Eliason A.L., *Online Business Computer Applications*, SRA, Chicago, 1987.
Opperman R., User participation: some experiences and recommendations, *Systems Objectives Solutions*, **4**(3), 157–168, 1984.
Saldarini R.A., *Analysis and Design of Business Information Systems*, Macmillan, New York, 1989.
Senn J., *Analysis and Design of Information Systems*, McGraw-Hill, New York, 1984.

15
System development control and management

Software development and testing

The translation of detailed system design specifications that have been agreed with users into fully functional, tested software is a crucial stage of the development process. Creating software is a major activity and there are a number of options to be considered. Choices among high- and low-level programming languages, 4GLs and packages have been discussed in some detail in Chapter 12.

The details of the software development process will depend on the development method chosen, but using a high-level language as an example, the steps involved could take the following form.

1. *Program specification.* With the use of detailed design specifications, program specifications are created; these define the language to be used and all aspects of input, output, files and processing steps for each program, and specify any special attributes such as data restrictions and control checks. The program specifications are prepared in the form of narrative description, decision tables, flowcharts or statements in structured English.
2. *Program coding.* This step involves translating the program specification into high-level language statements. Working from detailed flowcharts or structured English the programmer writes statements on special coding forms in structured format (or according to the organization's house style). The statements are then desk-checked for accuracy and completeness.
3. *Compilation and syntax correction.* The coding forms are entered into the computer and are used as input, called the *source program*, to the high-level language compiler. The compiler automatically checks the statements for syntactical errors (though of course it cannot detect logical errors or omissions) and reports these with a warning message. If there are no fatal errors, the compiler generates an *object program* in machine language; this is

stored on backing media until it is loaded into the computer for testing with input data.

4. *Program testing*. This involves selecting test data which is carefully designed to rigorously check the functions of the program. Data should be chosen to test all usual functions and decision steps, then to check unusual data and boundary conditions, and then to check error detection and fail-safe routines (see the section on software quality control, below).

5. *Suite, module and system testing*. Programs usually run in logically connected groups or suites within logical modules. Once individual programs have been checked, they can be run together to verify that the inputs and outputs between programs, and then between suites of programs, are handled satisfactorily. Rigorous software testing is a time-consuming and costly part of the development process; the care with which it is done will be reflected in the degree of satisfaction engendered by the system when operational.

6. *Acceptance testing*. Once the software is deemed to be technically accurate, the system undergoes acceptance testing by users. Systems tests are undertaken and evaluated by users who will eventually formally accept the new system for implementation. This marks another key decision point in the development cycle.

7. *Documentation of programs*. Accurate and complete documentation of software is another vital task. Program maintenance is a time-consuming and costly task at the best of times; if software is poorly documented then the problems involved in amending programs may become all but insurmountable because the software simply cannot be understood. The documentation used in the design and development phases of software development can form the basis of useful program documentation. Some programming languages (RPG for instance) are self-documenting to a certain extent, in that the format of the language enforces a self-explanatory, descriptive style; but most are not. Most programs will require very careful and full descriptions if they are to be understood later by somebody other than the programmer who wrote them.

SOFTWARE QUALITY CONTROL

Software errors can cause major disasters for the organizations that depend upon working systems; even minor hiccups can cause embarrassing delays and may necessitate very costly remedial action. In principle, programs must be tested to prove that they achieve their defined outputs under all conditions of input. However, in an absolute sense, this may not be possible: total proof that a program will perform absolutely correctly under all circumstances is not at present achievable. The essence of computers is their ability to make complex decisions very rapidly. Even the simplest computer program may be capable of taking many different logical alternatives and complex programs may potentially have millions or tens of millions of different feasible alternative routes through their logic. Predicting all the possible paths is quite impossible, let alone testing the correctness of them.

There is as yet no theoretical basis for proving the absolute correctness of computer programs; neither is there any generally accepted method or procedure which tests a given piece of software completely. This has been advanced as a powerful argument against the star wars Strategic Defense Initiative (SDI) technology being developed by the USA. The star wars technology depends crucially upon computers, controlled by complex software, both in space and on the ground; testing the software fully in battle conditions is hardly possible and so the reliability of the defence system must always be in doubt.

So, in an organizational context, the problem of software errors is an ever-present one and can be dealt with by employing three main strategies: *error prevention*, the thorough testing before the system goes live; *error detection*, performing rigorous control checks during live running to detect errors; and *error tolerance*, whereby the systems are designed so that failure is not catastrophic.

1. Error prevention is the objective of thorough software testing procedures performed during system development and maintenance, and *before* live system running starts.
2. Error detection is performed after software has been implemented, and is achieved by control procedures which are executed whenever the software is run; when errors are detected by manual or automatic procedures, the system is investigated to find out the cause.
3. Error tolerance is achieved in two ways: by designing systems which fail-safe, meaning usually that the system stops running so that remedial procedures can be carried out before any real harm is done; or by designing the system to fail-soft, meaning usually that the system can continue running despite a failure, perhaps by isolating a failed software module and switching automatically to alternative routines or procedures.

Managing system implementation

The creation of well-designed and tested software represents a major achievement in systems development. Making the system operational in its organizational setting requires the successful management of a number of other activities as well:

- site preparation,
- data conversion,
- defining manual procedures,
- staff training,
- selecting a changeover strategy,
- managing the behavioural aspects of change.

Site preparation involves ensuring that new computer equipment can function properly, and that people can use it comfortably. In the case of large mainframes purpose-built facilities may be required, with special fire and secure access arrangements, closely controlled air-conditioning (dust, temperature and humidity are important), special power supplies and false floors and ceilings to carry cables, air-conditioning ducting and fire prevention systems. On the other hand, a PC may require very little more than a normal office environment, a three-pin socket and a sturdy desk. Attention to ergonomic factors for people using computer equipment is very important: this means paying special attention to heating, lighting and noise factors, and ensuring that properly designed chairs and desks are available. Recent research into phenomena such as 'sick building' disease show that the physical nature of the working environment plays a crucial part in people's health, morale, comfort and working efficiency.

Most new systems require that a body of data is converted into machine-readable form. For example, implementing a new order processing system requires loading computer files with customer names and addresses, account data, product data and so on. Suppose there are 5000 customers and 100 products. Assembling this data, checking it for accuracy and then converting it to a suitable format for machine input is a surprisingly expensive and time-consuming task, and one which is sometimes overlooked when evaluating system proposals.

A new system means that people have to work in new ways. Creating new procedure manuals which define what people should do under different circumstances, and especially in an emergency or under unusual circumstances, is an important activity. Even more important is the *training* that must be given to everybody who will be involved in the new system. Attempting to implement a new system without giving the people involved adequate instruction, together with the time and facilities to practise the new routines, is a recipe for disaster. A wide range of training techniques is available, for example:

- reading procedure manuals,
- programmed learning,
- individual tutorials,
- classroom teaching,
- seminars and group discussions,
- task simulation,
- on-the-job training,
- information centre.

The training techniques range from reading manuals alone, through group discussions, to direct on-the-job or simulation training and, clearly, they afford the opportunity for quite different learning experiences, and selecting the appropriate one(s) for the situation at hand can be critical.

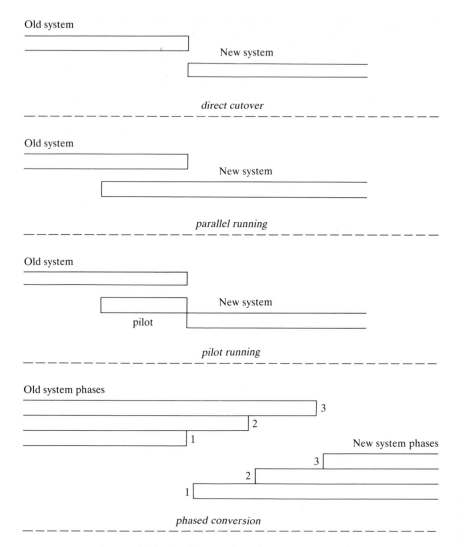

Figure 15.1 Implementation changeover strategies

SELECTING CHANGEOVER STRATEGIES

When the software is tested, people are fully trained, all data files have been converted and all the other tasks completed, how should the changeover to the new system be organized? There are four main options: direct cutover, parallel running, pilot running and phased conversion (Fig. 15.1), each with different advantages and disadvantages.

Direct cutover

This means that from an agreed time and date, the new system will start and immediately become fully operational; the old system, if any, will be abandoned from that time. If for any reason the system does not work properly, the problems must be resolved at once because the old system is no longer available. This is something of a bold 'do or die' approach, but it does represent a low-cost option which is appropriate under certain circumstances. There really may be no alternative (for example the system may be completely new, with no preceding manual equivalent), or the risks may have been carefully weighed up and considered to be acceptable under the circumstances.

Parallel running

This involves running both the old system and the new system together for a while, say one calendar month, until there is certainty that the new system is fully effective. While both systems are running, the outputs from both are carefully monitored and compared. Usually, the new system is used as the 'real' one, with the old one retained as back-up. If things go wrong, then the old system is still available and up-to-date. Parallel running provides a means of checking that new system outputs are identical with the old, and that new procedures are effective, under live operating conditions. It is commonly used with critical financial and accounting routines, where fixed time periods and predictable outputs lend themselves to the technique. The approach requires doubled operating costs so it can be very expensive in terms of staff and other resources. There is also the well-known tendency for staff to carry on with the old system for longer than is strictly necessary, because of fears that the new system may develop snags later. 'Just another month, till we're really sure', may be the cry; IS folklore is full of stories involving surreptitious destruction of old system files 'in the dead of night', in order to force in a new system which is 'sticking' long after it should have gone live.

Pilot running

The new system is introduced directly, without any parallel back-up, but involving only a subset of the organization. For example the system is made available to one department only, or with only one product category operational, or to a small segment of customers. This provides the opportunity to check that the system works well under live conditions, but with only a segment of the organization at risk. Piloting has the very great advantage that the new system can be directly experienced in real circumstances, and the consequences properly evaluated, without the costs or risks of parallel running or full-scale direct cutover. The method has much to recommend it, particularly where advanced technology is being employed so that human and technical responses are difficult to predict in advance.

Table 15.1   Changeover strategies compared

Changeover approach	Advantages	Disadvantages	When used
direct cutover	cheap, fast	risky	no alternative, risks acceptable
parallel running	very secure	very expensive	risks unacceptable
pilot running	limited risk, realistic	takes time	advanced technology inexperienced organization
phased conversion	allows time for change	takes time	very extensive systems

Phased conversion

Where a large system is to go live, it is split up into segments and one segment implemented at one time. Sufficient time is allowed between each implementation to check that the segment is working satisfactorily before the next segment is implemented. As with pilot running, only part of the organization's operations is at risk at one time. Organizations can cope with only so much change at one time; the phased method allows time for the organization to change and adapt before the next segment of implementation is undertaken.

The advantages and disadvantages of the four main approaches are summarized in Table 15.1.

These options are not mutually exclusive. For example, a realistic strategy for implementing a large-scale project might be one of phased implementation, where most phases are piloted separately first; one particularly sensitive component may be run in parallel for a period after piloting to ensure the new component is satisfactory while another, low-risk, component is implemented by direct cutover without piloting.

SYSTEM MAINTENANCE

Virtually as soon as a system is up and running it will need changing, however well it has been designed. People's information needs change as the organization reacts to changes in its environment; and the very fact of a new source of information will itself cause people to rethink their needs and request new or altered information. Altering systems to suit people's new needs, plus correcting minor errors and bugs in the system as they arise, all come under the heading of maintenance. A surprising amount of an IS department's development capacity may be taken up with maintenance: perhaps 50 per cent or more in a mature organization. As a system ages, so its maintenance costs tend to increase. This is due partly to changes in the organization causing more changes to be needed, and partly because of the increasing inefficiency of modifying already changed parts. Eventually, the time comes when it will be cheaper to redesign and redevelop the system from scratch rather than to continue to patch it up with maintenance work.

PROJECT MANAGEMENT

Successful system development and implementation calls for expert, sensitive management of groups of people working on very different aspects of the development project; systems analysts, programmers, users, management, clerical staff, data preparation staff, operations staff and so on. Coordinating these groups, which may be made up of people who have very different perceptions of the nature of the project, represents a very significant management challenge. Other management problems have been discussed during this chapter, but here they include, especially, the difficulties of estimating, in advance, the likely effort required to complete the phases of the project, and then planning for the completion of these phases to occur at the right time.

Estimating the manpower resources required, planning and coordinating the work of staff, and ensuring that the overall project is completed on time is a major management task. System development projects are notorious for overrunning on time and cost budgets. There are many reasons for this, but one reason is that time slippage on one element of the project, say, during the system design phase, cannot always be corrected simply by throwing more staff or money at the problem. The design process involves skilled personnel engaged in perhaps delicate negotiations with user departments over a period of time. As the design personnel have to be continually aware of the progress of their close colleagues, adding more staff at a late stage may only cause more delays while the newcomers gain an understanding of the current state of play.

The constraints and other factors that have to be taken into account in project planning include the following:

- achieving the project completion deadline,
- minimizing project costs,
- maximizing use of people resources,
- accurately estimating the resources and time required,
- coping with unexpected delays and slippage.

The unit of measure for systems work of all kinds, including analysis, design and programming, is the *person-day*. Estimating the number of person-days required to complete a development activity is a difficult area. Essentially, the planner needs to know in advance how much effort is required to complete a certain task: for instance, analysing the information needs of one department of the organization, or coding statements for a particular suite of programs. Estimating is done partly by utilizing staff experience of how long these things have taken in the past, and partly by reference to standards or yardsticks for that particular task. Unfortunately, systems projects tend to be 'new' for the organization that tries them, so extrapolating from past experience is difficult.

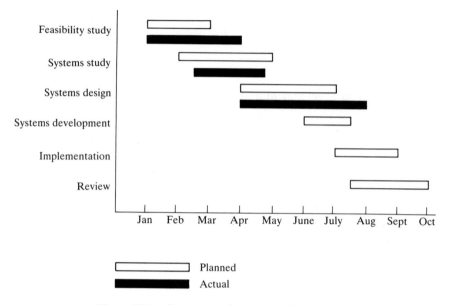

Figure 15.2 Gantt chart for systems development

One yardstick for measuring work output is the average number of program statements that can be produced per person per day. For example, 50 tested COBOL statements per day may be a reasonable average under certain conditions. However, such an average may hide very wide extremes of performance depending on the experience of the programmer and the difficulty of the work. It is not unusual to find that an experienced programmer can produce four or five times as much useful output per day as a programmer just out of training. Similarly, an experienced and talented systems analyst may be able to fact-find, discuss and negotiate system requirements with a user group in just a few days, whereas somebody less experienced or skilled may take weeks or months for the same task. IS mythology calls for planners to evaluate a reasonable time-scale using scientific estimating yardsticks, then, according to the 'folk wisdom', it is best to double the estimate to allow for the unexpected and then double it again to make it more realistic!

Successful project completion requires detailed and meticulous planning, careful monitoring of the state of the project against the plan, and the capacity to reallocate resources and replan when necessary. Techniques which support project planning and monitoring include the use of activity schedules, bar or Gantt charts (Fig. 15.2) and PERT networks (Fig. 15.3). PERT stands for project evaluation and review technique; the technique is also called CPA: critical path analysis. Large and complicated projects may be virtually impossible to control adequately without the use of these techniques.

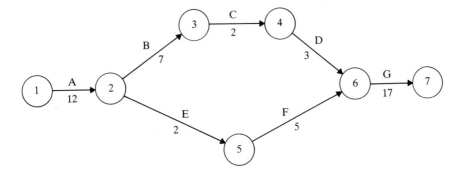

Activity	Preceded by	Followed by	Duration
A	–	B, E	12
B	A	C	7
C	B	D	2
D	C	G	3
E	A	F	2
F	E	G	5
G	D, F	–	17

Figure 15.3 A simple PERT chart

MANAGING THE BEHAVIOURAL ASPECTS OF CHANGE

There are many reasons why systems fail at implementation time. Potentially one of the most serious of these is the failure to take sufficient account of *human reactions* to the organizational changes involved in the implementation of information systems. This topic is discussed in depth in Part Six. For now, let us say that it is essential that all people who may be affected by the new system are fully involved at all stages of systems development, and that a carefully thought out education and training program must be implemented, supported by sensitive counselling and advice given by skilled personnel.

Structured methodologies

Awareness of the tremendous problems inherent in creating working information systems from the complexities of large modern organization has led to the evolution of a *structured approach* to systems development. The emphasis is on a logical, standardized approach which introduces a consistent discipline into the systems development process. Perhaps a minority of organizations have so far seriously taken structured methods fully to heart, but an understanding of the approach is gradually spreading through the IS community. Some British Government departments insist upon the full employment of structured methods in the shape of SSADM (structured systems analysis and design method) when commissioning software.

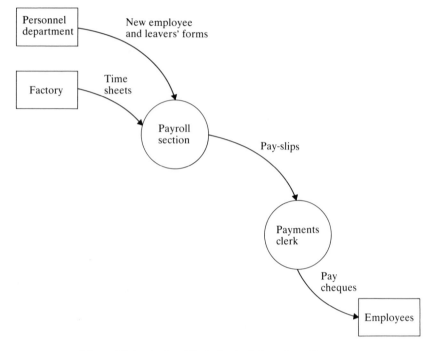

Figure 15.4   A simplified physical data flow diagram

Structured analysis is a commonly used means of creating precise, modular systems definitions. The main idea is to use a standardized analysis method which copes with the complexity of large-scale systems in a consistent way. Essentially it involves a *top-down approach* which breaks down complex systems into manageable modules, starting from the highest, abstract level and working down in increasing detail. The main tools of structured analysis are the *data flow diagram*, the *entity relationship diagram* and the *data dictionary*. The data flow diagram is similar in concept to the traditional systems flowchart, but it concentrates on the data, which is the heart of the matter; it shows specifically how data move from and to a system module, the processes which change the data, and where and how it is stored. Figure 15.4 shows a physical data flow diagram for staff payments.

The *entity relationship diagram* shows the 'things' (products, equipment and customers) which the data is about, and how these are related. The main idea is to rigorously document, in a straightforward way, the multiple relationships that may exist among entities. The technique is mostly associated with database design.

The *data dictionary* contains definitions of pieces of data shown in the data flow diagram, together with information on the format of the data and its frequency, security requirements and, most importantly, who uses it. Data dictionaries are used throughout the system analysis, design and implementation processes, and help with database design and management. Structured analysis is an evolutionary development of traditional systems analysis techniques, and is usually used alongside them.

Structured design is a system design method which is closely associated with structured analysis. It consists of a set of rules and techniques which are intended to promote simplicity and clarity in program design. As the cost of changing and maintaining software in complex systems is very high indeed, any techniques which facilitate program development and maintenance are very important. Structured design involves a top-down approach which looks first at the main, overall function of a system or program and then breaks it down into subsystems or modules which themselves are further broken down into ever-increasing detail. Only when the logic of the top level has been specified does the designer move to a lower level. The logic of the design is represented on a *design structure chart*. This shows each level of design and its relationship to other levels, and represents the principal item of documentation associated with the method.

Each subpart of the design on one level represents a module. Systems (and then programs) are carefully split into modules each of which represents a coherent and convenient unit of logic. Modules are deliberately chosen to be a manageable size, but also to be as *independent* of each other as possible. This is done to avoid problems arising from units that are to closely coupled. Data links between modules are kept to a minimum, and logical connections are kept simple to avoid unwanted knock-on effects if changes are needed.

Structured programming follows logically from structured design. The aim is to avoid the 'spaghetti' program, whose logic follows complex and obscure paths and whose statements cause control to leap backward and forward throughout the program. The bane of any maintenance programmer's life are programs which are complex, incomprehensible, or whose links with other programs or systems are obscure. The solution is a standardized and consistently logical programming style. This is achieved by using a top-down, modular approach to program development in the same way as for systems module design, together with standard principles of program writing. Structured programming uses only three standard program control constructs: *sequence, selection* and *repetition*. The sequence construct defines the logic as flowing from one statement to the next unconditionally; the selection construct tests some condition and chooses one of two paths as a result; the repetition construct causes a group of instructions to be obeyed while a condition remains true (a 'do-while' loop for those familiar with programming). These three constructs alone are sufficient to achieve any desired program control effect, and using only these can greatly simplify program logic.

The initial program design is prepared using a traditional flowchart, or using a special programming notation called Semi-formal English (SFE) or *Structured*

Process name: Employee Overtime Calculation

Process description:

1.0 If actual hours worked are less than or equal to standard hours then no overtime is payable

1.1 If actual hours worked is greater than standard hours then overtime pay equals standard pay times 1.2 for actual hours less standard hours

1.2 Add overtime pay to standard pay

Figure 15.5 Fragment of structured English

English; this is independent of any particular programming language and facilitates documentation of the resulting program code (see Fig. 15.5).

DRAWBACKS TO TRADITIONAL DEVELOPMENT METHODS

Classical systems development methods, including structured methods, are used successfully in many situations where large, well-structured systems are to be developed, and where tightly controlled formal management of the development process is required. But the classical methods have a number of well-known drawbacks. Some of these drawbacks stem from the rather inflexible requirements-elicitation → analysis → design sequence which calls for users' needs to be strictly predefined before software development takes place.

In general, the traditional system life cycle approach tends to be a lengthy and costly process. Much time is spent gathering information, and for large projects the development time may stretch over years and be very expensive in terms of the human resources involved. It is not unknown for large projects to become obsolete before they are even implemented. User dissatisfaction with excessive delays is also a major stimulus in the search for new methods. The traditional development process is inflexible: it calls for users to know their information needs, to state these unequivocally and to stick with them.

Unfortunately, the reality is that users usually cannot immediately state their requirements in straightforward terms, often for very good reasons. Information needs so often depend on subtle interactions between people and systems and it is expecting too much for them to be fully aware of the scope and limitations of current IS technology as well as the potential of IS in their working environments. As IS project unfold, people can arrive at a better understanding of their needs, and so an element of iteration in the development cycle is desirable: needs-elicitation and analysis cycles are repeated to refine the statement of requirements. But each iteration takes time and raises the level of cost and delay, so the ever-present temptation for management is to freeze the process as early as possible in order to place a limit on time and cost expenditures.

These considerations particularly apply where management decision-making is to be supported. It is often very difficult for managers to define their information needs in the concrete terms required by the systems analyst. And the higher the management, the worse the problem becomes, because at the higher levels decision-making is at one and the same time both less structured and more changeable, and this makes the rigid definition of information needs all the more difficult and inappropriate.

ANALYSING SYSTEMS ANALYSIS

Perhaps the most challenging aspect of systems development is the difficulty of gaining an accurate understanding of people's information needs. Traditional information needs-elicitation methods essentially rely on asking people to describe their requirements, and then these descriptions are put together with information from observation and from other sources. Problems arise for several reasons.

Firstly, difficulties arise with people as information users:

- people may not know their own needs;
- people find it difficult to articulate their needs;
- people's needs change over time;
- people's perceptions about information may conflict with others;
- unresolved *conflicts* may exist between individual people and between organizational groupings.

Secondly, difficulties arise with systems analysts and with the analysis process:

- analysts may elicit information from the wrong people;
- analysts may not understand people's needs;
- analysts' information elicitation techniques are imperfect;
- analysts may have perceptions about the organization which, due to their background and culture, are different from other people's.

There really are no straightforward antidotes to these problems. Some individuals seem to have a natural talent for eliciting and understanding people's needs, and resolving human difficulties; others apparently do not have these gifts. Training can help but most professional courses concentrate on technical matters and do not, unfortunately, address the human skills involved. As people and organizations gain experience in IS, an organizational learning process takes place which gradually improves IS success.

Alternatives to classical system development

Against a background of steadily evolving principles and practices in information systems development, new approaches have emerged for avoiding the traditional system development route, and some old methods have been revised.

PROTOTYPING

Prototyping involves building an approximate working version of a system as

1. Users' basic (or approximate) information needs identified
2. Prototype developed as rapidly as possible
3. Users gain experience with prototype system
4. Users refine their requirements in the light of experience
5. Prototype modified as quickly as possible
6. Repeat steps 3 to 5 as necessary
7. Redevelop system for efficiency and completeness

Figure 15.6 Applications development by prototyping

quickly and as cheaply as possible, and then asking users to try out the system in order to see how well it suits them. It is assumed from the outset that users will ask for modifications to be made. Changes are made as quickly as possible, and then users are again asked to assess the system to see how well it meets their needs. This process of trial and error, followed by modification and retrial, is undertaken several times over as users experiment with the system and ask for changes. A summary of the steps involved in prototyping is shown in Fig. 15.6. The system can go live in prototype form or, in some situations, the prototype may be an experimental version which is implemented using traditional change-over methods. Once the system has settled to a final version, it can be redeveloped in a technically more efficient and more permanent form.

At first sight, prototyping negates many of the principles of good system design: for example, users' needs are not closely investigated or defined in the first instance, and there is no great pressure to 'get it right first time'. Indeed, changes to the system are *expected and encouraged*—a far cry from the tradition-al systems life cycle! Yet, the method has been found to be very effective and efficient in certain situations. Where user needs are not known, or where there is substantial uncertainty about the usefulness of certain design solutions, then prototyping is likely to be a suitable design methodology. The use of 4GL software tools also plays a role in rapid development of prototype systems.

A major benefit of prototyping is that users can shape the design of their system as it develops, and can try out the effects of different alternatives. This has been found to be a much more accurate way of identifying users' needs than the traditional methods of interviewing and other forms of needs-elicitation which are undertaken in the absence of a working model of the complete system. Users find it much easier to say what they like (and perhaps even more impor-tantly, what they do not like) about a real, concrete, working system which they have used, than to express opinions about planned, imaginary systems which may exist at some time in the future.

PACKAGED SOFTWARE

A well-chosen package may be the best alternative to in-house development. See Chapter 12 for a discussion on the merits and de-merits of packaged software in comparison with in-house development. Where information personnel resources are slim or non-existent—and this may apply particularly in the case of small businesses—then packaged software may be the main or only choice of software acquisition. It should be noted that packaged software does not, of itself, eliminate all the functions of system development. There is still the need to identify users' needs, to undertake implementation management including data conversion, personnel training and system implementation steps, and to monitor and maintain system performance thereafter.

END-USER COMPUTING

The phenomenon of end-user computing (EUC) has become far more important in recent years. EUC means that computer users who are not themselves IS professionals are involved in the development of their own systems. Often this means using fourth-generation programming tools (4GLs). (See Part Three for a discussion on 4GLs.) EUC is particularly useful where users know what their needs are, and where the system under development is not particularly large or complex. For example, specialist business modelling staff developing decision support systems and executive information systems may devise these data accessing systems themselves using appropriate 4GL software linked to pre-existing databases. Apart from these specialist activities, software for the PC is most usually manipulated by its owner and PC database and spreadsheet software lends itself particularly to the self-development of systems by the user. Because the user is in complete control over the whole of the development process, his or her activities usually bypass the classical system development cycles.

THE CRITICAL SUCCESS FACTORS APPROACH

The assumption of this approach is that the progress of the organization can be identified and measured in terms of certain key variables which are sometimes called *critical success factors* or *key performance indicators*. These variables include indicators such as share price, return on investment (ROI), market share and other management measures. The basic idea is that these critical success factors are in some sense absolute indicators of organizational success, and are therefore independent of individual's idiosyncratic information needs. This idea is used in the design of executive information systems (EIS) for senior management, and the approach avoids a lengthy analysis of information flows: a process that might be impossible in the context of top management.

Summary

This chapter has completed our review of the systems development life cycle, involving the development and testing of software, the implementation process including the changeover process and system maintenance. Structured methodologies and alternatives to the classical systems development life cycle, such as prototyping, have also been considered.

All businesses must undertake systems development. This may entail no more than purchasing a turnkey system from a vendor, but even such actions must be taken on the basis of a rational, systematic analysis of the organization's needs.

KEY TERMS   Critical success factors   Data dictionary   Data flow diagram   Direct cutover   End-user computing (EUC)   Entity relationship diagram   Error prevention, detection and tolerance   Fail-safe   Fail-soft   Object program   Parallel running   Person-day   Phased implementation   Pilot running   Prototyping   Source program   Structured analysis, design and programming   Structured English   Top-down approach.

Further reading

Ashworth C. and Goodland M., *SSADM – A Practical Approach*, McGraw-Hill, Maidenhead, 1990.
Olle T.W. *et al.*, *Information Systems Methodologies*, Addison-Wesley, Wokingham, 1988.
Opperman R., User participation: some experiences and recommendations, *Systems Objectives Solutions*, **4**(3), 157–168, 1984.
Martin C.J., *Senior Managers and Computers*, NCC Press, Manchester, 1988.

Summary to Part Four

Part Four has investigated systems development, the life cycle that is used to describe the process and the controls and management issues necessary for successful project completion.

PART FIVE

The management of information systems

16
Managing system security

This section is about managing and controlling key aspects of IS in the organization. Until recently, the principal aim of information systems management was to control the *technology* of computing. This approach emphasizes the financial investment and developmental control aspects of computer systems. The nature of IS has changed dramatically over the last few years, and the rate of change appears to be speeding up rather than slowing down. These changes have resulted in shifts in the necessary focus of management attention. Managing the information resources involves taking careful account of these shifts. Part of the change is due to the recognition that information is a *strategic resource*, a resource that in its own right is vitally important to the future well-being of the organization. The successful management of the information resource involves actively controlling several key aspects of IS which will be discussed in this part.

Information systems hazards

Information systems are vulnerable to the wide range of security problems shown below and these problems must be recognized and planned for:

- human errors in system design and implementation
- human errors in data capture and system operation
- software errors and failures
- hardware errors and failures
- hacking, and other privacy violations
- viruses and other forms of deliberate software sabotage
- criminal activity, including data and equipment theft, and fraud
- vandalism and physical sabotage
- electrical supply failures
- accidental magnetic media erasures

- fire
- water flooding and pollutant damage to equipment and media
- gales, floods, earthquakes and other natural hazards

Many organizations have suffered substantial losses due to IS security failures of one sort or another, and there can be little doubt that those reported in the media represent the tip of an enormous, and largely unrecorded, iceberg. Prominent among the reported IS disasters are failures occasioned by errors (that is, human and system errors) and the financial losses due to unrecovered data loss.

Unauthorized access to sensitive data is an expanding problem for two reasons: firstly, data stored is increasingly of a strategic nature and, secondly, the enormous expansion of PC use means that many more people potentially have access. Data which could be of interest to business rivals, financial predators or speculators includes: accounting data of all kinds, especially management accounts and financial plans; price lists, customer and supplier lists, sales and marketing analyses; internal memoranda, position papers, and board minutes, contracts and third party dealings; new product designs and formulae. Critical data which falls into the hands of competitors may cost a company very dear.

Computer fraud, which involves using a computer to steal a company's money or assets, is an expanding criminal activity and although the absolute number of crimes is relatively low the amounts involved are often high. A significant proportion of computer crimes are committed from the inside, and often these crimes involve employees who are disgruntled and would like to 'get back at' their organization, or who are unable to resist an opportunity to steal. The criminal methods employed vary from entering false input data to payment systems, through to altering software so that payments are automatically made to the benefit of the fraudster. The following measures are specially designed to minimize the risk of unauthorized data access and fraud.

1. *Personnel selection procedures.* Fraud and other crimes have been perpetrated by criminals who successfully relied on inadequate checking of references and previous job histories, therefore procedures should be thorough.
2. *Audit trails.* As well as the normal accounting procedures, audits should include analysis of any significant deviations in data or business patterns that may signal a fraud in operation.
3. *Segregation of duties.* This can be done by reducing the authority of one individual over a sensitive area and enabling independent cross-checking.
4. *Effective input/output controls.* The prevention of unauthorized tampering with data inputs and outputs can be achieved, especially by passwords and other security measures.
5. *Effective system maintenance controls.* When live systems are being altered there should be independent checking to ensure that no illegal or fraudulent changes have been made.

6. *Job rotation.* Prevents a person from becoming entrenched in one position for too long which can encourage tampering with system procedures with which no one else is familiar.
7. *Follow-up on access violations.* Attempts to gain access to secure areas, or multiple password attempts should all be investigated in case they represent attempts at fraud.

Security breaches by hackers, who regard mainframe security procedures as a challenge to their technical skills, represent the lighter side of illegal computer access. A recent *cause célèbre* involved a hacker who infiltrated the Telecom Gold electronic mail network and accessed the mailbox belonging to the Duke of Edinburgh. The most recent technical threat to IS are *viruses*: programs which reside unnoticed in memory and cause various unwanted effects ranging from humorous screen displays at random intervals through to the destruction of data and programs. Some viruses have the ability to transfer themselves from machine to machine via floppy disks or other transferable media. These programs are written by mischievous software specialists for the technical challenge which they represent. There is little hard evidence that they represent a widespread threat.

More serious to firms than hackers and viruses are data losses due to fires, floods, earthquakes and other natural disasters. Until the data and the systems have been recreated those operations cannot continue, and in the case of crucial customer-orientated systems the firm may have to suspend trading until the systems have been restored. Human and computer errors can also achieve data losses by deleting or otherwise corrupting key data files. More than one firm has gone bankrupt through the loss of crucial business data such as accounts receivable, because there was no way to recreate the data once it had been lost.

Although far less newsworthy or glamorous than major disasters or technically sophisticated skullduggery, most IS calamities owe their provenance to good old-fashioned unintentional human errors. These together with a smattering of software bugs and the odd hardware failure make up the common daily round of computer calamity. However, it is the unexpected and rare event, like a major fire, which really tests an organization's contingency plans.

How is the organization to be protected from all these hazards? Establishing comprehensive system security means planning for errors and disasters of all kinds in a way that prevents data misuse and enables recovery from disaster.

Most organizations are dependent on their information systems to a greater or lesser extent. Because IS are increasingly taking a stategic role in the operations of the organization, it is even more essential that steps are taken to ensure that the systems operate reliably and that the organization will not be harmed when disaster strikes. Notice the 'when' and not the 'if' in the last sentence. *If something can go wrong, then sooner or later it will*; and there is always *a lot* that can go wrong with an IS. Table 16.1 shows measures which can be taken to enable recovery from disaster.

Table 16.1 Disaster contingency: strategies for recovery

Strategy	Measures/methods
On-site standby duplicate systems	systems which *must* be available at all times can be physically duplicated within the organization: the duplicate exists only to take over in the event of the primary system being unavailable for any reason
Off-site standby reciprocal agreements	two or more firms with compatible systems can offer mutual support if either firm has a disaster
vendor hot-site agreement	a compatible back-up facility offered by the computer vendor which can be made available if needed for a limited period of time
commercial computer bureaux	service bureaux with compatible equipment can contract to provide standby facilities
Power back-up emergency power supplies	in response to power failures, uninterruptible power supplies (UPS) utilize electronically switched battery power, followed by automatically started diesel generators
Financial recovery insurance	insurance can be arranged against losses due to equipment and data loss, for the extra costs of recovery, and for any trading losses incurred due to the system being unavailable
Planning detailed recovery plans	it is necessary to have detailed plans which show (a) how personnel are to react during a disaster, (b) how to restore systems to full running and (c) how the organization will operate during the period before system recovery

Controls

Controls are the preventative techniques, procedures and policies developed to guard against the hazards that befall operational IS. Some controls are preventative; others are designed to detect problems as they occur or have already occurred. There are many different types of control which can operate at all the different stages of IS development and use; controls can be developed to operate wherever there is the potential for something to go wrong. The important thing from a material point of view is that effective and comprehensive controls are an essential component of a successful IS, and without them the organization is at risk from one or more of the ever-present hazards listed earlier. Controls are designed and built in to the system at the system design stage; this means considering all the likely problems in advance and ensuring that the controls can cope with them. It is likely that developing the necessary control mechanisms for a sensitive commercial system will occupy as much system design effort as designing the system itself.

In general, controls can be considered in seven groups:

1. System design controls:
   (a) formal reviews and development audits,
   (b) user and management approval stages,
   (c) development walk-throughs,
   (d) standardized program and system testing procedures,
   (e) documentation review.
2. System maintenance controls:
   (a)–(e) as above, but with intensified care because systems are especially vulnerable when they are being altered.
3. Data capture controls:
   (a) input authorization checks,
   (b) pre-numbered forms,
   (c) batch and hash control total reconciliation,
   (d) transaction count reconciliation,
   (e) transaction logs,
   (f) key verification,
   (g) program vetting for invalid data, including check-digit verification.
4. Processing controls:
   (a) transaction count reconciliation,
   (b) control total reconciliation,
   (c) audit trail creation and review,
   (d) crossfooting,
   (e) sequence checks.
5. Output controls:
   (a) transaction count reconciliation,
   (b) control total reconciliation,
   (c) recipient authorization checks,
   (d) pre-numbered forms.
6. Database and file controls:
   (a) physical media write-protect devices,
   (b) magnetic labels,
   (c) database concurrency checks,
   (d) data encryption,
   (e) transaction count reconciliation,
   (f) control total reconciliation.

7. Hardware controls:
   (a) memory parity checks,
   (b) read/write check sums,
   (c) media/file label checks,
   (d) component duplication checks,
   (e) data transmission controls.

Security back-up of files and databases

Retaining back-up copies of files and databases is a straightforward and essential part of IS management. It must be assumed at the outset that sooner or later (probably sooner) important data files will be lost or corrupted. There are so many reasons why this can happen since just about every hazard on the list might be responsible for data loss or corruption, but by far the most common causes are human and computer errors of various kinds. Most people who have used a PC for any length of time will have had the experience of losing an important file for one reason or another, perhaps through a hard disk failure or other unexpected cause (or from overenthusiastic use of the *delete* or *format* commands!) and thus will have faced the prospect of having to reproduce many hours of work. It is usually after such an experience that the need for effective back-up is truly brought home to the PC user! Organizational IS usually have far greater consequences when they fail, and so designing file back-up is an important aspect of IS management.

The objective of a back-up file is to provide a replacement for lost data so as to minimize the costs of recovery (in terms of time and reprocessing costs) from the data loss. At its simplest, back-up means keeping a spare copy of a key file. But how often should the back-up copy be renewed? Usually, a back-up file can be used to replace a lost data file only after any transactions which have occurred since the back-up was last taken have been reprocessed to bring the back-up file to the same state as the original data file. So transaction data must be backed-up as well as the master-files. To copy files too frequently is expensive in terms of the computer time involved: large files may take several minutes to copy and there may be scores or hundreds of such files. But, on the other hand, if a file is lost and large amounts of transaction data have to be reprocessed then the time taken to recover from the loss may become unacceptable. This latter point becomes very important in the case of real-time systems where on-line data must be continually available. In general, a trade-off must be established between the costs of back-up and the costs of restoration.

A simple back-up procedure which is very commonly used for sequential master-files involves the traditional *grandfather–father–son* routine shown in Fig. 16.1. On Monday master-file A is processed using Monday's transaction data, and a new file B is created which represents the current state of the data. At this stage file A is still available; if anything goes wrong it can be used again

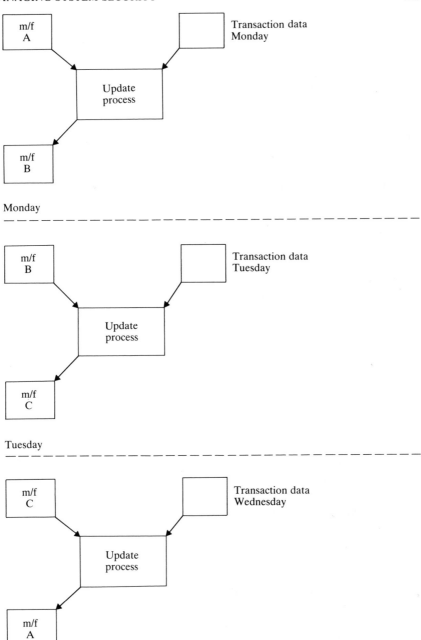

Monday

Tuesday

Wednesday

Figure 16.1 Grandfather, father, son: three generations of master-file back-up

with the transaction data to reproduce file B. On Tuesday, the current file B is used with Tuesday's transactions to create a third file C which represents the current status of the data. At this stage there are three versions of the file available, which, with the appropriate transactions, could be used to recreate the current data. The three files, grandfather, father, son, represent three generations of the current data. Together with the transaction data (which must also be retained) they provide two extra opportunities to recreate a lost master-file. On Wednesday, file C is used with Wednesday's transaction data to create a new file; but this time the old file A is reused and its data overwritten. To add to the security, the oldest file (grandfather) can be retained at a different location. Versions of this back-up routine are commonly used to provide security copies of all manner of IS files.

Where the master-file is updated *in situ* (i.e. a new file is not created as a result of processing) then a slightly different approach must be used; a back-up copy must be taken as a separate exercise, and stored together with appropriate transaction data. Real-time systems which involve the continuous updating of on-line files are a special problem, and several back-up strategies can be used. The simplest of these involves taking a file copy, *file dumping*, before processing starts in the morning, and then keeping an automatic record during the day of all transactions which have updated the file, *transaction logging*. If a problem occurs and the file is lost, then the previously dumped file is used together with the transaction log to recreate the file up to the moment at which it was lost: this is referred to as *roll forward*. More sophisticated methods involve dumping only those parts of the file which have altered since the last dump; this is called *residual dumping*.

Other physical security techniques for protecting the information systems installation are reviewed below:

- External building safeguards and barriers:
  - boundary fencing
  - supervised gates
  - restricted access to keys
  - alarm systems
  - guard dogs
  - CCTV and floodlighting at night
- IS installation access:
  - access restricted to authorized personnel
  - card key or key-pad controls on access
  - retina and handprint scan systems
  - identification cards with photographs
- PC security:
  - password access controls on software and files
  - data encryption
  - physical keyboard locks

- infra-red and indelible marking
- chaining the PC to fixtures
- software and datafiles on floppy disks to be stored securely (see below)
- Media protection:
  - lockable fire-proof cabinets
  - special-purpose fire-proof sales
  - off-site
  - back-up storage
  - multiple copies of files retained in different places
  - restricted access to media
- Output security:
  - secure printouts to be shredded
  - printers and VDUs which can display sensitive information in secure areas to prevent passers-by from inadvertently gaining access
  - exceptionally sensitive applications may require VDUs screened to prevent electronic eavesdropping
- IT equipment protection:
  - telecommunications equipment
  - on-line terminals
  - FAX
  - Telex and other IT devices require secure controls as for computer equipment.

Optimizing system security

The costs of developing and operating full-scale control systems, back-up procedures and security arrangements can be very high. Not all IS warrant on-site duplicate systems, or extensive control and back-up procedures; and clearly not all the outputs from an organization's computers are absolutely vital: some are simply more important than others. Then there is the risk level: how often should we expect a fire to destroy key computers and media? It is necessary to judge just how important data and systems are, and to develop controls and countermeasures which are cost-effective and appropriate to the risk level expected. There are thus three factors to be considered:

1. the expense of operating the control or security measure;
2. the risk of the controlled activity failing;
3. the costs which result if the controlled activity fails, data is corrupted or security is compromised.

For example, key-verification of input data is a commonly used data-input control which ensures that human transcription errors are reduced to a very low level, so the risk of these particular errors is small, perhaps 0.001 per cent or less. However, the costs of data input by this method are virtually doubled and there will be some types of input data for which it is simply not worth the expense.

For example when keying in customer order data, the customer's own order reference may be of far less importance than product codes and order quantities, and so the customer reference field may not be verified for accuracy. Some of these reference data will probably be in error (let us say that the risk increases to 1 per cent) but because the accuracy of this particular item is not crucial to the running of the system these errors are acceptable. On the other hand, errors in order quantities would result in wrong customer deliveries and these errors would definitely not be acceptable; so order quantity data are key-verified (and may be checked by other controls as well).

Similar decisions need to be taken about the controls employed in the organizational IS, as well as about back-up frequencies and about the organization's disaster contingency plans.

Summary

Information systems are valuable organizational assets, both for their intrinsic and physical worths. Security is crucial, but recovery procedures from unforeseen disasters is necessary. Controls are a set of techniques, procedures and policies which attempt to guard against possible IS hazards; these controls may be preventive, detective or recoverative. The costs of controls must be balanced with the costs of disaster, and hence realistic levels of security applied which do not compromise too much the normal operations of the system.

KEY TERMS Audit trail   Back-up   Computer fraud   Controls   Disaster recovery   File dumping   File generations   Grandfather–father–son   Hackers   Job rotation   Key-verification   Residual dumping   Roll forward   Strategic resource   Transaction logging   Viruses.

Further reading

Baskerville R, *Designing Information System Security*, Wiley, Chichester, 1988.
Chambers A.D. and Court J.M., *Computer Auditing*, Pitman, London, 1986.
Cornwall H., *Data Theft*, Heinemann, London, 1987.
Finlay D., Don't wait until you get burned, *Administrative Management*, March, pp. 16–22, 1988.
Hearnden K. (Ed.), *A Handbook of Computer Security*, Kogan Page, London, 1990.
Lane V.P., *Security of Computer-Based Information Systems*, Macmillan, London, 1985.

17
Controlling the IS function

Information systems personnel

Information systems personnel have been in short supply for many years. The more commonly found IS titles and roles are shown below and a typical organizational chart is depicted in Fig. 17.1. Especially sought-after are those people who have proven experience and skills in systems development and IS management generally, although some of the more technical roles (such as systems programmer) are also often in short supply. Although the number of people involved in IS has increased substantially in recent years the increase in supply is still not enough to meet the demand, which is growing at something like 15 per cent per year. Some categories of staff, in particular analysts and systems programmers, have enjoyed extreme temporary scarcity value which has resulted in dramatically enhanced salary potential, as firms compete for the scarce personnel.

- IS director: together with board colleagues, develops IS strategy in line with organizational strategic goals.
- IS manager: responsible for liaising with user departments, and for day-to-day running of all aspects of the IS department.
- Systems manager: heads systems analysis, design and implementation functions.
- Programming manager: heads programming staff, development and maintenance functions.
- Operations manager: responsible for day-to-day running of all implemented systems, heads computer operators and data preparation staff.
- Database administrator: responsible for controlling and maintaining the organizational database.
- Systems analyst: working with users, designs new computer systems and

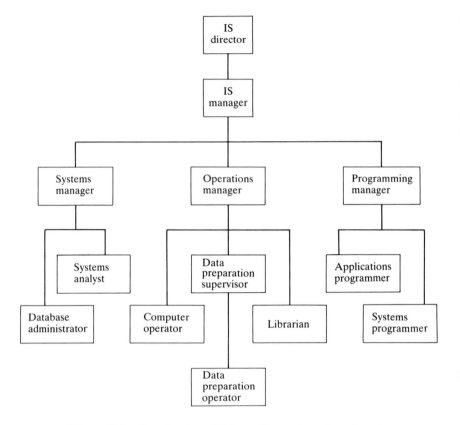

Figure 17.1   Organization of information systems department

produces system specifications.

- Applications programmer: working from detailed system specifications, produces tested computer programs.
- Systems programmer: responsible for technical support of the computer system software.
- Computer operator: working from job control procedure specifications, initiates computer activities and loads peripherals.
- Librarian: responsible for controlling the storage and issue of disk and tape files.
- Data preparation supervisor: responsible for data capture and conversion, including data control and data accuracy and also heads data preparation operators.
- Data preparation operator: converts data into machine-sensible form, usually by keyboard entry on key-to-disk devices.

Research into career and work motivations of IS personnel indicates that they

Table 17.1 IS management parameters at different stages of IS development history

Parameter	Initiation	Contagion	Control	Maturity
management objective	single application	facilitate growth	control growth	match supply/demand
slack	moderate	high	low	moderate
control	lax	very lax	formal	sophisticated
centralization	local	decentralization	centralized	decentralized
development/maintenance ratio	100 : 0	80 : 20	50 : 50	20 : 80

have higher *personal achievement* needs, but lower *social* needs than the average. This implies that they tend to prefer the impersonal, technical aspects of the world of computing and its intellectual challenges, but they also need a continually changing and developing environment which will enable them to learn new skills, meet new challenges and enhance their expertise.

It is not always possible to offer progressive career paths for IS personnel. For example, often the only promotion prospect for the skilled programmer or analyst is to become programming manager or systems manager of his or her group. Clearly, not everyone can (or should) follow this route. Neither is it always possible for IS personnel to change to alternative career paths in other areas of the business. This can result in a perceived lack of career progress and dissatisfaction.

A more specific motivational problem is that of systems maintenance. As the IS function develops over time, more and more of the work of the systems development team is occupied in updating and modifying old systems, and less time is spent in creating new ones (see Table 17.1). However necessary and important system maintenance is, the increasing emphasis on old systems work is highly demotivating for systems analysts and programmers who would much rather work on new, exciting and challenging projects, and preferably those on the leading edge of technology.

The result of these factors is an industry that is renowned for high turnover of skilled personnel. Average annual turnover for all IS staff is as high as 20 per cent with some categories of staff at very much higher levels than this. System development staff in particular tend to have a cosmopolitan outlook and show more loyalty to their profession than a particular firm or organization. Because the technology of computing changes rapidly and continuously, there is a constant need to update skills and training costs are a significant element of IS budgets.

There are no quick and easy solutions to these problems. In larger organizations, career paths can be designed so that there are progressive technical and/or professional ranks for personnel to proceed through, as well as the managerial routes. Promotion through these professional stages rewards effort and skills, and enables more staff to make progress. Creating these career paths may be more difficult in smaller organizations.

There is an increasing tendency for the distinctions between IS and other personnel to be somewhat blurred, as end-user computing gathers pace. This may in the future result in more crossovers between IS and careers in other parts of the business. But at present it is still unusual for IS personnel to move completely away from their original profession. Alas, it is even more unusual for senior IS staff to move up to non-IS senior management roles in the organization. Senior management, and especially board-level management, are still usually drawn from the traditional functional backgrounds of finance, marketing, engineering or production. The managing director or chief executive who was originally an IS specialist does exist, but he or she is still rather a rare bird. This may seem surprising in view of the fact that working in the IS area provides a unique opportunity to gain a valuable overview of the workings of the organization, together with crucial insights into the nature of its information and decision flows. It is likely that more IS people will gain the upper levels of management as IS is generally perceived to be of strategic importance. Education can help here: there are already a number of postgraduate and post-experience IS conversion courses which offer routes into IS for managers from other disciplines; there are also more opportunities for IS specialists to convert to general management via DMS, MBA and similar courses.

Controlling information systems costs and activities

The growth in the activities, influence and above all *expenditure* of the IS department has long been a concern of management. Although the costs of hardware have reduced steadily, this is usually more than matched by increasing IS utilization and hence greater expenditure. But hardware costs are usually a minor element of total IS costs: personnel costs will be the biggest element of most IS budgets. The way in which an organization utilizes and controls its IS resources changes over time because the organization learns from its experience. As organizations develop their information systems, a pattern of increasing expenditure—followed by attempts to control and constrain growth—emerges. That many organizations follow similar paths was first discussed by Nolan, who described a four-stage model of IS development.

How does the IS function in an organization evolve? Figure 17.2 shows some typical patterns of IS expenditure against time. (Expenditure includes the costs of IS staff, equipment, software and the other overheads associated with IS operations.) The spending line for each of the firms a,b and c shows a more or less consistent S-curve. Starting from some base figure, expenditure rises rapidly as systems are developed and the organization strives to automate and modernize its systems; later, the curve flattens off at a much higher level of expenditure as systems growth diminishes.

Nolan identified four key stages of IS growth (Table 17.1), each stage

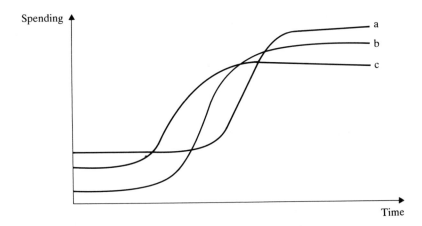

Figure 17.2   Typical IS expenditure pattern

associated with a part of the IS life history. The way in which management attempts to use and manage the IS resource is different at each stage. Changes in IS management objectives and style occur as part of the organizational learning process. A key feature of each stage is the nature of the *control* exerted. Figure 17.3 shows a generalized S-curve for expenditure against time, and the position of the four stages.

INITIATION

The need for IS development is perceived, usually in respect of one or two specific applications. Usually the organization has reached some critical point

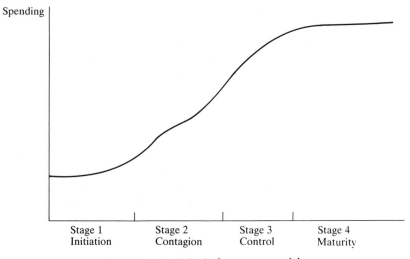

Figure 17.3   Nolan's four-stage model

whereby investment in limited equipment and software makes economic sense. Because there is no experience of IS in this particular organization (even though some individuals may themselves be experienced) there is a tendency to regard it as being of limited importance.

CONTAGION

The limited introduction of IS in the first stage results in success; perhaps even spectacular success. Automated data processing is seen to be efficient, cost effective and controllable; new and accurate management information results in shifts in management attention from old problems to new horizons. A beneficial impact is seen on customer service, on communications, on growth and on other key organizational factors. Suddenly, the race is on to automate and computerize everything in sight in order to maximize the benefits that the new technology can bring; little attempt is made rigorously to evaluate new applications. IS expenditure grows exponentially as the organization invests in more staff, equipment and software to meet the frantic demand for new systems. The concept of management slack is important here. Slack refers to spare management resources: money and, especially, time. By committing more resources to a project than are strictly necessary for planned outcomes, management encourages creativity. Slack is necessary for innovation to occur; it enables people to experiment, to discuss and communicate and try alternatives not ordained by fixed objectives.

CONTROL

This stage is entered in response to the explosive growth of stage two. Management realizes that IS growth and expenditure is out of control and desperately seeks measures which will limit further growth. Formal project and budgetary control methods are implemented. New applications for development are rigorously investigated and judged against strict economic criteria. Strict budgetary limits are imposed, together with charge-out systems to user departments in an attempt (usually unsuccessful) to stifle further demand for IS. Slack is reduced or eliminated. The structure of the IS department may be changed, usually with a move to a centralized structure which appears to provide more rigorous control.

MATURITY

This stage involves a basic re-think of the role of IS in the organization. The rather rigid control mechanisms of the third stage are replaced by more realistic and apposite ones which link IS to overall organizational objectives. The structure of the IS resource is decentralized so that users have more direct control over their IS resources. Further application growth occurs, but in a planned and moderate fashion.

The foregoing description of the stages of IS growth is clearly an idealized one, and each organization will have its own unique destiny. Nevertheless, it is most useful to look at one's organization and ask: where do we fit on this four-stage model? Identifying the current phase of development will give important insights as to what to expect and will provide clues on selecting a suitable management control strategy. Nolan went on to rework his hypothesis to show six stages, and various authors have developed his work further; but for our purposes the original four-stage model is sufficient to illustrate the main concepts associated with the organizational learning which occurs over the life history of IS developments.

Information systems in a strategic role

Where the future of an organization depends critically upon the success of its IS activities, then IS can be described as having strategic impact. Increasingly, for many organizations, IS are critical to their key operations: banking and finance are obvious areas where IS have become essential to survival. In general, there is evidence from US and UK sources that firms which are leaders in IS investment and use are more profitable than others (although there is not a straightforward connection between IS spend and profit—clearly it is possible to spend hugely and erroneously which could have a deleterious effect on profit).

   In general there are several different ways by which IS can play a strategic role: providing competitive advantage, improving productivity, creating new business opportunities, restructuring the organization.

PROVIDING COMPETITIVE ADVANTAGE

Firms which utilize IS as a means of providing significantly better products or customer service than their competitors can increase their market share at the expense of competitors. There are many examples of this use of IS by banks and building societies, for instance, in the provision of home banking services via a telephone link to a computer network. A group of estate agents in the north of England combined resources to install a network system which linked computers at all their branches. House hunters were offered instant access to houses for sale at all the branches connected to the network, saving them the trouble and expense of visiting many different agents in their chosen area. House sellers knew that their house would reach a much wider potential market than was possible with a single estate agent. This facility provided a distinctly better service to customers than rival estate agents could offer, and the group who first provided the service achieved a significant *competitive advantage*. Any new estate agents who wished to compete in the area faced the problem of this in-built technological advantage of the existing group; thus the IS created a *barrier to entry* into the market for new competitors.

IMPROVING PRODUCTIVITY

This has always been an important role for IS and reducing data processing costs was one of the first justifications for introducing data processing systems in the early days of computers. However, cost reduction has become a far more critical concern for many large firms as competition in home and overseas markets becomes more intense. Becoming more productive meant becoming more competitive, which became essential for survival. In the 1980s the UK chemical giant ICI was able to dramatically reduce staffing levels and hence improve its productivity through the application of a deliberate strategy of technological investment. Other large firms have initiated similar high-investment IS strategies in order to survive in the 1990s.

CREATING NEW BUSINESS OPPORTUNITIES

The opportunities offered by IS to create new information products and services is truly enormous. The role of IS in the financial and banking world has already been mentioned, but in many other areas the marketing of *information* is a rapidly expanding business. Communications technology especially, with its potential for value-added networks, has enormous promise. Mass data storage and retrieval is another sector; on-line databases covering a huge variety of business topics, and world and financial news services are obvious examples. The rapid expansion of the market in expert systems is the latest in a stream of IS-based innovations.

RESTRUCTURING THE ORGANIZATION

A large proportion of the workforce is involved in information processing or knowledge working of some kind. Communications and networking technology provide the means to locate people with great flexibility, because the ability to transmit and process information has virtually eliminated the need for fixed concentrations of people. In future, more and more people will work from home, or be involved in transmitting work to remote locations. Networks, electronic mail, Fax, enhanced voice communications and teleconferencing are the technologies which will make *telecommuting* a reality for information workers. These changes, as well as enabling staff relocation and reductions in office overheads, provide the opportunity to restructure tasks and management frameworks in new and more flexible ways (see also Chapter 22).

Information systems strategy and application selection

A key task for management is that of developing a strategic plan for IS in the organization. This plan will include, especially, a programme of IS development which will reconcile the many conflicting demands for IS into a coherent, organizationally optimal strategy. In principle there may be hundreds or even thousands of IS projects which could be undertaken. Choosing the wrong ones to develop could be disastrous because of lost business opportunities and wasted development effort. Some of the potential applications will be obvious non-starters because the technology for them does not exist, or because they would be hopelessly uneconomic. But that will still leave a large number of potential applications from which to choose the key ones for the IS strategic plan.

Given that choosing which IS applications to develop is a crucial decision, how is that decision to be made? Management needs to consider four sets of criteria:

1. *The strategic importance of the application.* Whether or not the application directly impacts upon the organization's strategic plans. Applications which confer competitive advantage will clearly rate highly on this criterion.
2. *The likelihood of organizational acceptance.* Organizations are made up of power-holding individuals and groups; political considerations will necessarily influence application choice. For example, if an application is likely to meet strong opposition from powerful unions, then this fact must detract from its viability.
3. *The economic validity of the application.* The full costs of developing the application must be considered against potential benefits. Not all applications can show direct cost savings or other economic advantage, but wherever possible these should be evaluated.
4. *The risk/benefit profile of the application.* Some applications are more risky than others, particularly very large projects which take a long time to develop and rely upon the success of advanced technology (see portfolio analysis below).

When choosing applications to make up the strategic plan for the IS resource, management will select projects which rate highly on most of these criteria.

PORTFOLIO ANALYSIS

Chapter 14 discussed cost/benefit analysis as a means of choosing among system alternatives. Also described were the limitations of this method. Many systems provide intangible benefits, i.e. the benefits are difficult or impossible to quantify in economic terms. The more sophisticated decision supporting applications such as DSS or EIS are especially difficult when it comes to demonstrating tangible benefits, even though their usefulness is generally accepted. One very important aspect of application selection is the potential risk of failure. Chapter 18 mentions the high failure rate of new IS applications, and discusses one very important source of difficulty: the human dimension. But there are other risks. McFarlan identified three major elements of potential risk:

1. *Project size.* The bigger the project, the higher the risk. The greater the number of people and departments involved, the higher the expenditure; the longer the time span before completion, the greater the risk of failure, essentially because there is more to go wrong and more time for events to overtake plans.
2. *Organizational experience with new technology.* The less experience there is in the organization of dealing with the proposed technology, the greater the risk

	High structure		Low structure
Low tech.	big	low risk	low risk
	small	v. low risk	v. low risk
High tech.	big	med. risk	v. high risk
	small	med./low risk	high risk

Figure 17.4 McFarlan's matrix of risk elements

of unexpected technical problems arising. The risk applies to new software as well as to new computers or communications equipment.

3. *Project structure.* Some applications are fully defined at the outset; elementary accounting applications, for example, have clearly defined inputs and outputs and are thus highly structured. They are far less risky to develop than, say, a new executive information system for which top managers' information requirements may be very hard to determine and whose needs may also shift rapidly over time.

Figure 17.4 shows the consequences of the three risk factors; 'low tech.' and 'high tech.' are relative to the organization. For example, a large, unstructured IS project requiring the use of technology which is advanced for the organization will represent a very high risk of project failure.

Evaluating the applications portfolio involves examining potential applications, deciding on the likely organizational net benefits (economic and otherwise) and matching these against the likely risks. Applications can be roughly grouped in four categories (see Fig. 17.5):

1. High benefit–low risk: these applications should be developed first.
2. High benefit–high risk: these applications are attractive but should be approached with caution.
3. Low benefit–low risk: these applications are not very attractive but do not constitute a high risk either, and therefore should be developed after other, more attractive, applications have been completed (put on the back burner).

Potential risks

		low	high
Potential benefits	high	1. develop	2. caution
	low	3. back burner	4. avoid

Figure 17.5 Evaluating the applications portfolio: risks vs benefits

4. Low benefit–high risk: these applications are unattractive and risky and should be avoided.

A reasonable IS strategy would be to develop the applications in cell 1 of the matrix first, then examine applications in cell 2. Only then would it make sense to look at items in cell 3, and applications designated in cell 4 would be developed last of all or avoided altogether. In this way it is possible to develop a strategic plan for IS development which will maximize the short- and long-term benefits for the organization. Technology is changing rapidly and the strategic plan needs to be reviewed at frequent intervals to take advantage of developments that make viable applications which, previously, would have been uneconomic or technically non-feasible.

Summary

The computer system is but one part of the organization's information system. There will be a set of people charged with running, maintaining and developing the system. As a strategic business tool, the information system will need to take account of its costs and benefits. Part of this will rely on the choice of appropriate projects to tackle and the knowledge of which project types are unlikely to yield much return.

KEY TERMS Applications portfolio Barriers to entry Competitive advantage Management slack Portfolio analysis Risk/benefit profile Stage model of IS growth Strategic IS

Further reading

Buss M.D.J., How to rank computer projects, *Harvard Business Review*, Jan./Feb. 1983
Grey P., King W.R., McLean E.R. and Watson H.J. (Eds), *Management of Information Systems*, Dryden Press, Chicago, 1989.
Keen J., *Managing Systems Development*, Wiley, Chichester, 1987.
Wetherbe J.C., Dock V.T. and Mandel S., *Readings in Information Systems*, West, St Paul, Minnesota, 1988.

18
Managing behavioural aspects of system implementation

The need to manage people problems

A key area of management concern in the IS field is the problem of system implementation failure. Although detailed figures are hard to come by, it can be estimated that perhaps 50 per cent of all IS development projects fail to meet all or part of their original objectives. This represents an astonishing waste of expensive resources. Examples of IS implementation failures are legion, and range from small-scale accounting systems which never get beyond the parallel-running stage through to major government departmental systems which are never properly implemented, resulting in the loss of millions of pounds worth of development effort. (For example, a report in *Computer Weekly*, 24 May 1990, cites a government report which refers to the failure of a £2000 M Department of Social Security computer project.) The consequences of failure to successfully implement an IS project can be very expensive indeed.

1. *Loss of development effort.* Where the system has absorbed a substantial amount of the organization's development effort, then the loss could be very significant. For the smaller business perhaps the majority of the IS department's resources for a year or more could be tied up in one major project.
2. *Loss of anticipated system benefits.* If the system is not implemented, then all the anticipated benefits which were planned to flow from the system will not be realized; these may include vital strategic benefits.
3. *Inhibition of sequential development.* Systems are often developed sequentially. For example in order to introduce stock control, it is usually necessary first to computerize stock recording in order to have the basic data available. If the stock recording system fails, then the stock control cannot be developed, and neither can any other systems downstream of the initial development, such as stock analyses for the MIS.

4. *Loss of credibility and morale.* Where a major system fails, then the competence of the IS department may be called into question. It may then be more difficult for personnel to gain acceptance for any new proposals. Failure breeds loss of confidence and morale and this may also impair future projects.

The reasons for implementation failures are many and varied, and three major risk areas were discussed earlier (see Fig. 17.4). Perhaps it is true to say, as of marriages, that all successful ones succeed in a similar way, but each unsuccessful one fails uniquely. The causes of failure can include various aspects of technological difficulties, together with lack of proper planning and management control (see Chapter 17). However, a most important source of difficulty concerns the reactions of people to new systems: quite simply, people resist change, and IS developments are in themselves a crucial source and catalyst for organizational change.

Surprisingly, the nature of this problem is not always fully recognized by IS specialists, even though the consequences (resistance, and a failed implementation) are usually clear enough. The solution to the problem is *actively to manage the introduction of change*, and so control the parameters of the implementation problem.

The nature of resistance to change

Individuals will resist change if they feel that they may lose out because of it. This is natural and logical, and applies to all of us. If change is in the offing (and people very soon get to hear about it via the organizational grapevine which is by far the quickest means of organizational communication yet known) then the first thing that people will ask themselves is: how will I be affected by this? Unless the nature and consequences of change are discussed openly and thoroughly, people will think for themselves and imagine (rightly or wrongly) what will happen. If accurate information is lacking, there is a natural tendency to fear the worst. Indeed, there are very many things to worry about, the following are just some of the factors which may be perceived to be at risk:

- job security
- personal skill and experience assets
- work roles and job status
- interpersonal relationships
- pay and other economic conditions
- future job expectations and prospects
- group membership and status

A natural worry is that one's job is at risk. Apart from the obvious immediate threat to one's economic livelihood (and all that that may entail for the individual and his or her family) there are a number of other issues. People gain in knowledge, experience and skills throughout their working lives, and these attributes are rightly valued as an important part of an organization's resources. But what if an individual's hard-won skills, i.e. his or her *personal assets* are to be made redundant by a new computer system? Naturally, an individual will feel that his or her *personal security* is threatened. In reality, involvement in IS may well enhance the individual's skills, but this may be not at all clear at the outset.

People do not go to work just for the money. Research has consistently shown that there are a number of very important *psychological and social rewards* which people obtain from working in organizations. Among these are the benefits of social interchanges from working with other people: over time people form relationships with others which are valued for their social benefits. People also gain important psychological rewards from achievements at work and from the status which their work roles confer upon them. Work provides a life-long source of interest and involvement, and the psychological problems of those unfortunate to be out of work for any length of time include depression and other forms of mental malaise due to the lack of intellectual and social stimulus which work provides.

The effects of group behaviour have already been touched upon in Part One. In the context of change, groups may develop attitudes *against* the acceptance of change; the group situation may act as a powerful reinforcer of *group norms* which resist change. Where there is poor communication about the new system and its consequences, then people will naturally fear the worst. All too often, IS personnel have a sanguine view of a new system and its consequences which is not shared by the people who actually will be affected. The views and understanding of the implementing IS group thus steadily diverge from those of the affected group, without anybody being properly aware of it. The result can be a situation where misunderstanding and mistrust between groups become the norm.

Some individuals welcome change and perceive it as adding challenge and spice to their lives. These people may change job roles frequently, or move from job to job and from town to town. But this is not true for everybody. Others do not welcome change; rather, they feel especially threatened, and require extra time and perhaps careful counselling before they can come to terms with it. These individual differences are not age-related (as people often wrongly assume), but correlate more with personality factors and childhood experience. *Organizational history* is also important. If there have been changes in the past where the company has imposed its will, or where the change has been badly handled in other ways, then people will naturally assume (with some logic) that the same processes and results will recur this time. People may resist the implementation of an information system because they perceive that factors which are vitally important to *them personally* are at risk.

The consequence will be resistance, which can take a number of more-or-less subtle forms. Figure 18.1 indicates the range of responses which may be expected. It is important to realize that resistance may be an entirely rational response to a very real threat felt by individuals, and unless the threat can be

acceptance	enthusiastic acceptance cooperation cooperation under pressure passive acceptance
rejection	apathy passive resistance refusal to cooperate sabotage

Figure 18.1 The range of responses to technological change

genuinely reduced or eliminated in the eyes of the people concerned, then resistance should be expected.

It is perhaps natural for IS personnel to feel that 'their' new system must be wholly beneficial to the organization and ought therefore to be welcomed by others with open arms. Yet there is no real reason to expect any such thing. On the contrary, the desired range of acceptance responses must be worked for, and may involve as much care and planning as the technological aspects of the system. Unfortunately, this aspect of system implementation is rarely even discussed, let alone properly covered in IS specialist training.

Facilitating system implementation

There is a *range* of behavioural techniques which management can bring to bear on the implementation problem. Essentially, successful implementation is achieved in the long term by carefully planning the behavioural aspects of the implementation. This especially means involving all the people who will be affected by any changs so that they can take a full part in the development and implementation of the new system. In this way, they influence the nature and progress of the new system and can therefore share control over the changes which will affect their lives. This latter point is perhaps the key to the issue of implementation resistance; after all, nobody likes to be in the position where they have no control over the events which may crucially affect them.

But this is not the only way to achieve change. Circumstances may dictate that other techniques are used. The following list illustrates the range of techniques which can be used to enable change to occur.

1. *Education.* This means increasing the knowledge and understanding of individuals in order to facilitate their involvement in events. It can be achieved by internal and external courses, and by various other formal and informal methods.
2. *Communication.* This means making people fully aware of the nature of the new system, and its implications for individuals and for groups. This can be achieved by briefings, seminars and discussion groups, and by various

written methods. Information should be accurate and complete, and there must be provision for people to ask questions.

3. *Participation.* The involvement of people in the planning, design and implementation of the systems which will affect them. This is a crucial point. Successful involvement avoids ill-conceived designs and encourages commitment to the new system.

4. *Assistance and support.* As the change takes place, people will need help (facilitation) in order to cope with the unexpected, and perhaps extra effort is required to operate the new system until things have settled down.

5. *Agreement by negotiation.* This involves bargaining with individuals or groups who have interests in the outcomes of the new system implementation. It may be that the new system creates unavoidable losses of an economic or social nature which can be offset by some other negotiated outcomes, such as increased pay or other benefits.

6. *Manipulation.* This means deliberately arranging affairs without fully involving the people concerned; they do not know the full picture and may be led into situations where they do not know the true extent of possible outcomes.

7. *Coercion.* This means forcing people to accept change against their will. The coercion may be explicit, in which case people may be threatened with direct consequences of non-compliance (say dismissal, or loss of salary), or implicit, in which case the threats may be veiled (but are none the less real to the people concerned).

At various times management may attempt to apply any or all of these techniques with more or less success. Experience shows that to achieve long-lasting positive implementation success then the techniques at the top of the list —*education, communication, participation* and *facilitation*—are by far the most beneficial and are by far the most likely to achieve success in the longer term.

However, there is a penalty. Education, communication, participation and facilitation, although very worth while in the longer term, are all highly expensive and time-consuming. The time usage and financial costs of the techniques must be allowed for in assessing the viability of any proposed IS project. There may be circumstances when non-communicative or even coercive techniques at the bottom of the list have to be employed. For example, a firm may need to implement a strategically important system, perhaps one which matches that of a competitor and without which markets will be lost, resulting in the failure of the firm. This situation has arisen more frequently in recent years as information systems provide direct competitive advantage. A section of key personnel may resist the new system if it appears to threaten their personal interests; but by doing so they threaten the livelihoods of everyone in the firm. In these circumstances, senior management may employ coercive methods in order to force the system quickly into place. Situations of this nature occurred frequently in the UK print industry in the 1980s when press managements were attempting to implement advanced computer-based text processing systems against the opposition of the powerful print unions. One press baron forced through changes in working practices by dismissing the entire workforce and then re-employing only those people who would sign a contract acknowledging their willingness to accept the new methods. The resulting industrial show-downs (which included strikes, picketing and mass dismissals) received considerable media coverage.

Choosing an implementation strategy

There are two common errors in implementation management: one is habitually to utilize only one or two implementation techniques regardless of the situation; the other is to respond to resistance on an *ad hoc* basis as it occurs, rather than to plan for it in advance as part of a considered strategy. The situational factors which affect the choice of implementation techniques to employ include the following considerations:

1. *Level of resistance.* If considerable resistance is expected, then special efforts must be made to ensure that potential resistors are properly involved, and that the necessary facilitation techniques are employed. The power-attributes of resistors should also be considered; clearly the managing director has a different resistance potential to a junior clerical assistant.
2. *Knowledge and information sources.* Information systems often depend crucially upon the knowledge of key personnel; it is all the more important that these personnel are properly involved, and that sufficient time is spent on facilitating the exchange of information.
3. *Organizational needs.* Where the requirements of the organization (and perhaps its very survival) demand that the system must be implemented quickly, then there may be no choice but to limit the involvement and participation of others and to have a very precise plan of action.

Successful IS implementations are achieved by carefully planning a strategy, in advance, which takes a realistic account of the nature of likely resistance. Assessing resistance and selecting appropriate facilitation techniques is clearly a very skilled and important task. This aspect of the implementation should be managed by a suitably adept individual who is usually referred to as the *change agent*. It will be his or her job to select an appropriate strategy and to manage the behavioural aspects of the implementation through to completion. Not everybody has the necessary interpersonal talents to make a success of this role, and the identification and training of skilled change agents should be a key organizational priority. Top management support for the IS project is a vital component of a successful implementation strategy. People in organizations tend to look to higher management for cues as to their own behaviour; in other words to see which way the wind is blowing. It is essential that the proper positive messages about the IS development are given. Where people can see that the project has enthusiastic high-level support then this will signal that it is to be taken seriously.

Ethical considerations

Clearly there are important ethical issues to be considered in IS development and implementation. Implementing information systems involves changing the nature of work, and affects the lives of all the people involved. Behaving in an ethical manner essentially means not harming either individuals or organizational assets. IS professionals wield enormous power and need to be fully aware of their responsibilities in the matter. Professional organizations such as the British Computer Society and the British Institute of Management require their members to act in accordance with clearly defined ethical standards. It is incumbent upon everybody involved in IS development carefully to consider these issues and to act only in a socially responsible way.

Summary

The behavioural aspects of information systems arise because people form a major part of the total system. Implementation of new systems has to be managed in order to be effective. Management should ensure acceptance and use in the face of genuine or ill-founded concern from those affected.

KEY TERMS   Sequential development   Personal assets   Psychological and social rewards   Group norms   Facilitation   Change agent

Further reading

Bennis W., *Organizational Development: Its Nature, Origins and Prospects*, Addison-Wesley, Reading, Massachusetts, 1969.
Buchanan D.A. and Huczynski A.A., *Organizational Behaviour*, Prentice-Hall International, London, 1985.
DSS fails to see the benefit of £2bn system, *Computer Weekly*, 24 May 1990.
Kotter J.P. and Schlesinger L.A., Choosing strategies for change, *Harvard Business Review*, **57**(2), 106–114, 1979.
Willcocks L. and Mason D., *Computerising Work*, Paradigm, London, 1987.

19

Legislation: the Data Protection Act

The need for legislation

Rather surprisingly, perhaps, there is very little legislation which directly impinges on IS development and use. The principal item of new legislation to appear was the Data Protection Act of 1984. Despite its title, the Act aims to protect people from any harm which might occur to them from computer-processed information about them as individuals. The DP Act was created in response to fears that in an increasingly automated society the powerful capabilities of electronically processed data might lead to the escalating abuse of the rights and privacies of individuals. (In fact, there is little evidence of widespread abuse of this kind.) A second reason for the Act involved the government's desire for conformity with our European partners, a number of whom had already enacted similar legislation. The fear was that UK trade would be hampered by restricted data transmission if our Data Protection legislation was not in place.

The heart of the data protection act

The principal elements of the Act involve the registration by all organizations of any personal data they hold about people, together with a set of eight principles of data processing and a new set of rights for individuals. The heart of the act involves the eight *Data Protection Principles* which data users are required to comply with. In summarized form, these require that personal data shall be:

1. Obtained fairly and lawfully.
2. Held only for one or more specified and lawful purposes declared by the data user.

3. Used or disclosed only in accordance with the data user's declaration.
4. Adequate, relevant and not excessive for the declared purposes.
5. Accurate and, where necessary, kept up-to-date.
6. Not kept longer than necessary for the declared purposes.
7. Made available to data subjects on request, and corrected or erased where appropriate.
8. Properly protected against loss or disclosure.

A key principle is item seven, which requires that individuals who suspect that an organization has data on them can request a copy of that information, and, if it is inaccurate, can demand that it be corrected or erased. Normally, a request for access to personal data must be met within 40 days. A fee (currently maximum £10) may be charged for each data entry registered. The other principles all have important consequences for individuals and for any organizations which hold personal data.

The technical terms used in the Act are of key importance, and summarized definitions of the major terms are included here:

- *Data*: information recorded in a form in which it can be processed automatically (i.e. not restricted to computer-based information, although this is the major form).
- *Personal data*: information, facts or opinions relating to a living, identifiable individual.
- *Data subject*: an individual about whom personal data relates (so firms are not protected by the Act, only individuals).
- *Data user*: a person or an organization who controls the contents and use of a collection of personal data.
- *Disclosing information*: making available information, or extracts of information, from data held; the medium of disclosure may be oral, handwritten, printed or screen display (so looking over somebody's shoulder at a VDU or printout could result in disclosure).
- *Computer bureau*: a person or an organization who processes data for data users, or allows data users the use of equipment for such processing (the definition is not restricted to commercial bureau businesses).

All data users who hold personal data on individuals are required to register their holdings with the *Data Protection Registrar*. The registration of personal data includes details on the name and address of the data used, a description of the data held and the declared purpose for which it is held and the identification of persons to whom it may be disclosed. Operating without registration is prohibited and is a punishable offence. The majority of data processing applications have to be registered. Data users must also operate in accordance with the principles and other provisions of the law and are liable to sanctions and prosecution for failing to do so. The Act has also created a *Data Protection Tribunal* to hear appeals by data users against decisions of the registrar.

EXEMPTIONS

There are a number of exemptions from parts of the Act. In summarized form these include the following three categories of data:

1. All data which is processed and stored *manually*.
2. Data which poses no threat to the individual, such as accounting, payroll and pension data, data used in word processing and data held on home computers. (However, the definitions of these activities are very restrictive and most organizations would in fact have to register their payroll and accounting systems.)
3. Data held for state purposes, including data in respect of crime, national security and tax affairs.

Implications for IS development and management

Complying with the Act creates a number of important implications for the design and operation of information systems. All personal data must be registered, and then processed only in accordance with the eight principles. The design of systems must include the provision for data subject access and for indicating the source and date of creation and amendment. Processing techniques must be developed which ensure the necessary accuracy and security, and which also ensure that the data is not held longer than necessary. Operational procedures and controls must be developed so that unauthorized disclosure is prevented. Most organizations will find it useful to appoint a *Data Protection Administrator* (that need not be his or her *only* role, of course), who has specific responsibility for coordinating the organization's compliance with the Act.

Summary

Information systems, just like any other business function, require management. This management encompasses all the behavioural aspects usual in other functions and a number of technical issues absent from other functional areas. These include the security of the organization's data and the legal requirements derived from the Data Protection Act.

KEY TERMS   Computer bureau   Data Protection Act   Data Protection Administrator   Data protection principles   Data Protection Registrar   Data Protection Tribunal   Data subject   Data user   Information disclosure   Personal data

Further reading

Data Protection Registrar, *The Data Protection Act 1984: Guidelines 1–8*, Office of the Data Protection Registrar, Wilmslow, Cheshire, 1985.

Summary to Part Five

Part Five has tried to place all the management issues described above in an information systems context.

PART SIX

Towards the future

20
Artificial intelligence

Developments in new electronic and optical technologies proceed apace, with the result that faster and cheaper devices are arriving in a constant stream. Previous chapters have indicated that we can expect these developments to continue for the foreseeable future, and probably we can expect the pace of change to intensify.

However, these technological changes do not, of themselves, contribute towards new ways of *utilizing* computer power. There are very many classes of problem which computers cannot at present touch, especially problems that require common sense or the ability to cope with the unexpected; in an organizational context there are many areas of activity, particularly in management decision-making, where current IS do rather little to support human judgement. Also, at present, we can say that computers are awkward to use, and those systems considered now as 'user-friendly' can be described as such only in comparison with older, even less-friendly systems. Today, if we want to interact with a computer we have to follow its rules, use its limited in-built facilities and communicate in its artificial language via a keyboard or other machine-oriented device; the machine will make no allowances for our minor illogicalities, slips of mind or hand, or linguistic idiosyncrasies and it does not have the world knowledge to anticipate even the most trivial want but must have every detail of every requirement spelt out for it. Why do we still labour under these well-known computer deficiencies?

Simply improving the technology will not of itself bring new solutions to the problems. So where are the new ideas to come from which will provide the pathways towards better techniques and methods? The study and practice of artificial intelligence provides a rich source of ideas for improving the human/computer interface, and for generally extending the range of things that computers can do.

What is artificial intelligence?

The study of artificial intelligence (AI) is concerned with building systems that behave intelligently: systems with the ability to simulate aspects of human behaviour or human cognition. However, there are many different definitions of intelligence and attempting to *define* the precise scope of AI research and practice simply means running into semantic entanglements. Instead, it is better to examine the *topics* that are actually being studied by AI workers as this gives a useful feel for the scope and direction of the subject.

So why study artificial intelligence? As has been pointed out, there are very many areas of human activity where computers have so far made little contribution. In an organizational context, for example, there are still a great many situations where human judgement is the only possible means of making decisions, and this is particularly true where common sense skills are required. Nevertheless it is hoped that AI will, in the future, enormously extend the range of things that computers can do. There is a second reason for AI research. Our understanding of the human mind itself has been enormously enhanced by attempts to simulate cognitive behaviour on the computer. Psychologists trying to unravel the mysteries of the human brain have turned to computer models in order to explore the processes involved in cognition. These two research avenues —one leading to cleverer computers and the other leading to a better un- derstanding of the mind—are very much intertwined, and research from each avenue enriches the other.

A famous example of the dual nature of AI research is found in the work of computer scientists Simon and Newell, who explored the cognitive psychology of human problem-solving by studying how people solved cryptarithmetic problems under experimental conditions. As a result of these experiments the scientists developed a computer program called GPS (general problem solver) which attempted to simulate human problem-solving. From studies of the way in which the GPS program behaved, they were able to describe more accurately the way in which their human subjects solved problems in terms of solution search within a search space, and their work has made a significant contribution to the development of enhanced computer search techniques as well.

Artificial intelligence research mainly involves creating clever software. Advances in robotics have also occurred which, to some extent, match the advances in cognition and software research, but these hardware systems are outside the scope of this book and we will stay with the software side of AI.

Expert systems are a subsidiary topic in AI research because they utilize AI software techniques; these systems attempt to reproduce human expertise, often in a form which provides a consultation facility. Expert systems have already achieved a significant commercial stature and have such an important practical potential for management that we will consider them as a separate topic in their own right in Chapter 21.

AI ANTECEDENTS

The idea of synthesizing human capabilities has fascinated people since classical times. Pygmalion made a female statue out of ivory, Galatea, which came to life, and Guiseppe's puppet Pinnoccio eventually acquired the human capabilities of a real boy. In later centuries, automata and mechanical marvels of various kinds were on display. An early chess-playing robot was displayed by its inventor von Kempelen in the late eighteenth century; this took the form of a wooden sculpture of a chess player which worked by clockwork and moved the chess pieces on top of a large plinth, and played an excellent game. This marvel was displayed to admiring (and fee-paying) crowds until, one day, the chess robot was heard to sneeze. It transpired that the 'works' were a sham: instead of a complex mechanical computer, a chess-playing dwarf was secreted inside the base of the chess machine!

In the nineteenth century, Mary Shelley's novel *Dr Frankenstein* describes how the good doctor fabricated a human body from bits and pieces of corpses (the forerunner of modern spare-part surgery perhaps). The body was 'given life' by a high-voltage jolt from a passing thunderstorm, but then later escaped from the laboratory and proceeded to wreak havoc in the world. In line with the moral and philosophical moods of the day, Frankenstein's creation was an offence against nature as mere mortals were not supposed to experiment with the god-like activity of creating human capabilities, and the doctor's fabrication became a monster which haunted and eventually destroyed its creator. *Dr Frankenstein* is subtitled: *A Modern Prometheus*; in Greek mythology Prometheus stole fire from the gods in order to bring rationality (intelligence) to mankind.

Ideas about robots as mechanical replications of humans go back to the early years of the twentieth century. In fact the term 'robot' entered the language in 1923 when Karel Capek's stage play, *Rossum's Universal Robots*, was translated from the Czech. Fictional accounts of robots have provided a rich source of ideas ever since. Isaac Azimov's novel *I, Robot* described a world in which robots were commonplace companions for humans; Asimov defined three rules of robot life:

1. A robot may not injure a human being, or through inaction allow one to come to harm.
2. A robot must obey all commands given by human beings, except in the event that they conflict with the first law.
3. A robot must protect its own existence as long as such protection does not conflict with the first or second laws.

Hollywood has also made much of the robot idiom. Space fantasy films such as *Star Wars* and *The Empire Strikes Back* portray idiosyncratic robots, R2D2 and C3PO, with endearing personalities. A more sinister being was HAL, the psychopathic spaceship computer in *2001: A Space Odyssey*, which attempts to kill its last human fellow traveller in an intriguing battle of wits before it is switched off. A more recent film genre has seen machines pitted against humans, with the portrayal of highly sophisticated robots such as the one programmed to annihilate the heroine in *Terminator*. Science fiction fantasy serves a very useful purpose in that it shows the way things might go in the not-too-distant future; in some respects science fact is not very far behind the fantasy and may even be a little ahead in some fields.

So how near are we to creating computer systems that can chat with us, understand our needs and wishes and then, in robot form, move purposefully off to set about doing things for us with better-than-human mental and physical powers? Or, if that sounds too futuristic, what is there to stop us building systems that just have the normal human capabilities of speech comprehension and visual image perception, coupled with some elementary knowledge of the real world? In view of the benefits these capabilities would bestow upon computer users surely it is worth an all-out attempt to provide them? In fact, these latter skills were part of the objective of the fifth-generation computer development effort initiated by Japan in the 1980s.

In practice, creating intelligent artefacts turns out to be very difficult indeed, and a prominent message from AI research and development has been that human cognitive and perceptual mechanisms are very much more subtle and clever than was at first thought. Commonplace human activities such as reading a book, talking to a neighbour, walking through a crowded building or even just standing upright involve cognitive memory and processing capabilities which are extremely difficult to reproduce (even ignoring the hardware/robotic components of these activities for the moment). That they are so difficult to recreate is because even these 'simple' human activities represent enormously subtle computing tasks which have matured over millions of years of genetic evolution.

However, despite the monumental difficulties, AI research has found ways and means of simulating at least some human capabilities, and we will examine these from a management point of view in the next pages. The following are significant milestone events in the progress and development of AI.

- 1950   Turing test proposed
- 1956   'AI' term first coined
- 1957   Newell and Simon's GPS
- 1964   Dendral: the first expert system
- 1971   First commercial microprocessor
- 1972   Winograd's natural language system
- 1980   Japanese announce fifth generation
- 1985   Commercial expert systems available
- 1990   Fifth-generation products appear

AI has been a serious research and development issue since the very earliest days of electronic computing, and the idea of intelligent machines has been discussed even earlier, notably by Lady Ada Augusta when considering the

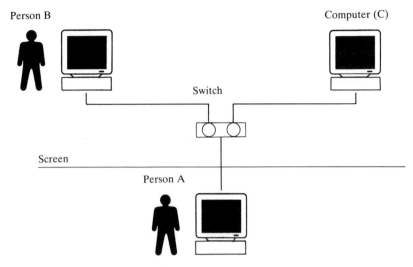

Figure 20.1 Turing test

potential capabilities of Babbage's analytic engine (see Chapter 5). She took the view that a machine could do only what it had been told, and could not originate anything. Can a machine think? Can it know things, be creative, be truly intelligent in the sense that we usually reserve for human beings? The mathematician Alan Turing asked this question directly in a famous paper, *Computing Machinery and Intelligence*, in 1950. For him, the question was unanswerable because of the difficulties of clarifying what is meant by thinking and intelligence, but this has not stopped others discussing the issues. Humans tend to be egocentric, ethnocentric and human-centred; perhaps we take altogether a too precious view of man and his abilities and the question is not really worth answering.

To clarify thinking about intelligent machines, Turing suggested his famous proposition about the intelligent machine and it has since become known as the *Turing test* (Fig. 20.1). Imagine a person (A) in a room seated before a computer terminal; he can enter anything he likes on the keyboard and can view the response on the teletype or VDU. A wire from the terminal goes to the next room where there is a switch; on one route there is a computer (C), on the other there is another person seated before another terminal (B). Person A cannot see which way the switch is set, and so does not know initially whether he is talking to a machine or to another person. Is it possible for person A to type messages and ask questions such that he can detect which way the switch is set, and therefore whether he is talking to man or machine? Person B must tell the truth, but the computer can be programmed to lie and do whatever is necessary to fool A into thinking that it is a person.

Would you be fooled? Could you ask questions that a machine could not

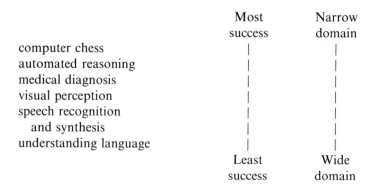

Figure 20.2   AI research and application topics

possibly deal with? This is an interesting philosophical point. It is also an important practical one because language processing systems are a key goal of AI, and surely we would check up on our invisible companion's knowledge of the world? Turing's point is that if it is not possible to tell the difference, then we truly have an intelligent machine. After 40 years, the Turing test is still a tough one for a machine because of the depth and subtleties of human language, and also the implied social behaviour which it would have to cope with. Later we will consider a language processing program called ELIZA which has fooled people into talking to it just as if it were truly intelligent.

Artificial intelligence topics

In order to illustrate the range and diversity of AI research we will examine six topics that have been addressed by AI researchers over the years (Fig. 20.2). The reasons why items at the top of this list have seen very successful computer application, while items at the bottom have not, should become more apparent by the end of this chapter.

Chess-playing programs

Computer games have become part of a major entertainment industry. Developing strategic game-playing abilities also has important consequences for AI. Playing games usually involves working to a clearly defined set of rules and also requires evaluating strategies and seeking solutions among the myriads on offer; these properties of games provide a fertile environment for the development of artificial cognitive skills. Limiting the extent of the problem search space is an important technical topic for AI researchers. One of the first AI workers in this area was Samuel who, starting in the early fifties, spent 20 years developing draughts(checkers)-playing programs. By 1961 a version of the program was playing at masters level and could beat its inventor with ease. Samuel wrote the program so that it would learn from its successes and failures (although in a fairly mechanistic way) and to modify its play accordingly; this may be the first recorded example of 'machine learning'.

Chess is a significantly more complex and subtle game than draughts. It may be considered to be at the top of the tree for strategic subtlety and the depth of knowledge required. The number of possible moves from a starting position is of the order of 2^{67}, while the number of atoms in the entire known Universe is a mere 2^{47}! Clearly, the computer cannot figure out its next move by merely calculating all the possible moves ahead since this would involve it in calculations which would take more time than several ages of the Universe! Chess programs work by utilizing *heuristics*, rules of thumb which suggest the best sort of strategy to follow in a given situation; this is similar to the way people act. Chess-playing programs and small dedicated chess computers are commercially widespread. The programs often incorporate several levels of playing difficulty and other features, such as suggested moves, tutorial sessions and chess problems. What may be so surprising is how good they have become; even low-cost commercial programs can beat club players, and the very best programs play at international masters level. However, it is interesting to note that the best programs are still beaten by people, even after several decades of work in this field.

Automated reasoning

This is another long-standing item of AI research. The idea is to utilize rules of inference together with problem-solving strategies to draw conclusions about a particular problem. The classic example is Newell and Simon's general problem-solver (GPS) which was designed to explore a generalized problem-solving strategy which could cope with a very wide variety of initial problems. Solving very narrowly defined problems is often straightforward for computers; coping with a wide range of unusual circumstances is very human-like, and relies upon 'common sense', which is another name for a generalized problem-solving capacity that is very hard to reproduce in a machine. GPS was designed to do exactly this; it worked by identifying the differences between the goal state and the present state, and then tackling the first difference. This led to other subgoals to be tackled, and so the problem was broken down into subproblems and sub-subproblems until elements were found that were solvable. A drawback of this method was that the single-minded concentration involved with searching the next logical step tended to exclude more attractive solutions which were lurking close by. A crucial feature of the GPS development was the exploration of different ways of restricting the solution search process, so that only reasonable lines of thought were pursued.

A closely related form of problem-solving involves mathematical theorem-proving, on the basis that given a set of axioms and suitable rules of logical inference, complex mathematical problems can be solved. In practice, theorem-proving programs relying only on formal logic tend to generate large numbers of irrelevant theorems to check before stumbling upon the correct one, and so search strategies guided by informal heuristics have been developed. There is an important distinction to be made between formal, complete methods of logical proof and the informal *ad hoc* heuristics which people use so successfully.

Research into automated reasoning has produced important results including successful solution-search optimizing techniques and has helped to define the predicate calculus. Work on these approaches led to the development of expert systems, which often use a mix of predicate calculus and other techniques. Another avenue for automated reasoning research is *automatic programming*. Here the idea is to use formal and informal logic techniques in order to enable programs to create other programs according to the programmer's specifications. These methods have a particular use where the object is to create highly efficient program codes for very complex logical problems.

Interestingly, automated reasoning has by no means solved the problems of recreating intelligent thought, despite the time and effort put into it. An interesting feature is that researchers have turned to informal heuristic-based methods when the formal, logic-based ones cannot achieve their goals.

Medical diagnosis

Computer-based medical diagnosis has been under development for many years, and is one of the best-researched and tested fields of expert systems. Medical diagnosis is a direct analogy for many consultation situations found in management, and the field is well worth looking at.

When you go to see your general practitioner, you meet a person who is both a trained diagnostician and has been exposed to an extensive period of theoretical training together with probably many years of diagnostic experience. When the GP looks you over, he or she may decide on the general area of problem and then, if the problem is complicated or obscure, will send you to a specialist. But the sheer volume of medical knowledge in the world is so vast that no one person can ever hope to master even a small fraction of it, and new breakthroughs in medical knowledge, drugs and surgical techniques are so widespread that even following a very small segment of the field is difficult enough. The result is a system of medical specialists: people who are experts on one narrow aspect of medical knowledge. By concentrating all their learning capacity on the theoretical and experiential aspects of one narrow field they become, not surprisingly, far better diagnosticians in that narrow field than their non-specialist colleagues. Such expertise is, by its nature, a scarce and very valuable resource; if the knowledge of the expert could be incorporated into a computer program it could be made available to a far greater range of patients, and at a far lower cost. The implications of this are far reaching because there are very many areas where individual personal expertise is at a premium, and management is surely one of them.

Table 20.1 Applications of artificial vision systems

Area of application	Target technique
weather and defence	analysis of satellite photo images
medical/industrial	X-ray analysis for problems
quality control	visual inspection of products by robot
general industrial	machine tool and robot assembly
general business	reading typed documents
security	recognition of faces, fingerprints, signatures, car number plates
defence	target finding and missile guidance
entertainment	TV image processing/special effects

Visual perception

Understanding what goes on around us is achieved to a large extent by our well-developed visual systems. These systems help us to interpret our world in so many ways, not the least in our ability to comprehend complex social non-verbal behaviours such as facial expressions, body language and the whole range of human physical activity. Only recently has it been realized how incredibly subtle and sophisticated human visual and perceptual systems actually are, especially as regards automatic colour adjustment under different light sources.

An essential requisite for the science fiction robots of films and novels is the ability to see their world and to understand what they are seeing. A vital requirement for present-day computers in business and elsewhere is to accept visual inputs in the form of documents, typed and handwritten, graphs, tables, pictures and a whole host of other visually presented data. Certainly, if we want to build intelligent robots they must be able to see and comprehend what goes on around them. Artificial vision systems have been developed which go some way towards achieving this, and a list of commercial applications, either in use or under development, is shown in Table 20.1.

Capturing visual data by machine involves several distinct phases:

1. digital image capture,
2. low-level image processing,
3. image analysis and enhancement,
4. object recognition.

The first phase is technically straightforward and involves scanning and digitizing a scene, which can easily be done using a device such as a TV camera. The scanner tracks across the scene to be captured and creates a continuous analogue signal which represents the *brightness* of the scene along the line of the track. At the end of the track, the scanner returns to its start position and scans the next track down.

The analogue signal is sampled by an analogue–digital conversion device which takes the value of the signal at discrete time intervals and passes these digital values to the computer via an interface device. The digital values are laid out in an array in computer memory. Each value in the array represents the brightness of the scene at that particular point, and each value represents a picture element or *pixel*. A typical array size might be 512 × 512 elements; the greater the number of pixels, the more the detail that may be analysed and hence the higher the *resolution* of the system. One pixel can be stored in 1 byte of memory, which provides for 256 (2^8) different values of brightness, so 1 pixel can represent 256 monochrome shades. In order to save memory, fewer levels may be used, and at the extreme of simplicity, binary (two value) pixels are used in some simple machine-tool guidance applications. Colour is taken care of by capturing three separate images using three scanners with different colour filters for red, green and blue. Monochrome images can be displayed in colour by assigning different colour shades to the monochrome pixel values; this is known as *false-colouring*.

The second stage involves processing the image to remove any 'noise' or camera and signal errors, and enhancing it to highlight desired aspects, perhaps by altering the contrast characteristics, or reversing the black and white tones. Achieving these effects involves the application of various mathematical algorithms to the pixel values in the image array in computer memory. For example, an algorithm to reduce noise errors which affect individual pixels would take the form: *for any pixel brighter than its neighbouring pixels, reduce its brightness to that of its brightest neighbour*. The same treatment is then applied with *dim* substituted for *bright*. More sophisticated statistically based algorithms are available which can highlight and sharpen the image in various ways.

The third stage, image analysis, is more difficult. It involves enhancing features of the image as a prelude to automatic recognition. The two most often used methods are *edge detection* and *region analysis*. Edge detection is a technique whereby the boundaries between differently shaded regions are emphasized; this is achieved by a statistical algorithm which alters the pixel values to highlight those between different regions.

A major problem in computer vision is that of establishing exactly where one visual object begins and another one ends. The edge-processed image strongly emphasizes the boundaries between different areas and is an essential first step towards identifying what those objects represent. The alternative to edge detection, region analysis, is a method which attempts to simplify the scene by combining regions of similar brightness, and also combining areas where one region is contained within another. The intended result is similar to that achieved by edge detection: a highly simplified outline of objects in the scene which can then be identified by a further automatic process.

The final stage, object recognition, is an order of magnitude more difficult than the processes described above. When confronted by a new visual scene, the human brain refers back to a vast store of reference objects which it uses to classify and identify elements in the scene. For example, on being given an out-of-focus family photo by a friend, you can recognize a sitting room, a group of people, furniture, pet dog and baby. You can draw a number of conclusions about the circumstances of the gathering and the relationships among the people from a variety of cues present in the scene together with the help of previously acquired specialized and general world knowledge. You do not have to have previously seen any of the specific objects in the photo in order to recognize and classify all the key objects.

A computer does not possess these abilities. Using a process called *template matching*, artificial vision systems attempt to match objects in the target scene with previously stored definitions or templates. This method works best with regular shapes, and much work has been done on recognition of three-dimensional cubes, cylinders, blocks and other regular geometric figures which can be easily defined in terms of angles and line lengths. Recognizing three-dimensional objects is more difficult still and involves detecting the orientation of the object, taking into account perspective and missing data from hidden surfaces, together with relative distances judged by stereoscopic image comparison.

The recognition of geometric figures can be extended to real-world object recognition by extending the template matching algorithms to look for other attributes of objects such as regions of certain size, relative location, light frequencies, the presence of junctions and other line characteristics, and the degree of region fragmentation. For example, a river will usually be sinuous with low-angle junctions or branches; a road will have low or medium sinuosity and with 90 degree junctions possible. The future for general-purpose vision systems seems to require the development of systems with the ability to handle an extensive knowledge base, together with *fuzzy logic* (for example, note that rivers are usually sinuous, but not always) in order to achieve successful real-world application. Although systems with the general capability of natural systems seem a long way off, more *specialized systems* requiring a limited knowledge domain are inherently easier and such limited applications will become increasingly common.

There are a number of difficulties which practical vision systems must overcome. For example edges may be blurred and shadows can cause changes in region intensity which do not signal the edge of an object; all the facets of an object may not be visible (any three-dimensional object must fall into this category) and the missing parts must be deduced; determining the orientation of an object may be very difficult; and classifying an object which nearly, but not quite, fits one of the stored set of template images is fraught with difficulty.

The fact that human vision systems continuously and effortlessly cope with an astonishingly varied mix of unknown objects under all conditions of light, shade, colour, orientation and semi-visibility should remind us of the fact that several million years of evolution have created a living system which is incredibly subtle and complex. Interestingly, human systems are by no means the most advanced: for example, the perceptual systems of predatory animals such as hawks must cope with subtle three-dimensional images at great extremes of distance and under very rapidly changing circumstances as the bird first locates, recognizes and then swoops on its prey.

Of course, the human brain and memory play a large part in human visual perception, and because of the ability of the brain to retain enormous numbers of scenes relatively few cues are needed to recognize particular images, or classes of images. This is not the case with artificial vision systems which are very crude by comparison and which labour under a tremendous disadvantage because of their relative simplicity.

Speech recognition and synthesis

A long-held goal of AI research has been to enable computers to be spoken to using natural speech patterns. The benefits this would convey are tremendous; simply relieving the enormous problem of having to input data via a keyboard would be an immense boon.

SPEECH RECOGNITION

When we hear somebody talking, our ears are receiving an analogue signal in the form of sound waves carried through the air. A good quality microphone can pick up all the information present in much the same way as the ear, so that the problem is entirely one of interpreting the signal. In much the same way as with vision systems, this interpretation problem becomes overwhelming if the artificial system is to achieve all that the human perception system can do.

In the fifties, an electronics engineer built a machine which came to be called the 'watermelon box'; full of electronics, it had a microphone in front and a red light on top. During the normal course of conversation nothing happened, but if the word 'watermelon' was spoken the light on the box would flash, indicating that the box had identified that word from all the other items of conversation. In fact, this word has unusual characteristics: it is the only English word with four successive vowels a, e, e and o in sequence, so constructing circuits to recognize this unique wave-pattern was reasonably straightforward. Unfortunately, constructing circuits to distinguish between all the other thousands of words in regular use is something more of a problem! Then consider that in normal speech, words are not spoken singly, but are run together and slurred in a continuous sound and it can be seen that this exacerbates the problem enormously.

Human speech recognition uses all kinds of non-verbal cues to assist understanding, together with extensive background knowledge of the nature and context of the communication. Experiments with compressed speech, in which tiny fragments of recorded speech are progressively removed, have shown that speech is intelligible to us when even up to 60 per cent of the total signal has been removed. However, artificial *continuous speech recognition* (CSR) for general data input still appears to be a long way off.

Speech recognition systems are available which can recognize up to several

REPORT	FORM	PERSONAL	FOR	EXPERT
key	key	report	key	field
word	word	name	word	name

Figure 20.3 Artificial language: a statement for dBase IV

hundred different words, when these are spoken separately. The systems must be tuned to individual speakers to allow for accent and intonation characteristics. Although these systems are obviously very limited when compared with natural systems, they still have an important role to play. There are many situations where even very limited recognition can be very useful, for example where the hands are occupied, as with some production processes, and in complex manual control tasks such as those managed by aircraft pilots.

SPEECH SYNTHESIS

Speech synthesis involves generating wave-patterns which correspond to specific words or phrases. This does not appear to be such a problem as speech recognition, and a number of speech synthesis applications have appeared. For example, cars which tell their drivers to fasten their seat belts are now commonplace, and some home banking systems will provide details of account balances and transactions over the telephone through automatic speech synthesis techniques. There are a number of applications where synthesis is useful, particularly where people are carrying out tasks that require their full visual attention; interaction with the visually handicapped is another important area. One reason why synthesis is relatively successful is that the recipient of the synthesized speech is a human being with a highly sophisticated recognition system, which can cope with even quite crude synthesis techniques.

Understanding language

In the previous section, we discussed artificial speech recognition, i.e. the ability of a computer to distinguish between, and identify correctly, spoken words. The next step, then, is for the computer to analyse the words and to ascribe meaning to the language thus received. Of course, a similar understanding task is involved if the words are typed in on a keyboard rather than received through a speech recognition system: the problem is that of understanding *natural language*.

ARTIFICIAL LANGUAGE

Computers can readily respond to *artificial languages*, such as FORTRAN, COBOL and PROLOG, i.e. languages that have been specially designed for them. This category includes all the programming languages which were discussed in Chapter 11. Figure 20.3 shows a phrase in the command language of the database processing language dBase IV. Each key word is one that will cause dBase to respond in a certain way. REPORT means that the report printing routines are required; FORM means that a format for the report has already been described to the system, and the next word is the name of the report format: PERSONAL; FOR is another key word which tells dBase that only certain records are to be processed, i.e. only those for which the logical code in the field called EXPERT is set to 'true'.

When processing a command, dBase will examine each word in turn and look it up in its vocabulary; either it is a standard key word, or it is a format or field name which has been defined earlier. Any other words will result in an error message. If the order of these words is changed, dBase will not be able to cope, and again will signal an error. Programming languages have an artificial *syntax* (structure), *grammar* (the set of rules which defines how words can be combined) and *vocabulary*, all especially designed so that commands can be recognized unambiguously. Computers 'understand' the language by parsing each phrase, i.e. each word is examined in terms of its position, and then looked up in a vocabulary which defines the action required.

NATURAL LANGUAGE

Early linguists believed that natural languages could be understood in much the same way as artificial ones, and that the problem was essentially one of defining the rules of grammar, together with an extensive vocabulary. This belief has been the basis of a number of attempts to create automatic translation systems, e.g. English into Russian and vice versa. Unfortunately, these automatic translators often produced unexpected and occasionally risible results. One famous (and probably apocryphal) episode describes how the biblical phrase: 'The spirit is willing but the flesh is weak' was translated into Russian and then back into English, whereupon it came out from the computer as: 'The vodka is fine but the meat is rotten'. On another occasion, an engineering description involved a 'hydraulic ram' which came back as 'water goat'!

Consider the translation possibilities for the word 'spirit': ghost, mind, alcohol, chemical, life-force, resolution, intention, a particular sort of person, essence and breath. Clearly, one-for-one vocabulary translation is not sufficient for any real understanding, or for translating one language into another. Neither are grammatical rules sufficient on their own to achieve understanding. The following lines from the famous nonsense poem *The Jabberwocky* by Lewis Carroll give the impression of being grammatically accurate and completely sensible: 'Twas brillig, and the slithy toves did gyre and gimble in the wabe'. The fact is that in natural language syntax, vocabulary and meaning are all bound up together in a rich tangle.

What was learnt from the early translation attempts was that natural language comprehension is a far more subtle and complex human activity than was at first thought. Not only are the rules of grammar subtle, flexible and dependent upon context, but much of the human understanding of language depends upon an extensive knowledge gained over decades of learning about the world. For example: 'My PC has had it; the disk's gone home I'm afraid. Yes, in my office now: can you replace it for next week?' The colloquial phrases in the first sentence are but a token of the choice of phrases available for common events in normal English usage. In the first sentence, is anybody really frightened? In the second sentence, what does the 'it' refer to: the office? Again, take the nursery rhyme: 'Mary had a little lamb': did Mary merely possess a small sheep, or did she eat a slice of mutton with mint sauce? Ambiguity, and richness and depth of meaning are a subtle part of English literature; but they make language comprehension by machine extremely difficult.

There have been several attempts to achieve some form of language understanding. A very famous example of a language system is a conversational program called ELIZA, developed by Weizenbaum. ELIZA responds interactively to sentences typed into a terminal, and talks rather like a therapist or social counsellor (sentences in capitals are ELIZA):

Men are all alike
IN WHAT WAY?
They're always bugging us about something or other
CAN YOU THINK OF A SPECIFIC EXAMPLE?
Well my boyfriend made me come here
YOUR BOYFRIEND MADE YOU COME HERE?
He says I'm depressed much of the time
I AM SORRY TO HEAR YOU ARE DEPRESSED
It's true, I am unhappy
DO YOU THINK COMING HERE WILL HELP YOU NOT TO BE
UNHAPPY?
I need some help, that much is certain

Some of the people who talked to ELIZA were convinced that the program was virtually human; and one student would not let the experimenter see her output, because it was 'private'! Has ELIZA passed the Turing test? If not, why not?

ELIZA uses several tricks to generate plausible looking responses. It scans the input for key words, rather like the dBase IV processor. For example, the key word 'my' causes ELIZA to repeat the phrase that follows, with 'your' tacked on the front. If ELIZA cannot spot a key word, then it will output a random content-free phrase, or arbitrary statement to keep the conversation going.

A genuine, and highly successful, language processor was created by Winograd. This program displayed a set of cubes, pyramids and boxes on a terminal screen (see Fig. 20.4): a block-world inhabited by a simulated robot called SHRDLU. A hand which can pick up and manipulate the objects is available. To have a conversation with SHRDLU you type requests about the blocks on the screen; SHRDLU will understand the English sentences even if they are not entirely grammatically clear, by referring back to previous inputs, or by making an assumption. If it is asked to do something that requires another

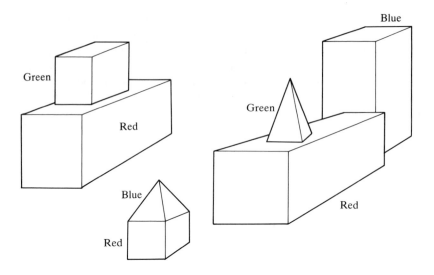

Figure 20.4 Block-world

step first, that step will be taken; it can also be taught new words which are used in future conversations. The capitalized words are SHRDLU's:

Pick up a big red block
OK
Grasp the pyramid
I DON'T KNOW WHICH PYRAMID YOU MEAN
(*there is more than one pyramid so the program does nothing*)
Find a block which is taller than the one you are holding and put it
into the box
BY IT I ASSUME YOU MEAN THE BLOCK WHICH IS TALLER
THAN THE ONE I AM HOLDING—OK
What does the box contain?
THE BLUE PYRAMID AND THE BLUE BLOCK

Does SHRDLU pass the Turing test? If not, why not? SHRDLU can obviously cope well with complex phrases and ambiguous pronouns. In fact the brief example above does not do justice to its abilities. However, it works well only as long as we are talking about the blocks in its scene. As soon as we talk about anything else at all, SHRDLU is lost. Within the very narrow confines of the block-world, language understanding by machine is demonstrable. Surely the next step is to broaden out this achievement so that a machine can cope with a wider knowledge base? Unfortunately, at present it does not appear to be possible to usefully extend language understanding beyond a minute knowledge domain because of the sheer enormity and complexity of the information that must be stored. The techniques used in the creation of SHRDLU do not appear to be generalizable to the world at large.

Summary

Although uses of artificial intelligence techniques in information systems are currently very limited, a knowledge of the opportunities which may be available in the future is valuable. Artificial intelligence involves building computer systems which exhibit intelligence. This intelligence may be of several forms, such as language and speech understanding, vision and automated reasoning.

KEY TERMS Artificial language   Automated reasoning   Automatic programming   Continuous speech recognition (CSR)   Edge detection   ELIZA
False-colouring   Fuzzy logic   Grammar   Natural language   Parsing
Region analysis Resolution SHRDLU Speech synthesis Syntax Template matching Turing test

Further reading

Bobrow D.G. and Hayes P.J. (Eds), Artificial intelligence – where are we?, *Artificial Intelligence*, **25**, 375–415, 1985.
Forester T., *Computers in the Human Context*, Basil Blackwell, Oxford, 1989.
Haughland J., *Artificial Intelligence: the Very Idea*, MIT Press, Cambridge, Massachusetts, 1985.
Rich E., *Artificial Intelligence*, McGraw-Hill, New York, 1983.
Simon H.A., *The Sciences of the Artificial*, MIT Press, Cambridge, Massachusetts, 1981.
Weizenbaum J., *Computer Power and Human Reason*, Penguin Books, Harmondsworth, 1976.
Winograd T., *Understanding Natural Language*, Academic Press, New York, 1972.

21
Expert systems

Introduction

By far the most successful practical application of AI techniques to date has come about from the development of *expert systems*. These systems show tremendous promise in diverse aspects of management, and many organizations are investigating their potential. A key field of AI research involves the representation and elicitation of *knowledge*. This is done in a number of different ways and for many different purposes; systems which employ knowledge-based techniques are generally called *intelligent knowledge based systems* (IKBS). IKBS may be found in all sorts of applications, for example, as a front-end to a database enquiry system; an IKBS differs from a conventional information system in that it utilizes human knowledge, heuristics or other AI-based technique in some way.

Expert systems represent a very important subclass of IKBS. An expert system is an IKBS with a knowledge base which is accessed by the user in *consultation* with it. The user provides details of a problem in the knowledge domain of the expert system through a question and answer dialogue led by the system; the system then offers a diagnosis of the problem and a suggested solution, or perhaps says it has none to offer. Expert systems reason heuristically: they use rules of thumb which experts think will work most of the time; and they can operate on incomplete or partially inaccurate data. Some expert systems will explain why they are asking a question, and, having provided a diagnosis, will offer a set of reasons to justify their conclusions.

MEDICAL DIAGNOSIS

Medical diagnosis systems have been a very well-developed and researched area of expert system evolution. One of the first (and perhaps most influential)

Name	Domain	Date
MYCIN	Blood infections	1976
CASNET	Glaucoma	1978
PUFF	Pulmonary infections	1978
IRIS	Ophthalmology	1977
PIP	Kidney disorders	1976
DIGITALIS	Cardiology	1978
ONCOCIN	Cancer	1981
SAM	Hypertension	1981

Figure 21.1   Medical expert systems

systems was MYCIN, created at Stanford University in the seventies. MYCIN was designed as an interactive consultation system to interpret clinical and judgemental data on infectious blood diseases. Patients in hospital can show symptoms of blood disorders after surgery or other treatment; fast and accurate diagnosis is necessary in order to treat a disease which might otherwise prove fatal. Because clinical tests which could positively identify the disease organism may take one or two days to process, it is necessary to make a best estimate of the problem immediately on the basis of the incomplete information available. Treatment involves drugs which have to be carefully selected to avoid adverse interactions on the patient. The diagnosis and suggested treatment depend primarily upon the expertise of skilled diagnosticians. MYCIN was developed to capture this diagnostic and prescriptive skill, and to provide it whenever required in a consultation form.

The heart of the MYCIN system is a set of *if. . . then* rules which captures the experiential knowledge of expert practitioners. A sample rule from MYCIN looks like this:

RULE 85

IF   1) The stain of the organism is gramneg
          and 2) the morphology of the organism is rod
          and 3) the patient is a compromised host

THEN   There is suggestive evidence (0.6) that the identity of
          the organism is pseudomonas

Note that the THEN part of the rule is expressed in terms of a *probability* (0.6) that the diagnosis is correct. MYCIN contains more than 500 rules, and these have been extensively altered or added to in the light of experience.

Because MYCIN was so successful, it has been used as the basis for developing other expert systems (Fig. 21.1). Stripped of its specific blood-infection knowledge, the MYCIN software was known as EMYCIN (empty or essential MYCIN) and the empty shell was used to create other systems. For example,

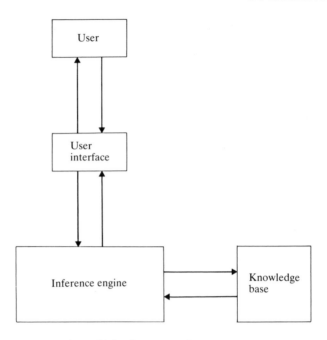

Figure 21.2   Structure of expert systems

a much smaller system called PUFF was developed from EMYCIN to diagnose lung disorders. Developing expert systems from scratch using specialist programming languages such as PROLOG or LISP is very time-consuming, so the idea of using a ready-made *software shell* to develop new expert systems is very attractive. Expert system shell software is now commercially available in a number of different forms for a wide range of potential applications, including management.

How reliable are expert systems? Rigorous research has been done on the reliability of medical diagnostic systems—something that is rarely done with commercial systems—for the obvious reason that the results are critical to human life (see Rogers *et al.* 1979). The systems are tested with cases which are diagnosed by panels of experts and then, where possible, checked against real outcomes. The very best of the medical expert systems such as MYCIN appear to be as good, or almost as good, as human experts. Significantly, the best systems are far better than human non-specialists, and this perhaps is the key to their practical acceptance.

Expert system structure

How does an expert system work? Typically, a consultative expert system contains the elements shown in Fig. 21.2. An input interface is needed to cope with the user's answers to questions: these answers can be in the form of free input of key words, but more usually the input takes the form of selections from a list or menu.

The outputs from the system are important; firstly, in terms of a series of questions, and then a diagnosis and possibly suggestions for action. The output diaglogue needs to be couched in suitable language for somebody who knows the topic area, but may know little about computers. Ideally, the system should be able to respond helpfully to questions such as: Why ask me that? and: How do you come to that conclusion? In some applications, it may be useful for the user to volunteer information, rather than simply react to the system's questions.

The knowledge base is the heart of the system, it contains the facts, heuristics and probabilities, together with their interconnections, which represent the system's diagnostic expertise. In most contemporary expert systems, the knowledge base is implemented in the form of a set of *if... then* rules, as described above. An elementary system may have a few dozen rules; a large, sophisticated one may have many hundreds or even thousands of rules.

Inference engine is a term that owes something to Babbage's early work. It is the 'reasoning' part of the system which infers new facts from those supplied to it. It consists of a mechanism for processing the knowledge base in the light of information received from the user. When a piece of information is received —usually in answer to a question—this information is compared to the left-hand side of the *if... then* rules, and where a rule is satisfied the right-hand side, or *then* part of the rule, comes into force. When this happens the rule is said to have 'fired'. The new information thus inferred may be used to examine the rules again, so that other rules can fire. This process of examining the left-hand sides of rules to draw inferences from the right-hand sides is called *forward chaining*, because the inference engine works forward from an initial state of knowledge and infers new knowledge whenever a rule fires.

An alternative strategy involves *backward chaining*. Here, the system looks at a goal state and works backwards to see which rules are appropriate for it. For example, considering MYCIN we might wish to establish whether or not the disease organism in question was *Pseudomonas*; in this case the inference engine would look at the right-hand sides of all the rules first to see which ones were involved (and rule number 85 clearly is); then it would ask the user questions to see if the rules were true. Some expert systems use a combination of forward and backward chaining techniques (termed mixed chaining) in order to seek goals and to make the best use of the knowledge available.

The logical and mathematical basis which underlies the rules of inference employed by most expert systems is called the *predicate calculus*. A predicate is simply a mathematical function whose value is true or false, and this is seen in the form of the *if... then* rules. Fortunately it is not necessary to understand the mathematical basis of logical inference in order to build an expert system. Table 21.1 shows expert systems paralleled with conventional information systems.

Table 21.1 Expert systems: parallels with conventional IS

Conventional IS	Expert systems
Content	
information	knowledge
Development tools	
high-level languages	LISP, PROLOG
fourth-generation languages	ES shells
Practitioner	
systems analyst	knowledge engineer

Software tools for expert systems

Early experimental expert systems were built using the AI specialist languages LISP or PROLOG which are designed to handle statements in predicate calculus. However, this is equivalent to building a conventional system using a high-level language and is both difficult and time-consuming. During the eighties a number of commercial expert system shells appeared; these shells are similar in concept to EMYCIN, i.e. they offer a ready-made expert system with a structure similar to that of Fig. 21.2, but which is empty of knowledge. The user acquires the shell, enters the rules which represent the knowledge for his or her application and makes use of the input/output user interfaces provided.

The appearance of shell software tools puts the development of expert systems within the reach of almost any organization, and many systems are currently under development. Expert system software has been devised to run on a variety of machines including PCs, mainframes and specialist AI workstations. Currently available shells which run on PCs are shown in Table 21.2; there is an enormous range of software available, and each package has its own

Table 21.2 Expert system development software

Expert system development tool	Comments
Automated reasoning tool (ART)	
ExpertEase	induction-based
Goldwords	
Guru	includes spreadsheet and other business software
Instant-Expert plus	available on IBM and MAC PCs
1st class Fusion	induction-based
KEE (knowledge engineering environment)	useful for engineering applications
Leonardo	
Nexpert-Object	runs on several machine types
Personal consultant	
RuleMaster	induction-based
VP-Expert	current market leader
XI-Plus	

particular strengths. The most comprehensive and flexible packages tend to require the most expertise on the part of the developer; tools that are easy to understand and use tend to be limited and inflexible in their capabilities. Choosing a suitable shell for a particular business application is not an easy task, and some organizations call on the advice of consultants who have detailed knowledge of the packages available.

An expert system called CAPE has been developed by one of the authors using the LEONARDO expert system shell. The problem to be solved concerns the relatively new PC user who would like to develop an application but is not sure which package type to use for it. See Chapter 12 for a discussion on the choice factors. The idea is for the expert system to suggest a suitable general purpose software package to suit various applications and circumstances. The users of CAPE include students and staff. The packages about which CAPE advises include spreadsheet, word processor, database, graphics, DTP, and decision support software. An edited example of a consultation with CAPE is shown in Fig. 21.3 (user inputs are selected from menus in practice, but are shown here in capitals). Suppose you wanted to create a file of 50 or 60 names which represent a club to which you belong; you are not sure yet exactly what you want to do with them, so which package should you use?

CAPE has about twenty rules in its knowledge base, including rules such as number 12:

> Rule 12
>
> | IF | calcs is small |
> | --- | --- |
> | AND | data is small |
> | AND | graphs is no |
> | AND | h_q_output is no |
> | THEN | package is wordprocessor |

CAPE uses backward chaining. Starting with the goal 'find a suitable package', the system looks at the rules and asks questions to see whether the rule fires and the goal is satisfied. CAPE is liked by its users, who are impressed by its solutions and its easy-to-use dialogue. The system can justify its conclusions to a limited extent by referring back to the rules it has used, but this is not entirely satisfactory from the user's point of view because the explanation is somewhat mechanical and unconvincing. CAPE was developed by one of the authors who acted both as the knowledge engineer and as the expert; but in most commercial circumstances this will not be the case and it is necessary for the system developer to elicit knowledge from somebody else. This turns out to be a significant problem area in expert system development, and is discussed in the next sections.

The nature of expertise

Expertise is a scarce and costly resource. Experts are people who have devoted

CAPE: Choosing an Application Package

CAPE will help you choose a general-purpose software package for a PC application you have in mind. A difficult choice to make is when you have a rough idea of what you want to do, but are unsure which software package to start with. A tricky choice! Simply answer the straightforward questions which follow as far as you can, and CAPE will suggest the most suitable package on the information available.

The *computer* type you are going to use may have some bearing on the issue. Select the type you will be using:

IBM PC or PS/2
IBM compatible
Apple MAC
BBC
Don't know

IBM COMPATIBLE

What level of *calculation* will be required?

small – no calculations, or perhaps limited summations
medium – calculations with straightforward rules or functions
large – extensive and complex calculations, perhaps with advanced maths/stats or financial functions don't know

SMALL

Do you need to create *graphs* as part of your output?

yes – graphs needed
no – graphs not needed
don't know

NO

How great is the number of *data elements* which the application requires?

small – up to about 50 pieces of data
medium – from 50 to about 100 pieces of data
large – more than about 100 pieces of data
don't know

MEDIUM

In my opinion the best package for your application will be a *word processor*. This will provide a flexible means of coping with your modest amount of data. A suitable package could be WORD, WORDSTAR or WORDPERFECT.

Figure 21.3   Choosing an application package

considerable time and effort to developing in-depth personal knowledge of a topic or phenomena, be it brain surgery or solving crossword puzzles. The knowledge may be acquired experientially, perhaps from working for long periods of time in the topic area and seeing a large number of instances or cases, or academically from formal training and study, and by utilizing the memories and experiences of others. Most expertise comes from a variety of different sources and is inextricably linked with the possessor's own general knowledge and view of the world. The way that people actually access and utilize their expertise cognitively is not at all clear; however, a model of expertise due to Dreyfus and Dreyfus (1986) suggests that there are several phases to the development of human expertise.

Stage 1: novice. The beginner learns about relevant facts and features in the expertise area, together with straightforward rules about how to cope. For example, when learning to drive a car there are rules about at what speed to change into fourth gear, and how many car lengths to be left between you and the car ahead.

Stage 2: advanced beginner. Performance improves as the beginner gains experience of real-world situations. The rules learnt are more complex and relate to specific situations. For example, changing gear when the sound of the engine appears to be correct, and leaving more or less space between you and the car in front depending on speed, traffic and other conditions.

Stage 3: competence. The competent driver is learning the extent of his or her acquired rules, and knows when they can be broken. His or her growing skills are based on concrete experiential knowledge which is stored unconsciously.

Stage 4: proficiency. Here the performer no longer consciously applies fixed rules all the time but makes decisions on the basis of an intuitive feel for the situation. On occasion, there will still be the need to consider the situation analytically, in terms of learnt rules, but generally there is no need to do this.

Stage 5: expertise. The expert copes with the task in his or her knowledge domain intuitively, without the need to make analytic decisions involving consciously realized sets of factors; the skill has become an ingrained, almost automatic response to familiar situations. The expert car driver responds successfully to ever-changing stimulus ahead by unconsciously processing the visual images in terms of a learnt and extensive database of similar scenes.

According to the Dreyfus model, human expertise cannot be directly captured in terms of rules because the genuine experts *do not work to rule.* Indeed, the very nature of their expertise means that they have gone beyond the rule-application phase, and their brains are employing a subtle pattern-matching technique which relies on a stored base of many thousands of particular, individual cases. When faced with a case for diagnosis, the expert says, unconsciously: I've seen this before, and I know from experience that the best thing to do is this .... Unfortunately, this sort of expertise does not directly translate into the rule-based format used by most expert systems. This is not to say that rule-based computer systems cannot *simulate* human expertise but that the computer analytical process is at least one step removed from the human, heuristic, cognitive one.

CHARACTERISTICS OF THE EXPERT

Experts come in all shapes and sizes, from piano players to jumbo-jet pilots. What they have in common is that they can perform some task with greater

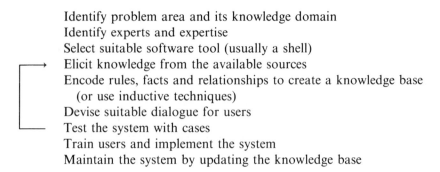

Identify problem area and its knowledge domain
Identify experts and expertise
Select suitable software tool (usually a shell)
Elicit knowledge from the available sources
Encode rules, facts and relationships to create a knowledge base
    (or use inductive techniques)
Devise suitable dialogue for users
Test the system with cases
Train users and implement the system
Maintain the system by updating the knowledge base

Figure 21.4   Expert systems development stages

facility and accuracy than most other people. In organizations, experts abound and it could be argued that the development of an organization is largely about the development of specialist expertise in its members. Experts are required who can make decisions about people, about financial and legal matters, about the management of general and specialist departments and about the working of particular machines and production processes. By its nature, expertise is scarce, and its acquisition costs time and money. When experts leave an organization, their expertise goes with them and their places must be filled by people who must acquire that expertise afresh. It is therefore a very attractive proposition to attempt to capture the expertise found in many aspects of organizational life, or to attempt to buy-in expertise in a field where this is lacking in the organization.

Developing expert systems

In some respects, developing an expert system is similar to developing a conventional system. Figure 21.4 lists the development stages which are usually required; even more than is the case with conventional systems development, there will be a need to *iterate* steps in the development process. However, eliciting knowledge and encoding it in rules is not at all the same as analysing and defining data paths in conventional systems analysis, and this area has proved to be fraught with difficulty in practice.

Prototyping (see Chapter 15) is a particularly suitable technique for expert system development because it allows the developing system to be viewed and tested early in the development process. Once the system has been created using a suitable shell it may need to be recoded using a more machine-efficient programming language in order to provide a suitable operational performance.

KNOWLEDGE ELICITATION

The knowledge that forms the basis of expertise comes in a number of different guises, but in practice it is available either from primary sources (human experts), or from secondary sources (including books and other static materials). The knowledge engineer must interact with the domain expert so as to elicit information which can be coded into the rules provided by the predicate calculus.

There are five main methods of direct knowledge elicitation:

1. Interviews: asking an expert to describe how he or she makes decisions, and agreeing rules which simulate expert behaviour.
2. Case walk-throughs: following the expert and talking through real or contrived case situations which demonstrate the decision-making capability.
3. Observation/case analysis: watching the expert make decisions, or analysing evidence of decisions which have been made.
4. Consulting textual sources: reading through published books, papers, articles, manuals and other secondary materials which contain information which yields expertise.
5. Development directly by the expert: the expert acts as his or her own knowledge engineer and translates his or her own knowledge directly into suitable rules.

Problems arise with all of these methods. But first, catch your expert. By its nature, expertise is scarce and even if you can locate the right person he or she may not have the time or inclination to develop a system which may perhaps be seen as threatening. There are other problems: the knowledge engineer may know little of the expert's knowledge domain, say chemical engineering or high finance, which can make mutual understanding difficult; the expert may find it impossible to express his or her ideas in terms of rules (bearing in mind the nature of expertise as discussed above); and, of course, the expert's time is probably at a premium. There may be several experts; in addition, one of the most certain things about experts is that they will disagree! The knowledge engineer may decide on a super-expert, referred to as a *knowledge-Czar*, because he or she is given an arbitrary stature and is correct by definition.

RULE INDUCTION

A completely different approach to knowledge elicitation is used in the *rule induction* method. Some expert system tools (see Table 21.2) have the facility to accept a number of cases, together with the expert's diagnoses or solutions. The software then uses these examples to *derive the rules* that can be used to solve other cases. This method eliminates the difficult task of eliciting or devising rules by the knowledge engineer. For example, taking CAPE, the package adviser discussed earlier, the inputs to a rule induction processor would take the form shown in Table 21.3. A hundred or so examples would be required to enable accurate rules to be inferred by induction.

Experience has shown that *expert system development is a very high-risk area in terms of costs and the likelihood of success*. This may sound a rather pessimistic statement, but it is as well to be aware of the limitations of present-day techno-

Table 21.3   Rule induction from solved examples

Item	Calcs	Data	Graphs	Q/o	Machine	Expert verdict
1	medium	small	yes	no	IBM	spreadsheet
2	small	small	no	no	MAC	word processor
3	small	large	no	no	IBM	database
4	large	large	yes	no	unknown	DSS
5	small	small	yes	yes	unknown	DTP
6	–	–	–	–	–	–
100	–	–	–	–	–	–

logy and expertise. Experience seems to show that expert system development may be successful where all or most of the following conditions apply:

1. There are clearly defined project objectives.
2. The objectives are limited and readily achievable.
3. There exists a very *limited* knowledge domain.
4. There exists a *well-defined* knowledge domain.
5. An expert is available, and is prepared to spend considerable time with the knowledge engineer during development.
6. The expert is highly articulate and can readily express his or her knowledge in terms of straightforward relationships.
7. The expert is highly motivated towards achieving the project objectives.

Having clear and, above all, limited objectives seems to be particularly important. As the scope and scale of an intended expert system increases, so the complexities and difficulties increase exponentially. When hundreds of rules have been extracted and encoded it is still possible for the system to be substantially incomplete because key concepts and principles have been omitted. It can be very hard indeed to de-bug an expert system because as the rules multiply it becomes increasingly difficult to see what is going on. (Experience with students working on expert systems for the first time shows that it is possible to have considerable difficulties with a system with only two rules in it!) As yet there are no established structured design methodologies available, and so programming expert systems is even more of a craft skill than is the case with conventional information systems.

Expert systems applications

There are very many situations in management where expertise is in short supply, and so it is hardly surprising that substantial efforts are being made in many organizations to create expert systems. The following is a list of topics where expert systems have been developed.

accounting advice	computer system configuration
career guidance	corporate tax advice
complex rules interpretation	Data Protection Act advice

fault diagnosis in complex machinery	medical training
fault recovery in on-line computer systems	military threat assessment
	mineral exploration
financial management	personal tax advice
industrial process control	personnel selection
legislation advice	raw materials sourcing acquisition
loan guidance	small business guidance
management negotiation	social services claimants advice
medical diagnosis	training salesmen

As can be seen, the list is tremendously diverse; the scope of expert systems seems to be limited only by our imaginations, and the time and effort required to develop them. However, it is worth reiterating the note of caution sounded in the last section: knowledge engineering is, as yet, a difficult and risky undertaking. Not all expert systems are successfully completed and implemented, and, as in any area of information systems development, much depends on the skill with which the development project is selected and managed.

Summary

Expert systems are the most successful artificial intelligence application available to businesses. They are now a used, and useful, tool in diverse areas such as medical diagnosis, legal interpretation and taxation. Although differing in detail all expert systems have a structure which includes a knowledge base of a particular expert domain and an inference engine which handles the reasoning or the application of that knowledge to the current problem. However, the development of expert systems is problematic and no clear, trusted development methodologies currently exist. Yet it is clear that information systems interacting with expert systems will become common as mutual benefits are apparent.

KEY TERMS   Backward chaining Domain expert Forward chaining Inference engine   Intelligent knowledge-based systems (IKBS)   Knowledge base Knowledge-Czar   Knowledge elicitation   Knowledge engineer   Predicate calculus Rule induction Software shell

Further reading

Alty J.L. and Coombs M.J., *Expert Systems: Concepts and Examples*, NCC Publications, Manchester, 1984.

Buchanan B.G. and Shortcliffe E.H., *Rule-Based Expert Systems*, Addison-Wesley, Reading, Massachusetts, 1984.

Department of Trade and Industry, *Expert System Opportunities: Guidelines for the Introduction of Expert Systems Technology*, HMSO, London, 1990.

Doukidis G.I., Land F. and Miller G. (Eds), *Knowledge Based Management Support Systems*, Ellis Horwood, Chichester, 1989.

Dreyfus H.L. and Dreyfus S.E., *Mind Over Machine*, Basil Blackwell, Oxford, 1986.
Feigenbaum E., McCorduck P. and Nii H.P., *The Rise of the Expert Company*, Macmillan, London, 1988.
Forester T., *Computers in the Human Context*, Basil Blackwell, Oxford, 1989.
Harmon P. and Maus R., *Expert Systems: Tools and Applications*, Wiley, New York, 1988.
Luger G.F. and Stubblefield W.A., *Artificial Intelligence and the Design of Expert Systems*, Benjamin Cummings, Redwood City, California, 1989.
Martin C.J., Expert systems in a managerial context, *Industrial Management and Data Systems*, Nov./Dec., pp. 6–8, 1985.
Rogers W., Ryack B. and Moeller G., Computer-aided medical diagnosis: literature review, *International Journal of Bio-Medical Computing*, **10**, 267–289, 1979.
Sell P.S., *Expert Systems: A Practical Introduction*, Macmillan, London, 1985.

22
Information systems and society

The impact of information systems

What effects will IS, or its slightly wider counterpart, information technology (IT), have on society in the future? Are we moving towards a post-industrial society where very few people are employed in making things, and most will be involved in the rising industries of information, knowledge, leisure and services generally? What effect will there be on the quality of our lives and our environment? Whatever else we can say about this, we can be reasonably sure that the effects will be dramatic. It is likely that IS will change the way we work, our leisure, the way we commute and travel, and especially the way we communicate with each other. Some of the effects of information systems on our lives are shown below. Not all of these effects will be benign, and some aspects of the new information systems will need to be closely watched.

- *National level*
  - improved international communications and enhanced visibility of state actions;
  - better governmental data processing systems (e.g. taxation, vehicle licensing, social services);
  - more information, and more integrated information, on individuals (the big brother syndrome).
- *Organizational level*
  - improved productivity through direct and indirect applications of information technology;
  - improved communications, decision-making and data access;
  - increased computer crime.
- *Personal level*
  - changed work roles and activities;

- job displacement and occupational changes;
- new leisure activities;
- increasing leisure time.

It is possible that the way nations interact with each other has already been profoundly affected by the shrinking of distances enabled by greatly improved communications. Would the democratic revolutions in Eastern Europe of the early nineties, or the Russian glasnost and perestroika, have happened without the communication systems which brought the actions of governments and peoples directly to public attention? Nations can no longer isolate themselves from the rest of the world, and this ever-increasing cultural exchange could be a strong influence on the political and cultural development of nations.

The effect on work and jobs

Increases in productivity have consistently reduced the amount of time the average person spends actually working, as a proportion of his or her waking lifetime. In the nineteenth century the proportion was over 40 per cent, in 1985 this had dropped to 18 per cent and by the year 2000 this could be about 15 per cent with the trend continuing into the twenty-first century. Information technology will continue to offer substantial productivity improvements, and so increasing leisure time will be something we can all look forward to. This may prove to be a mixed blessing; work offers people important social and psychological rewards as well as economic ones. It may be necessary to replace the work ethic with a leisure ethic, that is, one which recognizes the legitimacy of non-work activity.

The character of employment has also changed. Earlier this century we saw the replacement of agriculture by manufacturing as the major employer; now we are seeing the demise of manufacturing and the growth of service industries. This is not to say that the industries themselves have disappeared; rather that it now takes far fewer people to operate them. Now, more and more people are employed as information workers of one kind or another and the information services industry itself has burgeoned at the expense of other sectors. Over two-thirds of all employees now work in the service sector compared to less than one-third in industry and only 2.5 per cent in agriculture. It is a matter of debate as to whether this trend will continue, or whether service-related industries are dependent upon manufacturing to the extent that they can expand only so far before a balance is struck; naturally, the rise of information does not herald the demise of all that has gone before. The following are examples of growth in the service industries.

- Technological
  - computer services
  - software
  - computer and electronics manufacture
  - telecommunications, local and long distance

- Financial
  - banking and finance
  - insurance
  - accounting services
- Information
  - publishing
  - media industries
  - entertainment
  - education

Many information firms are changing and expanding within the information sector. Reuters, well known as a world-wide news agency until the eighties, has diversified into providing financial information on a world-wide basis; Dunn and Bradstreet, originally sellers of credit information, have diversified into providing computer-based marketing databases.

There is no doubt that automation has dramatically affected all stages of manufacturing and production, including, especially, the factory floor. Computers are now used widely in computer-aided design (CAD) and in computer-aided manufacture (CAM); the robot-manned production line has become almost a cliché of manufacturing technique. Robots can work in areas hostile to humans; they can perform boring and repetitive work for as long as is required, and they can be rapidly reprogrammed to do new tasks. Materials-handling technology has led to fully automated warehouses which can be programmed to select, locate and retrieve items from stock. Putting all these things together gives us a sight of the totally automated factory of the future. The following list shows the variety of occupations that are likely to be changed greatly by information technology.

- Factory and shop-floor
  - materials storage and warehousing
  - manufacturing
  - assembly and repair
  - supervisory and shop-floor management
- Office and clerical
  - financial and banking
  - information and clerical work
  - knowledge work
  - middle and junior management
- Professional and education
  - accounting
  - legal
  - medical
  - higher education

There are two forces at work. One which removes jobs and replaces them by automated (or alternative) electronic systems, and the other which creates new markets and jobs to exploit the information potential of the new technology. Unemployment as a whole seems to be more closely related to the general economic situation than to structural changes within industry. Work *displacement* from old jobs to new ones seems to be the main characteristic of the information revolution.

Human skills in the workplace

The impact of computers on people's working lives is undoubted; but is the effect generally beneficial or detrimental? There are many cases where the introduction of computers has resulted in the deskilling of traditional jobs. For example, skilled machine tool operators would normally undergo a long period of training and shop-floor apprenticeship, and then be rightly respected and rewarded for their experience and skills. The advent of computer-controlled machine tools has removed the need for these skills in many factories. In clerical work, there are many instances where human information processing skills and judgement have been replaced by automated data processing systems. In the office, the word processor has replaced the secretary's long-practised and hard-won skills in layout, centring, indenting, tabulating and spelling.

But is the trend inexorably one-way? A counter-argument to the deskilling problem is that factory automation by and large removes dangerous, boring and repetitive work and leaves more time and human capacity for work which really does require human skills. In the office, it could be argued that repetitive and mundane clerical operations are no better for people than their physical work counterparts, and that their replacement by data systems is no real loss. Because the new office systems eliminate repetitive data processing and filing, the work that is left is more varied and interesting and requires more human contact and more real human judgement. It is more likely that the few people operating the new system will be responsible for the whole of the system rather than just one small part, and therefore this will improve job satisfaction.

It used to be the case that possessing a skill or gaining a job in a profession was considered enough to last the working lifetime; now this may no longer be true and far greater employment flexibility will be required. The information society makes much stronger demands on individuals in terms of educational requirements; many more people are now required to understand the technology of information systems. People may have to train and retrain several times over during their working lives, perhaps in order to work in completely different disciplines.

Are any jobs safe? Surprisingly, it may be that unskilled and semi-skilled jobs such as cleaning and manual labouring, and service tasks such as restaurant waiting and hairdressing may be with us for the foreseeable future. Creative and imaginative jobs will also be hard to replace; artists, musicians, writers, designers, thinkers and performers will always be needed. The previous section on artificial intelligence came to the conclusion that we are a very long way off from reproducing real human skills in computers.

Computers for everybody?

When computers first became consistently reliable in the sixties, it was thought that information, on an organizational and national scale, would be concentrated in the hands of a few people, aided and abetted by the few technocrats who were trained in the mysteries of computer science. George Orwell's vision of the future in *Nineteen Eighty-Four*, in which Big Brother would control everybody's thoughts and actions, was thought to be a distinct possibility. Instead we have had the home computer, and now we have the PC: computers are for everyone. The rise of end-user computing and the general trend to decentralization of organizational computing power have both acted so as to diversify control of the technology out of the hands of the few and into the hands of the many within organizations. The increasing *visibility* of government activity in the modern state seems to act as a protection against the autocrat and the madman.

What of computers for individual's own use at home? Surprisingly, perhaps, the home computer has not yet had a very great impact. It was thought that there would be great demand for systems which could offer home banking and finance, personal tax analysis, share portfolio analysis, teleshopping (i.e. shopping interactively using television and telephone), and data and electronic mail services such as those offered by Prestel. Indeed, at first, British sales of home computers outstripped the rest of Europe. But those people who bought home computers did so out of curiosity, for the games, or for their children. Many parents recognized that both they and their offspring would benefit from exposure to information technology and bought home computers for their educational value. The home banking and other facilities have not become widespread; some people use a computer at home in preference to a typewriter, but this is still not a common use. Perhaps the last surge of home computer marketing was aimed more at the hobbyist and would-be programmer, and for its games and educational benefits, and when suitable software becomes available which really does cater for people's needs home use will become more widespread.

An exception to the general rule that home computing is not popular has occurred in France. Here, the electronic telephone directory system *Minitel* has become for some an electronic addiction. The most popular services on Minitel are the *messageries*, direct-dialogue electronic mail networks. Protected by a pseudonym, the caller sends a message to another, unknown recipient and a dialogue may then ensue. Conversations can be polite, flirtatious or outrageous, and many different human needs are offered and received. Some communicators swap telephone numbers and meet in person, but for many the main goal is purely emotional: risk-free communication with another human being.

The electronic cottage

Advances in electronic office products, and especially in communications technology, have given rise to the forecast that soon few people will need to travel to work, rather they will stay at home and communicate through their PCs to central computers. There may well be strong economic arguments (and environmental ones, too) against everybody physically commuting to the workplace when electronic links can be forged to their homes. This has not happened so far, except perhaps for some people involved in writing and editing, and indeed a switch to the electronic cottage may never happen for most. Social interactions at work are subtle, and are not limited to transmissions of data between individuals. As well as the work-based necessity for social and political communication, there are the human needs for personal interaction which are an important part of working life. Research shows that telecommuters tend to suffer from a range of psychological problems including feelings of isolation and loneliness, stresses and strains within the family, a lack of motivation and self-discipline, and an inability to organize their working lives effectively.

Summary

Information systems have an effect on society; this may be beneficial or not depending on how we control and use the tools on offer. It is clear that the nature and content of many jobs has already changed and will continue to in the future; our response to this needs to be flexible.

KEY TERMS   Deskilling   Electronic cottage   Labour displacement   Minitel   Teleshopping

Further reading

Clutterbuck D., *Information 2000*, Pitman, London 1989.
Forester T., *Computers in the Human Context*, Basil Blackwell, Oxford, 1989.
Forester T., *High-Tech Society*, Basil Blackwell, Oxford, 1988.
Handy C., *The Future of Work*, Basil Blackwell, Oxford, 1985.
National Economic Development Office, *IT Futures ... IT Can Work*, NEDO, Millbank, London, 1987.
Rowe C., *People and Chips: The Human Implications of Information Technology*, Paradigm, London, 1986.
Sherman B., *The New Revolution: The Impact of Computers on Society*, Wiley, Chichester, 1985.
Stonier T., *The Wealth of Information: A Profile of the Post-Industrial Society*, Methuen, London, 1982.
Toffler A., *The Third Wave*, Morrow, New York, 1980.
Zorkoczy P., *Information Technology: An Introduction*, Pitman, London, 1985.

Summary to Part Six

Part Six rounds off our analysis of information systems by looking towards the future. However, some of this future is already present. Certainly many of the technical problems are being addressed, but there is often a very long lead time between technology becoming available, being adopted, and then being used effectively. The pace of change is rapid in the information systems field, but the concepts introduced in this text should provide a strong grounding for tackling the development of information systems for managerial decision-taking. Often this will mean looking more at needs than technology. Businesses should be pushed by their information system requirements, not pulled by the technology on offer.

Index